BURIED
IN THE
BITTER
WATERS

BURIED
IN THE
BITTER
WATERS

*The Hidden History of Racial
Cleansing in America*

ELLIOT JASPIN

BASIC

BOOKS

A Member of the Perseus Books Group
New York

Published by Basic Books,
A Member of the Perseus Books Group

Books published by Basic Books are available at special discounts for bulk purchases
in the United States by corporations, institutions, and other organizations. For more
information, please contact the Special Markets Department at the Perseus Books
Group, 11 Cambridge Center, Cambridge MA 02142, or call (617) 252-5298 or
(800) 255-1514, or e-mail special.markets@perseusbooks.com.

Interior design by Brent Wilcox

Library of Congress Cataloging-in-Publication Data
Jaspin, Elliot.
   Buried in the bitter waters : the hidden history of racial cleansing in America /
Elliot Jaspin.
      p.   cm.
   Includes bibliographical references and index.
   ISBN-13: 978-0-465-03636-3
   ISBN-10: 0-465-03636-8 (hc : alk. paper)
   1. African Americans—Segregation—History. 2. African Americans—
Relocation—History. 3. African Americans—Crimes against—History. 4. African
Americans—Social conditions. 5. Racism—United States—History. 6. United
States—Race relations. I. Title.
E185.61.J37 2007
305.896'073—dc22

2006039307

10 9 8 7 6 5 4 3 2 1

For my grandsons
Samuel and Alexander Axton

Ah done been in sorrow's kitchen and Ah done licked out all de pots. Ah done died in grief and been buried in de bitter waters, and Ah done rose agin from de dead lak Lazarus.

—ZORA NEALE HURSTON,
JONAH'S GOURD VINE

So Moses brought Israel from the Red Sea, and they went out into the wilderness of Shur; and they went three days in the wilderness, and found no water.

And when they came to Marah, they could not drink of the waters of Marah, for they were bitter: therefore the name of it was called Marah.

—EXODUS 15:22–23

CONTENTS

Minutes after two black men were publicly executed in Forsyth County, Georgia, for the rape and murder of eighteen-year-old Mae Crow, a photographer apparently mounted the gallows and took this picture of the crowd. Although some blacks watched the hanging (lower right-hand corner), within a few weeks nearly every Negro had been driven from the county.

Introduction

The story of how I found America's racial cleansings begins in an unlikely place: the small town of Berryville in northwest Arkansas. I was visiting there in 1998 and, with time on my hands, decided to tour a small history museum in the center of town. It was a quirky place—one room was devoted to antique embalming equipment—with all sorts of bric-a-brac piled on tables.

As I wandered from room to room, a picture on one wall caught my eye. In the top of the frame was a photograph of a farmer and his wife taken some time before the Civil War. Below the picture was the farmer's will. On separate lines he carefully recounted his earthly possessions, parceling each out to family and friends. It was what you would expect until this line: Wedged between livestock and land were five slaves to be given away.

A friend once described walking into a vault in the New Orleans courthouse and seeing stacks of old record books listing the slaves that each person owned. He stood there in horror. Before him was row after row of moldering books with their ghastly roll call. I understood the shock he tried to describe because it was what swept over me as I stared at that will. How do you describe an encounter with the artifacts of slavery? It is the corpse at the funeral. In it we see both our own loss and the loss of someone else.

I stared at the will and as the shock drained away, a question began to form. I had been in the area for several days. For the first time it occurred to me that, in all the time I had been there, I had not seen a single African-American. Yet here in front of me was proof that at one time blacks had lived here. Were they still here? If not, when had they left and why? I walked out of the museum with the questions nagging me.

Over the next few days as I drove to my different appointments, I kept searching for even one black face. Tourism was one of the pillars of the local economy and the area was dotted with hotels, restaurants, and concert halls for country music fans. The people shopping in the stores were white. The people behind the counters were white. The people working in the motels were white. I began checking the people in cars as they passed. All white.

On my last day, I finally asked the person I was interviewing if there were any blacks in the area. "Oh no," she said, "the Klan keeps them out."

When I got back to Washington, D.C., I decided to take a closer look. Using 1990 census data I had downloaded from the Internet, I sorted the information from Arkansas to see how many counties had a black population of less than one percent. I soon had a list that included about a third of all Arkansas counties. I thought that Arkansas, as a slave-holding state, would have a more even distribution of its black population. Perhaps I had been mistaken.

I collected census data for other southern states. Tennessee. Georgia. North Carolina. Kentucky. Texas. Each time I found some counties that were either all white or populated by so few blacks as to be virtually all white. This was not what I had expected.

It was pure coincidence that, on one of the days that I was going over the census data in my office at Cox Newspapers in Washington, a woman from the Atlanta bureau was visiting. As we chatted I told her about the odd distribution of blacks in some southern states. She launched into a story about her brother, who is a cook. He had been recently hired as a chef in a restaurant in Forsyth County just outside of Atlanta. On the day she visited him there, she said the Klan was holding a rally on the courthouse lawn. She explained how all the blacks had been run out of the county around the turn of the century and had been kept out ever since. I went back to my census tables and found Forsyth County. In 1990, there were twelve blacks living in a county of over 40,000 people.

It wasn't until several months later that I had the time to drive to the National Archives in Maryland and copy data from census books from the turn of the century. At night I would sit at the kitchen table and pore over the columns of numbers. I would compare counties from one census to another looking for a sudden drop in the black population. Here and there I would see a strange gyration in the numbers. I had a gut feeling there was a pattern lurking in all these census tables, but the work was tedious and far too slow. There had to be a better way.

While I would frequently go on the Internet to find current census information, it had never occurred to me look there for census data from fifty or a hundred years ago. But frustrated with hunting through paper records, I did a web search for "historical census data." Almost immediately I found a database maintained by the University of Virginia. I began downloading census data from 1890 through 1930 for a small list of southern states. I then wrote a short computer program that would sort the data by state and county and compare the black population between each census. If there was a drop of fifty percent or greater between two decades, the data from that county would be saved in a separate file.

I punched the Enter key and in a matter of seconds the program had completed its work. I opened the new file I had created and began to scroll the list of counties where there had been a black population collapse. It was a moment of shock. Page after page of counties scrolled by. I had expected four or five counties, but I now had dozens. This could not be. I had made a mistake. I went back and checked the numbers. They were accurate. I downloaded data for more states from the University of Virginia and reran the program. The list grew. I started adding states outside the South, and the list grew even longer. What had happened?

I made a list of four or five counties that seemed to be the most suspicious and went to the Library of Congress. By cross-checking my list with the *New York Times Index* for the decade when each collapse occurred, I found the dates when there had been stories written about some of the counties. I mounted a microfilm reel and turned the crank. As I fiddled with the focus in the dark of the library's microfilm room, a headline appeared.

"ALL NEGROES DRIVEN FROM INDIANA TOWN."

The seven-paragraph story was to the point.

"Negroes began leaving this mining town early this afternoon, following the warning issued by white residents to be out of town by 7 o'clock tonight."

I mounted another reel and found another story:

"MISSOURI MOB'S WORK, Kills Three Negroes, Burns Their Homes and Drives Every Negro Out of Pierce City."

"For nearly 15 hours, ending at noon today this town of 3,000 people has been in the hands of a mob of armed whites, determined to drive every negro from its precincts."

I had found America's racial cleansings.

Like an archipelago, the counties where racial cleansings occurred form a rough arc that begins in North Carolina, crosses the Appalachians, and extends into the Midwest. In some cases more than a century has passed since blacks were driven out of these counties, and yet they still remain islands inhabited almost exclusively by whites. People pass through such counties on interstate highways never guessing at their history. If they were to stop and ask about a racial cleansing, it is likely they would be met with blank stares. History is what we choose to remember. But anyone who carefully digs through the history of these islands will often find the evidence of these long-ago eruptions.

These were not small, discrete events. The racial cleansing that struck Forsyth County, Georgia in 1912, for example, engulfed at least a half dozen surrounding counties in northern Georgia before it burned itself out in 1913. Because Forsyth County was the epicenter, the blacks there sustained the worst losses. More than a thousand people—97 percent of the county's black population—were driven out over a period of about two months. They owned 1,900 acres of farmland, nearly all of which they were forced to sell or abandon. The county's five black churches were burned. As the frenzy spread, whites in adjacent counties began ordering their black neighbors to leave. The numerical losses in Jackson County were the largest. The black population there dropped by 1,600, a loss of nineteen percent. Whites in Dawson County forced every one of its 152 blacks to go. In other counties like

Hall, Cobb, and Cherokee there were smaller but still substantial drops in the black community.

Racial cleansings occurred across the nation. They occurred in the North and Midwest as well as the South. The dozen cases described in this book took place in eight states including two in Indiana and one in Missouri.

In this book I focus specifically on racial cleansings that emptied entire counties, but there are many more cases where whites ordered blacks to vacate towns or villages. Typically the accounts of these racial cleansings are found as brief items in the back pages of old newspapers. The *New York Times* ran a two-paragraph story from Dothan, Alabama in 1912 that began, "After wreaking vengeance on the negro population of Dixie, a small town near here, driving every black from the village and killing one last night, a mob is searching the countryside for another negro." According to another story in an Ohio newspaper from 1919, "Columbus is sheltering many Negroes who made a precipitous exodus from Marion Monday evening following the posting of warnings for them to leave the city." Occasionally the account of a racial cleansing will appear in an oral history. A schoolteacher in Garrett, Kentucky reminiscing about the town's past, said that, after a local sheriff was killed by a black, the townspeople "got on every side of the hollow with high powered rifles and just riddled the [black] houses. The next morning there wasn't a colored person in Garrett."

These racial cleansings in rural towns and villages were so common that I would stumble across them just by leafing through old newspapers. But the tools to do a systematic search still do not exist. Census data that would point to sudden population drops is only computerized on the county level, a limitation that shaped my own research. But as more and more old census data is computerized, the list of racial cleansings is bound to grow exponentially. By just searching for counties where there was a drop of fifty percent or greater in the black population, I found 260 suspect sites. Because I limited the search to thirty-one states in the South, Midwest, and Mid-Atlantic where I thought I would be most likely to find racial cleansings, the search took in about 2,500 of the approximately 3,100 counties in the United States. While it is unlikely that there were racial cleansings in all 260 counties, the number of places to research was overwhelming. But that number pales in comparison with the possibility of looking at the census data for the approximately 18,000 towns and villages in the United States. If, as with the counties, about ten percent are suspect, the list of places will grow to 1,800. Even that number is probably understated. Driving people out of a town is far easier than driving them out of a county.

There is another indication of just how common these expulsions were. To make sure the examples of racial cleansings used in this book were as unambiguous as possible, I selected only those that were "the worst of the worst." I applied four criteria in selecting the cases for this book: the cleansing had to be countywide; it had to occur suddenly (taking a few months at most); it had to be documented through some kind of contemporary account, and, most important, it had to have been successful.

To be "successful" the number of blacks living in a county today had to be less than it was before the cleansing occurred. This standard represents a particularly high bar because it does not take into account population growth over the last hundred years. At the time that the approximately 1,000 blacks were driven out of Forsyth County, for example, its total population was about 12,000. Nearly a century later, the county has grown to 98,000 people, but there are only 684 blacks living there, and most of those have settled along the county's border. The same is true of the other counties represented in this book. The populations in counties with successful racial cleansings are less than one percent black as of the most recent census. In seven of the counties there are fewer than fifty black residents. In other words, these counties remain white preserves. Despite these stringent criteria, I was able to document a dozen such cleansings.

In addition to being numerous, possibly even common, what is striking about racial cleansings is that they were unlike the all-too-familiar lynchings or race riots. While people were lynched during some racial cleansings, there were expulsions where no one was killed. And, although the threat of violence always hung in the air, there were racial cleansings, unlike race riots, where no one was attacked.

What sets a racial cleansing apart from other kinds of violence against blacks is its intent. In every case whites would deliver an ultimatum: Leave by some deadline or die. Afterwards residents might post signs telling blacks not to enter a town or county—so-called sundown towns—but that was not always necessary. The reputation these places earned because of a racial cleansing was often enough notice.

However their "whiteness" was enforced, it has been an enduring legacy. These counties remain the "holes" in America's racial map. While Forsyth County has 684 blacks, neighboring Fulton County, which experienced lynchings and race riots but never a cleansing, has a black population of 363,000. In Marshall County, Kentucky, where a racial cleansing took place in 1908, there are only thirty-seven blacks. Next door in Graves County, the black population is 1,600. In Unicoi County, Tennessee, there are twelve blacks compared with more than 4,000 in adjacent Washington County.

The paradox of these counties is that while the fear remains, the histories are missing. Although blacks will warn one another that a particular town or county is dangerous, they will often have no idea of what happened there. By the same token, people who live in a county where there was a racial cleansing usually think their history is unique. They are unaware of numerous other racial cleansings across the United States. It is as if racial cleansings are a blank space in America's memory.

The vast majority of Americans have no knowledge of the nation's racial cleansings. They are so little known that when the 1923 destruction of the black community in Rosewood, Florida came to light in the 1980s, the public was astonished. The state formed a commission to investigate. Officials sought out survivors. The Florida legislature voted to make reparations. Hollywood made a movie about the event. It was treated as something unique. Unfortunately, it was far from unusual. What was unusual was that the history of Rosewood was resurrected.[1]

This book then is intended to begin the process of reconstructing and understanding what happened. Concentrating on twelve of the very worst racial cleansings throws this history into stark relief. Through these detailed accounts I also hope to give the reader a sense of what it was like for both whites and blacks to live through an expulsion. While all expulsions have their similarities, they also echo what Tolstoy said of families: "All happy families are alike; each unhappy family is unhappy in its own way." Each cleansing was unique in its origins. Whites feared that ex-slaves would become citizens. They feared blacks were a danger to the community. They worried that blacks would take jobs. In one case it was done supposedly to find a child molester. In some towns, whites opposed these expulsions, and there are accounts of white men fighting one another in the street. Other communities looked back on their racial cleansing with pride.

In the end these were justifications for a cleansing rather than their cause. Blacks were targets for a cleansing because, while they lived in a community, they usually did not belong to the place where they lived. The mark of citizenship is the right to vote, and that right was largely denied to blacks. Worse still, segregation widened the gulf between blacks and the community they lived in. Once whites walled off blacks, the lack of normal social contact gave rise to increasingly bizarre fantasies. Whites worried that armies of blacks were forming in the night waiting for the right moment to pounce. Even if they did not attack in groups, their bite was poisonous and they had unrestrained sexual appetites. The only reason for risking the presence of blacks in a community was economic necessity. Who else would pick crops or wash clothes? But black labor was a double-edged sword. Blacks represented a very real economic threat to the white workingman. When business interests were not training blacks to compete with whites, they were hiring them as strikebreakers. If some pretext could be found—a rape or murder— white laborers would benefit by driving off their black competitors.

As this history is resurrected, we are always left to grapple with the legacy of pain. Victims of the expulsion describe an abiding sense of shame. After a farmer was driven out of Forsyth County, he would forever after tell people he was from Chicago. For others the shame comes from a sense of helplessness. Black men, who would have liked to defend their homes, instead bowed to the inevitable. In flight there was safety, but it was also emasculating. The children and grandchildren of the victims talk about their fear and anger. The counties where racial cleansings took place loom large in black folklore. They are seen—and often for good reason—as dangerous places.

Again and again as I interviewed people for this book, I heard about "The Speech." It was the talk that black parents gave their children about where it was safe to go and where it was not, and what to do when, inevitably, you were stopped by the police. At the heart of "The Speech" was a memory of some place that had driven out its black population. The details of what happened are often sketchy or even nonexistent, but the terror endures. The result is that for blacks the country exists as a checkerboard with some squares that are safe and others that are not.

For whites, the memory of racial cleansings is, if anything, even trickier. At the time that these expulsions occurred, whites often applauded what had been done. As one chamber of commerce proudly noted in its marketing brochure, the town did not have "mosquitoes or Negroes." Today, when catch phrases like "multiculturalism" and "racial diversity" are national goals, that history makes whites uneasy. Faced with an inconvenient history, the first defense is silence. The official historian in one county acknowledged that something "terrible" had happened in her area but refused to discuss it because "it would only cause trouble." When Murray Bishoff, the editor of the *Monett Times,* wrote a series of stories in the 1990s about the racial cleansing in his Missouri county, it was the first time it had been discussed publicly in more than ninety years. Some newspaper editors decided that the less said the better. When blacks were forced to leave Sharp County, Arkansas in 1906, the editor of a paper there declared, "The *Record* does not know who is responsible for this exodus among the negroes. We have no desire to know." Even when a racial cleansing is mentioned, it is often cloaked in some euphemism. A local historian, trying to account for a racial cleansing that involved three murders, the burning of black-owned homes, and a military-style assault on the black quarter by more than a thousand men, only told readers that blacks left after "a disturbing situation."

When silence fails, the second defense is to blame someone else. The easiest targets are those who were driven out. After Bishoff published his history of the Pierce City racial cleansing, a reader objected in a letter to the editor. "Don't be deceived into thinking the black populace was totally innocent and totally law abiding being jumped on unaware by a bunch of bigots." The problem, the writer noted, was that there was "reputed lawbreaking by Negroes leading up to the mob action."

Comanche County, Texas put a slightly different spin on its expulsion. There had been two separate incidents where blacks had murdered whites, and whites used them as the justification for the racial cleansing. In its retelling, about twenty years after the event, the whites were being generous by only forcing all blacks to flee. "It may be supposed that this has grown out of unreasonable prejudice and without just cause, but it finds its origin in two terrible tragedies so atrocious and coming so near together that the forbearance of the people was manifest by a sentence so mild as banishment."

A third defense is to simply deny that the racial cleansing ever occurred. When Forsyth County was thrust onto the national stage in 1987, one resident explained on national television that, "I understand [blacks] weren't run out. I understand that they left over a period of time." The *Atlanta Journal-Constitution* echoed that revisionism when it ran a page-one story during the same period arguing that the expulsion was a "legend" because not every single black left. That article was followed by a local historian's "study" arguing against black reparations claims on the grounds that Forsyth County blacks had somehow managed to sell their land as they were being run out of town by a deadly mob. Picking up on the study, the Forsyth County Historical Society declared in a book it published in 2002, "Decades old rumors to the contrary, each and every parcel of land was sold, with the proceeds going to the African-American owners."

In fact these denials mask an economic reality. The land that Forsyth County blacks were forced to abandon has today become very valuable. Rather than deal with the thorny issue of compensation, it is far easier to pretend that blacks have no claim. Even when whites acknowledge that their forebears may have stolen black-owned land, they angrily dismiss the idea that anyone today should be forced to compensate the descendants. Those who own the land today clearly are blameless. But they also deny that the government, which, at best, did nothing while its black citizens were being robbed and persecuted, should finally be held to account.

That a community feels a need to either deny or shade its history is a measure of just how powerful these racial cleansings remain. In part, townspeople may want to edit the past as a way to protect the memories of their fathers and grandfathers who took part in these expulsions.

But by shading what happened, they are also protecting the legacy of these cleansings. Through a variety of devices, these communities continue the project their ancestors began—an all-white society—even though the rest of the country has moved on. By denying what took place long ago, they can claim that their racially "pure" world is a coincidence. In fact, it is not.

Over the last century, a variety of different tactics have been used to enforce the color line in these counties. Sometimes a county's reputation has been enough to keep blacks away. When that failed, the record shows that after a cleansing there was a long history of threats and intimidation. When threats failed, force was used. What permits this to continue is not the denial and hostility in these communities. It is that the wider world has chosen to remain silent, to maintain these racial cleansings as America's family secret. The silence surrounding these cleansings has had another, unintended consequence: It has robbed these communities of the example of those people who, in a time of great moral crisis, acted heroically. In nearly every racial cleansing there were whites who opposed what was happening. Towns like Cumming, Georgia, and Comanche, Texas, held mass meetings and passed resolutions condemning the expulsions. White employers in Harrison, Arkansas sheltered their black employees. Newspaper editors in Texas and Kentucky denounced the expulsions. A railroad superintendent in Tennessee faced down a mob that was ordering the blacks to leave. A judge in Kentucky almost single-handedly fought the vigilantes to a standstill.

This tradition of resistance continues to this day. Over the past decade mostly local historians or reporters in a few of the counties where there were racial cleansings have begun to investigate what happened. Murray Bishoff, unmoved by complaints of townspeople, wrote a series of stories and later dedicated a plaque to the memory of those killed by the mob in the Lawrence County racial cleansing. In Forsyth County, Don Shadburn, the county historian, has produced a thoughtful and carefully researched account of his county's racial unrest. And in Harrison, Arkansas newspaper reporter George Holcomb has written a series of stories describing the community's racist past.

But as encouraging as these efforts are, the fact remains that we are a nation with two histories: one white, one black. In our day-to-day lives, this may not be very important. But in times of crisis, our divided history exerts its hold on the national debate. At those moments, because they see the world in such different ways, whites and blacks find themselves talking past one another.

In the wake of Hurricane Katrina, black objections to the word "refugee" seem overly sensitive, even eccentric, to whites. When the poor in New Orleans, who are overwhelming black, are left to their own devices while the city is being evacuated, whites talk about a "class" problem. Blacks, with long and painful memories of being outcasts, decry what they see as yet another example of racism. The same is true when it comes to the debate over reparations: Whites, with almost no memory of racial cleansings, see reparations claims as a not-so-subtle attempt by blacks to get a handout. Blacks, who remember how their families lost all they owned in an expulsion, wonder why they cannot get justice. The list is almost endless because, as unsettling as it may be, Americans do not share a common history.

The problem grows more complicated when we talk about racial cleansings. Even when they are acknowledged, people stumble over how to talk about them. What words should we use to describe what we know? To worry about semantics may seem pedantic, but language is how we understand things. It is no coincidence that people used euphemisms such as "disturbing situations" to describe—or perhaps more accurately to disguise—what was occurring. And as we now try to uncover what took place, classifying what we see before us is a vital step in restoring our history.

In the few surviving accounts, the expulsions are described by the physical act that was occurring. In 1908, for example, Ray Stannard Baker, a crusading white journalist who wrote a prescient series of stories on race relations in his book *Following the Colour Line,* discussed how whites would terrorize their black neighbors into leaving a community. He called what he saw "Driving out Negroes." Others have used terms like "banishment," "forced to flee," or "expulsions." The problem with these phrases is that they describe only the act, not the policy. Nazis murdered Jews, but what was going on was not just murder. It was genocide, the policy of killing a whole class of people. To say that Nazis murdered Jews without also saying they were conducting a campaign of genocide is to miss the point of what was happening. And yet the word "genocide" did not exist when Hitler began his mass killings. It was invented by the Polish-Jewish lawyer Raphael Lemkin in 1943 and was ultimately used during the Nuremberg trials to punish Nazi crimes—not prevent them.

Words and terms are born out of a need to describe the world. But because the victors, who get to write the history, had little need to describe the fate of the conquered, the words did not exist soon enough to describe and ultimately prevent the wholesale destruction of black communities in America.

In 1991, however, the information revolution allowed victims of similar expulsions a chance to write their own history. It was during that summer that the Serb-dominated Yugoslav federal army marched through a large swath of Croatia sending thousands of Croatian refugees fleeing in terror. In a press conference the beleaguered Croatian government accused the Serbians of "ethnic cleansing of the critical areas that are to be annexed to Serbia." Within a year, the term "ethnic cleansing" was in almost daily use. But while it was used widely, it was not defined. In one sense events defined it. The daily reports of killings and rapes, the streams of refugees, and the bland denials of any wrongdoing described "ethnic cleansing" in a very graphic way. But it was left to the United Nations to give it a more formal definition. Ethnic cleansing, the UN decided, was "the elimination by the ethnic group exerting control over a given territory of members of other ethnic groups."[2]

If it were not for the fact that the term was coined by its victims, it would be especially unpalatable. The idea of cleansing brings to mind the idea of purifying. And as one critic has noted, there is nothing "pure" about driving innocent people from their homes. As it is, the term, because of its origins, has a sardonic ring to it. But sardonic or not, it gives us a way to describe what we see and know.[3]

These, then, are the stories of America's racial cleansings.

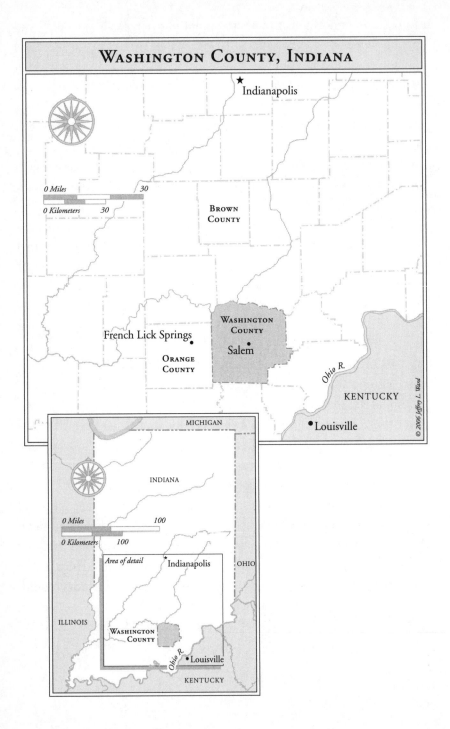

WASHINGTON COUNTY, INDIANA

★ Indianapolis

0 Miles 30
0 Kilometers 30

BROWN
COUNTY

French Lick Springs •

WASHINGTON
COUNTY

ORANGE
COUNTY

• Salem

Ohio R.

KENTUCKY

• Louisville

© 2006 Jeffrey L. Ward

MICHIGAN

INDIANA

0 Miles 100
0 Kilometers 100

Area of detail   ★ Indianapolis

OHIO

ILLINOIS

WASHINGTON
COUNTY

Ohio R.
• Louisville

KENTUCKY

CHAPTER 1

We the People

Washington County, Indiana
1864

Negroes are not citizens. United States Supreme Court Chief Justice Roger Taney was very sure of that. And if there was any doubt, Taney made it very clear why in his landmark 1857 decision involving Dred Scott.

When his master died while they were living in Missouri, Dred Scott petitioned for his freedom. Because Missouri had outlawed slavery, Dred Scott reasoned that he was a free man. But Taney and six others of the nine Supreme Court justices ruled that Scott was still a slave. And further: "The Declaration of Independence [shows] that neither the class of persons who had been imported as slaves, nor their descendants, whether they had become free or not," could be citizens. It did not concern the court, wrote Taney, if excluding blacks from citizenship was a question of "justice or injustice." He and his six fellow justices were just following the founding fathers' original intent.[1]

But there was a corollary proposition buried in Taney's argument. Because blacks, whether slave or free, were not citizens, they were not part of the community, and so the citizenry could dispose of them as it saw fit. Aliens can always be deported.

Reasons could always be found for driving African-Americans out of town. A black killed or raped a white. Black workers competed with whites for jobs. Whites didn't want blacks living nearby. Any reason would do. What really mattered was that whites thought they were entitled to drive out blacks. As long as blacks were not seen as citizens, racial cleansings were possible.

Seven years after the Dred Scott decision, blacks were driven out of Washington County, Indiana. The reason was citizenship.

————

Today Washington County is a sleepy farming community in southern Indiana as pleasant and unremarkable as any other collection of midwestern towns. In Salem, the county seat, the courthouse sits in the middle of the town square bounded on every side by small shops and offices just as it did during the Civil War. Beyond the boundaries of Salem lie only fields and farms spreading out for miles. Even the ubiquitous Wal-Mart does not intrude. It was built eighteen miles east of town near the interstate.

The only clue to what happened here is what we do not see. Although one hundred and forty years have passed, there are almost no blacks. Salem today has a population of 6,172, of which two are African-Americans. Blacks lived here once, but, when the Civil War came, angry whites formed a secret army, planned an uprising, chased most blacks away, and killed the few who stayed.

In 1860 the census found 187 blacks living in Washington County. A decade later only eighteen remained. But figuring out exactly what happened in Washington County between these two dates is like trying to read an old book with most of its pages torn or missing. Documents have been misplaced and newspapers destroyed. Witnesses have long since died.[2]

Much of what we do know about the collapse of the black community in Washington County comes from the pen of one man, Horace Heffren. That the history of a racial cleansing would fall to Heffren, a local newspaper editor, lawyer, politician and amateur historian, is supremely ironic for one reason: Horace Heffren hated blacks. When President Lincoln issued the Emancipation Proclamation in January 1863, Heffren editorialized: "Abraham Lincoln sent a long message to Congress, almost all of which he devoted to [*sic*] nigger."[3]

Heffren was a bear of a man. He had a full beard, stood over six feet, and, at his death in 1883, weighed nearly 400 pounds. The only known picture of him was taken in the 1860s when he was in his thirties. In it, he is already paunchy—the material around the top button of his ill-fitting coat is pulled taut. His high forehead and round shoulders give him a bullet shape. The hair on either side of his head sticks out.[4]

In the photo, Heffren stares down and away from the camera. The effect is unsettling. There is something disheveled and a little off about his posture—as if he paused a second to have his picture taken before rushing on. One of his enemies—and he had many—captured the man in nine words: "a disgusting compound of whiskey, grease, vulgarity and cowardice."[5]

Heffren had sided with the South before Fort Sumter, but, when war broke out, he joined the Union Army and got an officer's commission in a unit being formed by an uncle.[6] In letters home, soldiers described Heffren as a bully who delighted in forcing soldiers on sick call to dig trenches. Those who disobeyed were forced to march around wearing a barrel.[7]

His military career ended ignominiously in September 1862, fifteen months after it had begun: He was drummed out of the army after he commandeered a railway handcar during a skirmish and deserted, leaving his soldiers to be overrun by rebel forces. In later years his opponents called him Handcar Heffren.[8]

He returned to Salem to edit the Democratic newspaper there. And while he may have left the army, he did not leave the battle. Instead he secretly switched sides.

On May 6, 1864 at about eleven in the morning a man from Kentucky named J. J. Grundy stepped off the Louisville, New Albany, and Chicago train in Horace Heffren's hometown of Salem. He was headed for a crucial meeting in French Lick Springs about twenty miles away, and he got off the train thinking he could catch a stagecoach to his meeting. But Grundy soon realized there was no regular transportation from Salem to French Lick Springs. He would have to wait till ten for the night train.[9]

With most of the day to kill, Grundy had lunch and then explored the town square's shops. At a clothing store, he struck up a conversation with the owner, Simon Drom, a German-Jewish immigrant. Soon the two realized they belonged to the same fraternal organization, the Order of the Sons of Liberty. Grundy was on his way to French Lick Springs to meet a leader of the Sons of Liberty, Dr. William A. Bowles.[10]

Grundy's meeting piqued Drom's curiosity. The clothier explained that Heffren, who was lounging outside the courthouse, was the deputy grand commander of the order and was expecting a messenger from Kentucky. Drom apparently assumed that Grundy was that messenger.[11]

Drom called out to Heffren and introduced him to Grundy. A curious ballet of hints and gestures followed, as the two men, each with his own secrets, tried to sound the other out. Heffren said he was expecting a "commissioner from the rebel forces" in Kentucky. Since Grundy was from Kentucky, Heffren asked if he was that man.[12]

Grundy had no idea who or what the "commissioner" was, but he did know from a recent newspaper story that three Confederate regiments were being disbanded in Kentucky. It was rumored that the men from these regiments would become part of a secret army. It was a long shot, but Grundy, bluffing his way with a single newspaper story and a rumor, replied that three regiments of rebel troops were being disbanded.[13]

Heffren immediately answered that another four regiments would be disbanded as well. When that happened in the next few days, Heffren explained, he was supposed to be notified by a man from Kentucky. Unstated was that, at the right moment, these southern forces could be used to aid an insurrection in the North.

Pressing further, Heffren asked Grundy if he knew anything about the Democratic "organization"? Improvising and using the terminology of secret orders like the Masons, Grundy replied that he was a member of the "first degree."

Grundy might not be the "commissioner" from Kentucky, but Heffren was now sure the stranger he was talking to was more than just a fellow member of the Order of the Sons of Liberty. Grundy had to be a fellow conspirator.

In this the third year of the war, Indiana was restive. Bloody disasters like Fredericksburg had cooled the fervor of some Republicans, and Democrats, who had originally opposed the war, were now emboldened. Their opposition to the war, begun as a campaign of speeches, rallies, and pamphlets, turned violent. They attacked a Union rally in Brown County, killing a soldier. Elsewhere they assaulted draft officials and destroyed their enrollment books. These attacks came soon after the 1862 elections, which had demonstrated the growing strength of antiwar sentiment: The Peace Democrats in Indiana had won overwhelmingly.[14]

As discontent grew in the Midwest, rumors abounded of secret societies with shadowy ties to the Confederacy arming themselves for battle. The federal government had tried to infiltrate these groups with little success. It suspected the Sons of Liberty of burning federal warehouses. The Sons of Liberty was organized like the Masons, with various tests that you had to pass to earn different "degrees." The group presented itself to most of its members as a fraternal extension of the Democratic Party.[15]

But a few members, including Heffren, knew the group's secret plans to kidnap or kill the governor of Indiana, free Confederate prisoners of war, and take Indiana, Illinois, Ohio, Kentucky, and Missouri out of the Union. The Sons of Liberty were buying and stockpiling guns and ammunition. Heffren and others went from town to town organizing chapters and recruiting foot soldiers for the coming conflict.[16]

These were heady times, and Heffren saw Grundy's arrival in May as one more sign the uprising was at hand, and in July the Grand Council meeting in Chicago set the date. A Democratic rally in Indianapolis, scheduled for August 16, would be the cover. Posing as visitors to the rally, the Sons of Liberty would descend on Indianapolis, free Confederate prisoners of war at a nearby camp, then seize the state government. Other chapters would attack a government arsenal in Columbus, Ohio and free confederate prisoners held in camps in Illinois and Ohio. Then they would march to Kentucky and join with a Confederate army there.[17]

The two men chatted most of the afternoon. Heffren was concerned that Grundy had chosen to stay at the Faulkner House hotel because Joe Faulkner was a United States Detective. Men like Faulkner were everywhere trying to ferret out the conspiracy. Heffren suggested Grundy should in the future stay at his father-in-law's hotel—the Persise House—because it "was of a different stripe."[18]

Grundy was grateful for the advice. He was traveling in disguise because, as he later told another co-conspirator, "I had been watched on the street by United States Detectives." Grundy was also using a phony name—his real name was Felix Stidger. Throughout the summer of 1864 he shuttled around Indiana and Kentucky helping to organize the uprising. He became grand secretary of the Kentucky branch of the order. When a government spy was discovered, Stidger and three others tried, unsuccessfully, to kill him.[19]

Dr. Bowles, whom Stidger was planning to meet when he first came to Salem, started handing out wads of money to chapter members. In the county clerk's office one day Heffren saw a friend flash a roll of bills Bowles had just given him to buy guns. In Indianapolis the Sons of Liberty purchased four hundred revolvers and ammunition and stored them in crates marked "Stationery" in a printing plant. Meanwhile, men in the various chapters "drilled every week or two." Everything was in readiness.[20]

Then it all started to collapse.

On July 30 Union troops arrested Judge Joshua Bullitt, chief justice of the state's appellate court and the leader of the Kentucky branch of the Sons of Liberty, as he got off the ferry in Louisville, holding a satchel with $5,000 in gold that Confederate operatives had just given him. Harrison Dodd, an Indiana printer who led the conspiracy, was arrested in Indianapolis in August. Union soldiers swooped down on other leaders and raided the Indianapolis printing plant where the revolvers were stored. Some conspirators fled to Canada, but Heffren was not so lucky, and by October he and four other leaders of the order were in an Indianapolis jail awaiting court-martial.[21]

What Heffren and his fellow conspirators did not know was that a spy inside the Sons of Liberty was feeding information to Indiana's

Republican governor, Oliver P. Morton. After the Democrats won both houses of the Indiana legislature in the 1862 elections, they wanted to take control of the state militia away from the governor and then withdraw it from the war. When Morton and Republican legislators blocked them, they retaliated by refusing to appropriate funds to run the state government. Morton responded by borrowing from a New York financier and the federal government.

Now, in the machinations of the Sons of Liberty, Morton saw an opportunity to improve Republican fortunes. In an early version of the October Surprise, he carefully waited until a month before the 1864 elections to arrest the leaders of the Sons of Liberty and try them in a military court.[22]

The Republican press, ecstatic about the arrests, warned of "Jacobin conspiracies" and "revolution" while government prosecutors hammered at the ties between the Sons of Liberty and the Democratic Party. Morton was re-elected in November by the considerable margin of 20,000 votes. Republicans regained control of the state legislature and won eight of the state's eleven congressional seats.

The trial of Heffren and four fellow conspirators began in Indianapolis on October 21, 1864, but the government's star witness did not testify until a week later. On October 28, Felix Stidger, aka J. J. Grundy, walked into the courtroom and sat down in the witness chair. Stidger, who had worked so assiduously for the Sons of Liberty and gained the confidence of men like Heffren, had been working undercover all the while for the Union Army. Now he had a story to tell, a story that could send Heffren to the gallows.[23]

The next day, October 29, saw the first written indication of racial cleansing in the county, when the Blue River Meeting of Friends, an administrative unit of the Quakers that included Washington County, met to hear its committees' annual reports. The year before, the Committee on the Concerns of People of Color's report had been brief and unremarkable, but this year was different: "By inducements held out to enter the army and increase of prejudice and other difficulties surrounding them their population within the limits of our Quarterly meeting has been much reduced."[24]

In subsequent annual reports the committee would hint at the disaster that had befallen Washington County's blacks. In 1867 it notes that "but few colored people" now lived in the county, and the following year that "there are about 150 colored people within our limits nearly all of whom reside in Orange County."[25]

Sometime in the space of a year almost the entire black population of Washington County had disappeared. The county had never been particularly welcoming to blacks, but the African-American community had deep roots there. Heffren noted that in the 1850s there were "three settlements of negroes in the county, beside a large population of the colored element in Salem." He counted three black churches and recalled that, before the Civil War, one of the hotels on the town square was managed by Alexander "Black Aleck" and that "he would not receive those of his own color, but whites exclusively."[26] Washington County had been a place where blacks could prosper. When he died, the blacksmith John Williams was worth $5,500, approximately $100,000 in today's dollars.

Some whites sympathized with their black neighbors, particularly the Quakers, who donated clothing to blacks, helped educate their children, and found volunteers to aid the freedmen. Some local ministers preached in favor of abolition, driving Heffren to distraction. After sitting through an abolitionist sermon at the Methodist church on Thanksgiving 1862, Heffren thundered in an editorial, "Such preachers assume the place (and well do they fill it) of Annanias [Ananias, a liar in Acts 5:5]. They preach rebellion, negro equality and all its horrors and gradually bring the public mind as far up to their standard as possible."[27]

Heffren's racism probably reflected the majority view. Many of those who settled Washington County had come from slave states. In 1860 about a quarter of Salem's 1,370 residents were not born in Indiana, of these half came from slave states. They were not slaveholders, and they did not want to compete with black labor, and the Indiana Constitution of 1851 suited them perfectly: It prohibited slavery, and it prohibited any black or mulatto from settling in Indiana after 1851.[28]

At the same time southern Indiana's economy and geography bound it to the slave states, with the major trading center of Louisville, Kentucky, only thirty-three miles away from Washington County. At a public meeting just before the war the Washington County Democratic Party laid out this position with remarkable frankness. In February 1861 it approved a resolution that said Indiana's "commercial, agricultural, mechanical and manufacturing interests" were "fostered chiefly by the South." While the party abhorred the idea of secession, it took a practical view of the crisis. If secession was inevitable, "the line of division must run north of us."[29]

At the start of the war, men from Indiana flocked to enlist in the Union army, but soon military defeats, economic woes, and Lincoln's suspension of habeas corpus caused second thoughts. And then came the Emancipation Proclamation. It was denounced at political rallies, and army officers resigned their commissions, desertions shot up, and enlistments stagnated.[30]

Not surprisingly, newspaper editor Heffren greeted the Emancipation Proclamation as if it were the Black Death. He opposed freeing the slaves because, "We all know the brutish nature of the Negro slave. Do we expect that the mothers, sisters and daughters of southern men would be safe from continued outrage and insult?" And worst of all, he feared that blacks in the United States would gain equal standing with whites. "We speak what we know, when we say there are thousands upon thousands in Indiana and the North who would rather see the Southern Confederacy recognized than the slaves freed and turned loose amongst us."[31]

What exactly the Emancipation Proclamation meant for Washington County's blacks can be glimpsed in two brief items Heffren inserted in the *Salem Democrat*. According to the first story, from 1862,

Some of the big greasy buck niggers of Salem, since Lincoln's proclamation have been putting on airs. They get drunk insult both men and women, both steal, carouse and play the devil generally. Three even threatened to shoot a white man the other night, but got themselves decently thrashed for their impudence. There are some who attend to their own business, but there are three or four by the name of William Lucas, Dave Cloud and Rey Jackson, the oil of hickory would be of great benefit to if the truth is told on them, and we think it would be hard to tell anything else.[32]

The other item appeared in August 1863. "Dave Cloud, a 'free American of African descent,' was considerably injured by coming in contact with a half brick last Thursday evening."[33] It was becoming very dangerous to be a black in Washington County.

Just how dangerous became clear in October 1864 when the Quakers noticed that nearly all the blacks had left. Sometime between the attack on Dave Cloud and the autumn of 1864, there was a racial cleansing. During this period, two blacks, both prosperous and with substantial ties to the community, were murdered. And then the remaining blacks left.

Over the next few decades at least three sources would confirm what the Quakers had diplomatically described as an "increase of prejudice." In 1893, the black Indianapolis newspaper *The World* published a front-page story about places in Indiana, such as Salem, where "The Negro Dare Not Lay His Head."[34]

Shortly after the war there was a large settlement at Salem, and some of the members became quite wealthy, notably an old man named Williams. For some reasons, Williams who had large deposits in the Salem bank, drew out his money, consisting of several thousand dollars, taking it out in gold. On the night of the withdrawal, he was shot down while near his home, and money was stolen by the murderers. Immediately after this the entire colored population was driven out and since then none has been permitted to settle within the borders of that county.[35]

The article contains some errors. A well-to-do African-American blacksmith named John Williams was indeed murdered, but he was killed in December 1864, four months before the war ended. He did not withdraw his money from the bank, and in fact he left it to the Quakers for the education of black children.

A year later, a local historian, Elias Hicks Trueblood, writing about the underground railroad, notes that Washington County once had "fifty families of colored folk in and around Salem," then adds, "It is not our purpose in these articles to call up the changed condition, except as it may have a bearing on other matters we shall write. That persecution, intimidation and all manner of ill treatment was used against them is not doubted and from these causes they sought homes elsewhere."[36]

Trueblood does not say who was persecuting the blacks or why. He is silent about what this "ill treatment" consisted of. Nor does he explain what prompted such treatment. But thirty years after the event, he is very clear about one thing: Persecution forced blacks to leave.

Only in 1934, a full seven decades after the events, did a careful examination of the causes of the persecution and expulsion appear in print. In a story about John Williams's murder, another Washington County historian named Trueblood, Lillian D. Trueblood, wrote,

> A strong feeling against negroes existed among the pro-slavery element of Washington County during and just after the Civil War. Following the Emancipation Proclamation, this element felt sure that negroes would receive citizenship to which they were deeply opposed. Impelled by the heat of the situation, they proposed to destroy the colored people who would not leave the neighborhood.[37]

This final account at last describes how blacks were threatened and gives a reason for the expulsion. The Quakers said the blacks left following "difficulties." Elias Trueblood expanded this to "ill treatment." *The World* said they were "driven out." But now Lillian Trueblood describes the exact nature of the threat: "they proposed to destroy the colored people." The blacks of Washington County fled for their lives and, as the *World* story shows, thirty years later, blacks were still warning one another about Washington County. They had seen the racial cleansing, they had heard of the murder of a black who resisted, and they drew the only reasonable conclusion: A black unlucky enough to be in Washington County risked death. A racial cleansing drove blacks out and kept them out. In this the whites of Washington County had succeeded.

Lillian Trueblood's account is important because it gives a reason for the expulsion. Whites feared that blacks "would receive citizenship." It is on its face an implausible, irrational fear. Even if every black man, woman, and child in Washington County counted in the 1860 census was handed the vote, they would hardly have represented a political force then or in the foreseeable future. There were 187 blacks living in a county of 17,900 souls. Whites outnumbered blacks ninety-five to one.

There, was, however, one man who could have explained why it was so important for whites to drive out their black neighbors. As a politician, lawyer, historian, and keen observer of life in Washington County, Horace Heffren was uniquely qualified to make sense of what was happening. But in the cool autumn of 1864, as he sat in front of a military tribunal, guarded by Union soldiers and surrounded by fellow conspirators, Heffren was far more interested in cheating the hangman.

It could not have been pleasant for Heffren to sit quietly in an Indianapolis courtroom listening to his former confederate, J. J. Grundy, aka Felix Stidger. Within minutes of taking the stand, Stidger described Heffren eagerly awaiting news from Kentucky about rebel forces, his warnings about "United States Detectives," and Heffren's role as a leader of the Sons of Liberty. A year earlier in an editorial lambasting the tyranny of the Lincoln administration, Heffren had counseled his readers to "meet the grim monster death" rather than submit to tyranny. But after listening to Stidger's devastating testimony, Heffren now saw another alternative. In the middle of the trial, Heffren turned state's evidence and "peached" on his fellow conspirators. For his cooperation, he would get off scot-free.[38]

But Heffren, ever the opportunist, tried to have it both ways. While acknowledging the obvious—he had been a member of the Sons of Liberty—he tried to portray himself on the witness stand as an innocent who, once he learned of the group's treasonable plans, had quit the conspiracy. Heffren told the court that in February 1864 he and two other members concluded "the whole concern was a humbug and not worth a damn . . . and agreed to have nothing more to do with the order."[39] The tactic might have worked except that evidence kept turning up that Heffren was an active member after he had supposedly quit.

There was, for example, a letter signed by Heffren in September 1864, seven months after he said he'd quit, to the other officers of the Sons of Liberty asking what the group should do about the arrest of Harrison Dodd, the leader of the conspiracy. He also acknowledged on the stand that, in the weeks after he said he had washed his hands of the Sons of Liberty, he was busy organizing new chapters and inducting members. Years later Stidger still could not understand why the prosecutors had let Heffren turn state's evidence.[40]

In all of the damning testimony about Heffren's role, however, there was one brief anecdote that sheds more light on the Washington County expulsion. It came on the first day of Stidger's testimony and passed almost unnoticed. As Stidger described his first visit to Salem, he mentioned meeting Simon Drom, the clothing store owner. Stidger recalled Drom saying that Heffren wore a pin to show his support for the Confederacy. If anyone tried to take the pin away, Drom said, "there would have been 1,000 or 1,500 men ready to revenge the insult." Later that day Heffren boasted to Stidger that "he could call together within 24 hours from 1,000 to 1,500 armed men" in the county. The meaning was clear. Heffren, who championed slavery and considered blacks sub-human, was also the leader of what he apparently considered his own personal army—the Sons of Liberty.[41]

Heffren was a braggart, but this boast to Stidger has the ring of authenticity. As a Democratic Party leader he had a long history of organizing meetings, rallies, and political campaigns. And Heffren himself testified that he had personally inducted at least twenty or thirty men into the local chapter of the Sons of Liberty during 1864.[42] As head of the local chapter as well as a statewide officer, he was a leader in an organization that was buying weapons and preparing its members for combat. The numbers may or may not be inflated, but the idea that Heffren led a band of armed locals is not only plausible but likely.

If Heffren was indeed acting as a warlord, the timing and description of the racial cleansing begins to make more sense. Lillian Trueblood said the people who attacked the blacks were the pro-slavery element who feared "that negroes would receive citizenship." Her description fits Heffren perfectly. She also said they "proposed to destroy the colored people who would not leave the neighborhood." Again, Heffren's credentials as a bully were well established during his brief military career, and at the time of the expulsion he had an armed force at his disposal. But it is the timing of the cleansing that is especially interesting. Trueblood writes, "Following the Emancipation Proclamation, this element felt sure that negroes would receive citizenship." But the Quakers place the community's destruction sometime in late 1863 or 1864. The Emancipation Proclamation was announced in 1862 and became effective at the beginning of 1863. Why wait a year to drive the blacks out? Again we turn to Heffren's own account of those days. He says he was inducted into the secret society in the fall of 1863. Allowing for some time to get his chapter organized, it would have been in late 1863 or 1864 before he could have fielded a secret band of night riders.

As intriguing as the timing may be, it still does not explain Heffren's motives. Trueblood said those responsible for the racial cleansing were angry that blacks would receive citizenship. Yet Heffren the politician could count votes as well if not better than the next man and there were simply too few blacks to make any difference in an election. That is, of course, if one only considers voting as a political act. In fact, as the history of voting makes clear, it is far more than that.

There is an odd thing about the United States Constitution. It starts off grandly with "We the people" but nowhere does it say who these "people" are. As close as it gets is Section 2 of Article 1, which says that in choosing candidates for the House of Representatives "the Electors in each state shall have the Qualifications requisite for the Electors of the most numerous Branch of the State Legislature." In other words, the federal Constitution tosses the ball to the states. They would decide who constituted "the people."

For the white people of Washington County in 1864 this raised a ticklish question. If they understood the Emancipation Proclamation correctly, not only were men like Dave Cloud "free Americans," they could eventually be voters. And if they voted, they were by definition part of "the people" along with every other man in town including Horace Heffren. In other words, once Dave Cloud got the right to vote, he and Horace Heffren were social equals. Now that was something to think about.

Behind this uncomfortable prospect stood the evolving idea of what constituted "the people." In England the vote had originally been reserved for property owners, a formula borrowed by colonial America. But over time America radically reworked this idea. Who should vote shifted from extrinsic values such as property to measures of intrinsic worth. Adult white males, for example, were believed to be imbued with uncommon good sense. Finally, there was really only one good argument against giving someone the vote: That person's worth was somehow lacking or damaged, if he or she was morally or intellectually incompetent. Children cannot vote because they may not yet be able to form judgments necessary to making an informed choice. Convicted felons in some states cannot vote because they are considered morally damaged.[43]

Thus, the issue facing the whites of Washington County was whether they believed that Dave Cloud and his fellow blacks had the intrinsic worth to be part of the people. The same question would arise repeatedly all across America in the next decades and it would be answered in a similar fashion. For men like Horace Heffren, the answer was obvious. Blacks, who were not worthwhile people, did not belong socially and, to drive home that point, they would not belong physically.

What happened then in Washington County was an echo of the Dred Scott decision seven years before. Chief Justice Roger Taney had said that blacks were not citizens, and, no matter who won the Civil War, men like Horace Heffren clung to that belief. In time other elements would help fuel America's racial cleansings. Segregation would foster racial alienation, white paranoia, and a sense that blacks were dispensable. At other times, the economic threat posed by low-wage blacks would drive an expulsion. But as important as these other factors were, whatever happened always took place against the backdrop of citizenship. In Washington County it was important to drive out blacks who one day might become voters and, by extension, members of the community. But in time southern states through different strategies allowed blacks to stay while refusing them the vote, confirming precisely what Chief Justice Taney had said: This was white man's country. And, if for some reason, it was inconvenient to have blacks around, they could be dispensed with. Negroes were not citizens.

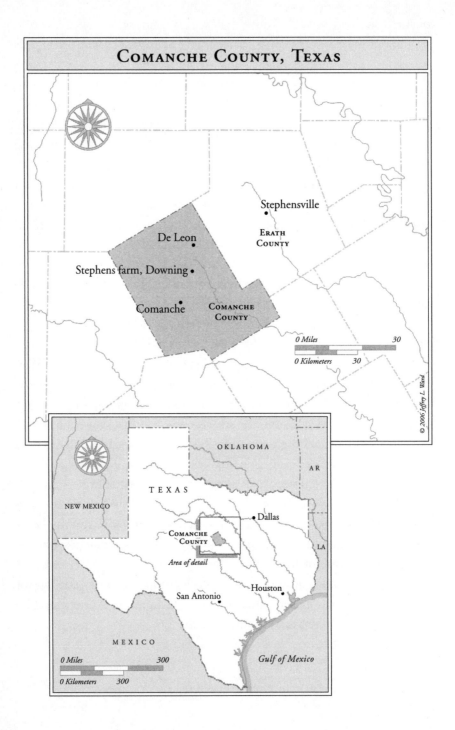

COMANCHE COUNTY, TEXAS

Stephensville

ERATH
COUNTY

De Leon

Stephens farm, Downing

Comanche

COMANCHE
COUNTY

0 Miles   30
0 Kilometers   30

© 2006 Jeffrey L. Ward

OKLAHOMA

AR

TEXAS

NEW MEXICO

Dallas

COMANCHE
COUNTY

Area of detail

LA

Houston

San Antonio

MEXICO

0 Miles   300
0 Kilometers   300

Gulf of Mexico

CHAPTER 2

McNeel's Feet

Comanche County, Texas
1886

"What's a nigger?"

Nicole Harlmon was puzzled. The other kids in her grade school in Comanche, Texas had taunted her with the word, warning everyone not to get too close. But she didn't know what it meant. They just shouted it and ran away. So Nicole did what any little girl would do. She went home and asked her mother, Evelyn Young.[1]

"The next time one of the kids calls you a nigger," Ms. Young told Nicole, "just ask them to spell it for you. And if they can't spell it, they don't know what it is. But don't blame them. It's not them who's really talking. It's the adults."[2]

Ms. Young knew all about the adults. When she found herself stranded in Comanche in 1983 with two kids and no husband, she soon learned just how hard life could be there. As one of her friends said, "Comanche is a hard town when you are black."[3]

A few nights after Evelyn Young moved there, she took her two daughters to the local store. Inside were two white woman, one behind the counter and the other shopping.

One of the white girls made the remark that there are two things I hate: and that's wetbacks and niggers. And the lady that was running the store just kind of laughed about it and of course I grabbed my daughters—Talila had just turned a year old and Nicole was like three. So I grabbed Nicole's hand and I picked up Talila and took them over to the chip counter and I tried to get them to ignore what the girls were saying. The lady walked over behind us and said it again and I just kind of turned around to her and told her, "You know you had better be careful what you hate because, if you check your family history, you may have some niggers or wetbacks swinging from some of your branches." She didn't like that at all.[4]

It wasn't until Ms. Young called home shortly after she arrived that she found out the truth about both the town and the county, which is also named Comanche. "When I first got there, I didn't know the history," she said. "My grandmother told me that years ago they had come through Comanche and saw some signs that said, 'Niggers don't let the sun go down on you.'"[5]

The Young family had unknowingly become the first black family in recent memory to move to Comanche County.

———

There had been an argument on the drought-stricken Stephens farm the summer morning in 1886 when Sallie Stephens was murdered. Sallie's husband, Ben, was going to the nearby town of Comanche, and Tom McNeel, the black teenage farmhand, understandably wanted to go along. During that summer the farms in Comanche County were burning to death. The relentless sun, which had already killed the cotton crop and the family gardens, was now scourging the livestock. The town of Comanche—two saloons, a few stores, and the county courthouse—was not much, but it must have seemed like it would be paradise after the tedium of fieldwork in the unremitting heat. McNeel begged to go, but Ben Stephens would not hear of it. Stephens hitched up his wagon and left, and Tom went back to work in the fields.[6]

What happened next is surmise because the only people left on the farm after the murder were the Stephens's three children, and the oldest, their daughter Doan, was only six. Most accounts agree that Sallie, who planned to make a cake for a friend's wedding, headed to the barn to get some eggs. At about the same time, McNeel came in from the fields, entered the house, and took down a single-barreled shotgun. The story passed down within the Hulsey and Stephens families is that McNeel waited by the back steps, Sallie saw him, tried to run away, and was shot in the back. The local papers simply said she was found shot in the back. The newspapers in Waco and Austin made the crime more lurid by saying McNeel had first tried to rape a pregnant Mrs. Stephens then killed her.[7]

However it happened, McNeel killed Sallie Stephens, dropped the gun, and ran. When neighbors found the body, a man rushed to the J. W. Greene store, where Sallie's husband was buying supplies, and cried, "Stephens, Tom has killed your wife!" Within hours between 250 and 500 men were hunting McNeel. Their quarry, alone and on foot, was pressing northeast toward Stephenville, gambling he could slip past his pursuers and out of the county.[8]

It was a simple murder, something all too common on the Texas frontier. In normal times McNeel would be caught and lynched, and there it would end. The lynching would have little to do with the fact that McNeel was black. On the lawless frontier, lynching was remarkably colorblind, and it was what passed for justice.

But this time race would matter, and the lynching would prove to be a prelude to something much more destructive. When he killed Sallie Stephens, Tom McNeel unwittingly raised the issue of black citizenship. It was the same question that the white people of Washington County, Indiana had struggled with during the Civil War. Were former slaves part of the community? How do we treat them? What are their rights? McNeel's irrational action forced the question.[9]

America in 1886 still had not found a safe harbor after years of tacking back and forth on how to treat its ex-slaves. Opposition to freeing the slaves—so evident in Indiana—had given way to a more difficult question: What was to be done with them? During Reconstruction they were full citizens, and southern whites rebelled. Night riders, Klansmen, and simple thuggery had made their point. But after federal troops were withdrawn in 1876, there was even more confusion. Should blacks be served dinner in a restaurant, allowed to ride with whites on a train, allowed to vote, and be treated the same way as white laborers? In Comanche County evidence of this confusion was easy to see. All you had to do was look at Tom McNeel's feet.

One account of the Stephens murder mentions a seemingly inconsequential detail. When McNeel dropped the gun and ran across the fields, he was barefoot. It seems unimportant until you walk a short distance across the Comanche County cemetery where Sallie Stephens is buried. The sandy soil of the graveyard, like the soil around much of Comanche County, is perfect for the sandbur. At every step small burrs from this weed seem to leap from the ground and cling to your clothes. Every burr is, in fact, a small ball of spines with each spine barbed like a fishhook. Try to pick them off, and they dig into your fingers. Try to knock them off your hands, and inevitably a spine will remain behind to burrow into your flesh. If you are wearing shoes, they are an annoyance. In bare feet, imagine a field of broken glass.[10]

With his feet bare, however, Tom McNeel ran across fifteen miles of Comanche County carpeted with burrs and nettles before he was caught. Even though he was running for his life, there is only one reason he could have covered that distance: McNeel *never* wore shoes. He went off to work in the fields that morning barefoot, and he was barefoot as he stalked Sallie. His feet were so callused, he could cross the Texas plains and, for two days, outwit men on horseback hunting him down.

But what did it mean that McNeel was barefoot? One of the things ex-slaves remembered about their captivity no matter where they were held was that they did not have shoes. "No sir, I never seen a pair of shoes until long after freedom," one former slave recalled. "I had on brown trousers and blue shirt when I married with great big bandana handkerchief around my neck, no shoes, no sir, I was barefooted. Negroes never wore shoes in them days." Another ex-slave remembered bitterly, "No shoes or socks. In winter occasionally the men would wear shoes but never the women or children."[11]

If slaves went barefoot, shoes were the mark of freedom. "I didn't knowd what shoes was on my own feet. I used to see white chillens with shoes and stockings and I wanted shoes and stockings. I 'members I got a pair of shoes and stockings when I was free. They was given to me. They was new, the stockings was."[12]

Slavery had been abolished twenty years earlier, but the Stephens family was still allowing its black farmhand to work without shoes. It was not that they were cruel or uncaring. In fact, McNeel himself later said his victim had been "best kind to me." But the Stephens's kindness was predicated on the conventions of what was being called the New South. In that world a black farmhand who went barefoot would be paid for his labor but still carried the mark of slavery. Was he slave or citizen?[13]

For McNeel the question was pointless now. Whatever his status, if he was found he would be lynched. But it was a more complicated matter for his fellow blacks. Their fate would be determined by the answer. Citizens had a right to stay in Comanche County while non-citizens could be dispensed with.

After the Civil War, far more pressing than the political question of citizenship for blacks was the simple, practical, and overwhelmingly important problem for whites of who would pick the cotton. If the crops were not planted and harvested, the South was doomed. Former slaves seemed the obvious answer, but their labor had been built on slavery, one of whose central tenets was that blacks would not work without physical compulsion. Some farmers sent their former slaves away and went looking for Europeans. Germans and Dutch were especially prized as racially sound workers. In one of those wonderful moments when a loony racial theory slips on the banana peel of reality, a South Carolina farmer hired Dutch workers. "They cost me $35 each to bring to Charleston from New York. I fed them far better that ever I thought of feeding my hands, even gave them coffee and sourkrout [sic], when, what should they do but demand butter for their bread and milk for their coffee, and the next thing the whole crowd left me."[14]

When the plan to replace blacks with Europeans fizzled, the focus turned to the former slaves. In 1865 and 1866 every southern state rushed through a series of laws that forced blacks back to work, the infamous Black Codes. While details varied from state to state, the laws rested on the proposition that blacks had to enter into labor contracts with whites; not to do so violated the law.[15]

Mississippi, the first state to enact Black Codes, made sure that freedmen would be landless by making it a crime for blacks to own, rent, or lease land outside of towns or cities. Having guaranteed a class of landless black peons, Mississippi whites then ordered that every black had to have proof of lawful employment. Idle blacks, which is to say those people without contracts, were defined as vagrants who could then be fined for their idleness. Blacks who did not pay the fine could be hired out at an auction and forced to work until they had paid off their debts. The postwar auction block was not quite the antebellum slave market, but it served the same purpose.[16]

Texas, which enacted its Black Codes in the fall of 1866, designed them as one observer described it to "make the Negro useful to society and subordinate to the white race" and required blacks to have a contract if the job they were working on lasted more than a month. Once under contract, laborers were at the mercy of their employers, who could fine them for everything from sickness to "idleness." If workers missed three consecutive days, they lost a year's wages. Employers could also be fined for hiring a worker already under contract to another employer. In addition, anyone convicted of vagrancy could be forced to work on public projects.[17]

One of the legends about the Texas Black Codes is that they were absolutely necessary because "Texas plantations were being overgrown with weeds." But the timing of their adoption suggests another motive. The 1866 cotton crop—at 359,000 bales—was a modest sixteen percent below prewar levels. After the harvest, the *Houston Telegraph* bragged, "Every station on the Central and Washington County railroads are [sic] crowded with cotton bales, and the railroads cannot ship it off as fast as it comes for want of sufficient rolling stock." Yet it was after this relatively successful crop, brought in by freed black labor, that Texas imposed the Black Codes. Under them, cotton yields reached prewar levels four years later, in 1870.[18]

White Texans touted the Black Codes as economic policy, but it is obvious they were also intended as an instrument of social control. It did not matter that the 1866 cotton crop was brought in with free black labor that worked without the goad of the Black Codes. What was important to whites was to reaffirm the belief that the Negro must be forced to work. The Black Codes did that. They also ensured that blacks would remain landless, dependent, and subordinate. As one of the delegates to the Texas Constitutional Convention put it, blacks had to remain "hewers of wood and drawers of water."[19]

For the North, which thought it had abolished slavery when it won the war, the Black Codes were seen for what they were: an attempt to continue slavery by other means. The codes could not be allowed to stand. In some southern states, federal officials overseeing Reconstruction efforts overruled state officials. In Mississippi and Alabama, state governors, realizing the Black Codes were a political blunder, abolished the worst parts of the laws. And in Congress the Black Codes spurred legislators to pass the Civil Rights Bill of 1866 and later the 14th Amendment, which overturned the Dred Scott decision and unequivocally granted citizenship to African-Americans.

But while the Black Codes did not survive as law, they continued as informal policy. With the end of Reconstruction in 1876, whites quickly created legal and extra-legal devices, such as convict labor and peonage, to fulfill the intent of the Black Codes and continue slavery by economic means. And it followed that, if blacks were stripped of their economic rights, it was only a matter of time before they lost their political rights. In fact, southern lawmakers would begin the campaign to strip blacks of their voting rights in 1890, and the U.S. Supreme Court would give its blessing to segregation in 1896. Who would pick the cotton had answered the question of who would be a citizen.

And what Tom McNeel amply demonstrated was that the future was at hand. As he loped across the drought-scorched fields toward what he thought was his salvation, McNeel represented the policy's success:

landless, a menial laborer, and, as his bare feet showed, little better than a slave.

Any murder is terrifying, but murder without motive is especially frightening. Absent motive and until the killer is caught, everyone is a target. Which may be why the killing of Sallie Stephens so rocked the community. There seemed to be no reason for Tom McNeel killing Sallie Stephens. Worse still, it echoed another murderous rampage. Years earlier and without warning, a black man in Comanche named Mose Jones had also turned on whites.[20]

In one of those odd twists of fate, we can read the details of what happened from those who were there. Their stories were captured in the 1940s by Billy Bob Lightfoot, a graduate student who was collecting oral histories for his master's thesis at the University of Texas. One of those he interviewed was Jim Nabers, one of the children who survived the attack by Jones. Nabers, who was then ninety-two, began his story in the flat, unadorned style of the Texas frontier. "My two brothers, Joe and Fleet, were murdered by a Negro called Mose."[21]

Up until the day of the attack, Mose Jones had been known for his studied deference to whites. "When he met whites, he at once held his hat against his breast and bowed and spoke with deep humility," one woman recalled. His obedience was, no doubt, a product of his upbringing. Born in 1830, Jones had been a slave most of his life. He had been owned by the Carnes family before the war and, following his emancipation, chose to remain in the county. He had a wife, two sons, a daughter, and a step-daughter, and he found work with one of the town's leading citizens, T. J. "Uncle Jack" Nabers. No one suspected that, beneath the elaborate manners, there was homicidal rage.[22]

When his wife died sometime in the 1870s, Jones became obsessed with marrying his fourteen-year-old stepdaughter. When she refused, he supposedly made "improper advances." Rebuffed again, he threatened the girl. The girl complained to Mrs. Nabers, who in turn tried to reason with Jones. The ex-slave showed his customary deference to a white woman, but the talk was fruitless. The next day she came upon Jones holding his step-daughter by the hair with one hand and waving a butcher knife with the other.[23]

"Mose, what do you mean?"

"I was just a playing," he told Mrs. Nabers as he released the girl.

The following morning Mrs. Nabers was awakened by banging in the kitchen. One of Jones's chores was to draw water and build the morning fire to make breakfast. He was up earlier than usual, but, aside from that, it seemed like a normal morning. Then Mrs. Nabers heard a crackling fire and smoke began filling the house. She raced for the kitchen, but the dining room door was blocked.[24]

What happened next is not clear, but Mrs. Nabers and her husband were able to escape. Others were not so lucky.

Jones had cut the rope to the well so there would be no water to put out the fire. To prevent anyone from getting to the kitchen, he blocked the door with benches from the dining room. He then ladled lard from a bucket—the banging sound Mrs. Nabers heard—and smeared it on the walls to make the house burn quickly. Using an axe he bludgeoned two of the Nabers children and finally murdered both his daughter and the object of his obsession, the step-daughter.[25]

When Mrs. Nabers realized the house was on fire and cried for help, Jones ran off. But it was only a matter of time before he was found. By chance, Nabers was there when it happened. "The next morning we were still hunting the Negro. Finally he stepped out on the road just as Hode Carnes was riding by with another fellow. Hode killed him."[26]

Now, as the posse, sweating and cursing, rode through the brush and searched along the sun-baked river beds for Tom McNeel, a terrible question was beginning to form in their minds: Was it too dangerous to have blacks living among us?

McNeel's capture was anticlimactic. As he emerged from a swamp, he was found by a man heading to church. Where exactly he was captured is unclear. Four different accounts give four different locations. When he was captured is also in dispute. One account says in the morning and another in the evening. But once captured, a county with a long history of lynching people, regardless of race, did the unexpected. It waited.[27]

It was not that anyone was uncertain about what to do. All accounts agree that the vigilantes wanted to take McNeel back to Downing and execute him on the spot where he had murdered Sallie Stephens. But unlike other lynchings, the killing of Tom McNeel was to be a public event. To ensure as large a crowd as possible, the lynching was delayed to Monday noon.[28]

A public lynching was unusual. The pattern in other vigilante hangings was to kill anonymously. The oral histories that Lightfoot collected are laced with accounts of masked men appearing in the night to drag off their victims. Tom Conaway, who grew up in the county, told Lightfoot about a lynching he and his brother witnessed as children in 1882. The sheriff arrested two brothers, who were accused of stealing cotton, and was bringing them back for trial in the town of Comanche when he stopped in Hazel Dell for the night. Conaway's mother made the party supper while the brothers were guarded in an old store. At nine that night, out of a driving rain, vigilantes in black slickers and wearing masks rode up and demanded the guards turn over their prisoners.[29]

"The younger boy about sixteen years of age started crying," Conaway said. "His older brother begged the mob to let him go. However, they didn't."[30]

The youths were led to their deaths and Conaway told Lightfoot that even after all the years, "I can still hear the younger boy crying."[31]

There were practical reasons for anonymity. One possibility was that the law might step in and try to punish the vigilantes. A month before McNeel was captured, William Pruitt, a white man, had been lynched in the county simply because he talked about some vigilantes he recognized from an earlier incident. When Pruitt was killed, the county attorney announced he was going to try and find the man's killers.[32]

Being caught by the law was unfortunate. But being caught by the victim's friends or family, who themselves wanted revenge, could be far worse. As one murder avenged another, the bodies quickly piled up. In 1839 when vigilantes were identified after a lynching on the border with Louisiana in Shelby County, there were revenge killings. Those murders, in turn, spawned a feud that, at its height, involved hundreds of men. It did not end until 1844 and was so ferocious that it was dubbed the Regulator-Moderator War.[33]

Lynching a black teenager, by comparison, was risk free. There is no record of Tom McNeel having any family or friends living nearby. By one account he was an orphan. And no one seriously considered that in a county of about 8,600 people the small black community—with less than a hundred people—would be capable of retaliating. It was equally unlikely that any sheriff or county prosecutor would try to hold a white mob accountable for killing a black accused of a horrific crime. During Reconstruction whites had murdered blacks as a way to intimidate other blacks into peonage or simply to "thin the niggers out." Now whites were both avenging a murder and sending a message to blacks about who was in charge. It was critical that the execution be as public as possible.[34]

McNeel was brought back Sunday from neighboring Erath County, through DeLeon, a town just north of Downing. He was held in chains overnight at the farm of Green Sanders, a local farmer and Confederate veteran. The next morning farmers and townspeople began streaming past the Downing graveyard to the Stephens farm. By about noon approximately 750 people had collected there. Even as they assembled, debate was raging. Jim Nabers, who had seen his two brothers murdered by Mose Jones, wanted McNeel burned alive. Sallie's husband, Ben, wild with grief, had to be stopped several times from shooting McNeel before he could be publicly executed. It ultimately fell to the murdered woman's father, Zack Hulsey, to decide how McNeel would die. Overruling Nabers and others, Hulsey said, "Now, boys, the laws of our land say hanging and not burning. So we'll just hang him."[35]

At about the time Hulsey decided how the youth would die, Deputy Sheriff D. W. Cox arrived. Unaware that McNeel had been captured, Sheriff John Cunningham was still out searching. That left Cox with the unenviable job of trying to wrest McNeel from the mob. By all accounts the hapless deputy did his best. He told the crowd that district court would be held in only three weeks. He argued that there was little chance McNeel would not be executed. He personally pledged to make sure McNeel would not escape. The crowd laughed. Green Sanders, who had guarded McNeel overnight, told the deputy his services were not needed. According to one account, Cox then "bade them a pleasant good evening" and rode away.[36]

A rope was thrown over a tree. McNeel was placed in a wagon and driven underneath. With only seconds to go, Hulsey turned to his daughter's killer for help in trying to make sense of what had happened.[37]

"Tom, We're gonna hang you, and in two or three minutes you'll be dead. I want to ask you some questions, and you'll be dead in three or four minutes so it won't do you no good to lie."

"Yes, suh," replied McNeel.

"Tom, did Sallie mistreat you?" Hulsey asked.

"No, suh," Tom said. "She's the best kind to me."

Did he plan to kill her?

"No, I took down the gun when I came into the house to kill a hawk but it flew off and I then shot the lady."

"Then what in the name of God did you kill her for?"

"Just for meanness."

For Hulsey it was too much. Someone asked McNeel if he wanted to pray. The teenager asked for a minister to help him. Hulsey snapped. "I can't hear no more! He didn't give my daughter time to pray! Pull him up!"

They botched the hanging.

Men in the wagon pushed McNeel out while another group yanked on the rope. They pulled so hard that McNeel's body went hurtling skyward, his head slammed into the tree limb holding the rope, the branch broke, and McNeel fell back to earth. A teenager climbed the tree, reset the rope, and McNeel was pulled up again and strangled to death.

It should have ended with the corpse in the tree. That was what people had come to see. For the last few days the county had been consumed with finding and killing McNeel. If there had been talk of punishing all blacks, no account mentions it. But as McNeel's body hung above the crowd, Green Sanders shouted to be heard. It was like a rock breaking glass.

There is nothing in Sanders's past to suggest he would play a pivotal role in the county's history. Born in Louisiana in 1847, he enlisted in the Confederate army in October 1864 five months shy of his eighteenth birthday. He was assigned to Company E of the 38th North Carolina Infantry, which at the time was trying desperately to hold a line of trenches around Petersburg, Virginia. A teenager going off to war, even a war that was clearly lost, could see it as a great adventure. But his descendants remember Green Sanders as an ornery man. Leo

Page, his last living descendant in Comanche County, says that his great-grandfather is remembered in the family as someone who would "fight a circle saw." Whether out of adventure or belligerency, he joined a unit that had been shattered at the Battle of Gettysburg and fought with an army in its death throes. Six months after he joined, the war was over.[38]

Following the war, Sanders married a woman ten years his senior and moved to Texas. It appears he prospered. By 1880 he had five children and owned a farm in Comanche County. It may be that he settled down. Still the picture that emerges is of someone abrupt and uncomfortable. Along with his prickly personality, he is remembered for his maxim that "Short visits make long friends." When his first wife died in 1900, he remarried and then two and a half years later divorced. He took a third wife in 1914 but left her little in his will when he died in 1919. Aside from his role in the lynching of Tom McNeel, he is remembered for little else.[39]

The lynching seemed to have energized Green Sanders. He had guarded the doomed youth before the lynching, faced down a deputy sheriff, and now, as McNeel's body hung lifeless in a tree, he jumped on a stump so he could be seen and heard.

"Boys, this is the second killing of white people by Negroes and it's more than people will put up with. I propose we give the Negroes a reasonable time to get out of this county—never allow them to return—and never allow one of color to settle here. All who are in favor of my proposition come about this stump."[40]

The crowd surged forward, and Sanders called for a vote. Nabers would later recall that "the crowd was unanimously in favor of this move." The Comanche newspaper reported that Sanders assembled a force of several hundred men outside of town that night and then, after dark, rode into town. This huge force delivered its ultimatum to the forty or so blacks living in Comanche and a similar number living around the county by going to each home. The message was simple. All blacks had to be gone in ten days.

The expulsion order had an unexpected result: It ripped the white community apart.

As the mob rode into Comanche Tuesday evening, it was met by Frank Sherrill. Sherrill and Nabers had pushed earlier in the day to have McNeel burned alive. Now Sherrill offered to point out for the mob where the blacks lived in town. Sherrill's offer says a lot about relations between blacks and whites at that time. In another few decades American society would become rigidly segregated. Negroes would be penned into ghettos in the cities and restricted to "little Africas" and "darktowns" in rural areas. But as the 1880 census rolls show, Comanche County's blacks lived wherever they wanted to. Generally they lived close to where they worked. Anyone wanting to intimidate the town's blacks would need a guide to take them to the different homes.[41]

Sherrill's offer is also a clue about the nature of the split that was about to develop in the county. Only about 700 people actually lived in the town of Comanche. In a town that small, just about anyone would have known exactly where to find the black families. That means Sherrill's offer only makes sense if the mob consisted mostly of farmers who went to town infrequently. These farmers, who had little or no contact with blacks, wanted to drive them away.

But townspeople, who lived with blacks, were adamantly opposed to the expulsion. The Comanche newspaper, *Town and Country*, which hit the streets on Thursday, denounced mob rule and the expulsion of blacks. "They [the mob] have been misled by the promptings of an outraged feeling into committing an act which civilization looks upon as a grave crime." In a front-page editorial, the paper reminded readers that blacks had worked alongside whites to found the county. "What connection is there between [McNeel] and the rest of the race in this community and especially those who are known to be as harmless as the most inoffensive white man?" the editor asked.[42]

Community leaders were also incensed. The day after the mob issued its ultimatum, fifty-five people including some of the town's leading citizens called a mass meeting at the courthouse. In what was to become known as the Law and Order Meeting, townspeople debated whether "ordering all the negroes in the town to leave the county is approved or condemned by this community." The resolution that was unanimously adopted read in part, "we regard the demonstration in the town of Comanche on last night in ordering the negro population out of the county as uncalled for, wrong, and lawless."[43]

If the ultimatum opened a rift between the town and the surrounding farms, it also exposed the personal ties that had developed between the races. Because blacks were scattered around the town, they were an everyday presence in the lives of whites. Now that they were being forced to leave, their white friends and employers were in a quandary because they relied on their black neighbors.

Businessmen faced the loss of valuable employees. Marthia Hanson, recently widowed, desperately needed the help of her hired hand. Mart Fleming, who ran a butcher shop, told the aged Horace Mercer and Dallas Dabness he would defend them if they wanted to stay. Dr. Paine balked at being forced to send his maid packing.[44]

In some cases white families were raising black children. *Town and Country* ran a small article shortly after the ultimatum.

> Mr. E. B. Riley lives a few miles to the northward of this place. Four years ago a negro woman died at his house leaving an infant. Mr. Riley and wife took care of it and have kept it up to this time. In the last week he has been warned several times that he must take that four-year-old child out of the county or risk the consequences. Mr. Riley, not knowing what to do, came to town for advice. The only advice that can be given in such a case consistent with justice and liberty is to keep the child and defend his rights with shotguns if necessary.[45]

The Streety family in DeLeon faced a similar problem. Their black servant had died soon after childbirth and the Streetys were caring for the dead woman's baby. Will Streety, a prominent businessman, was unwilling to bow to the mob's demands, but he faced a mathematical challenge: There was one of him and hundreds of the mob.[46]

At such a moment the community looks to its police force for protection. One of the resolutions of the Law and Order Meeting was to "uphold the sheriff in all his efforts to maintain law and order." But the sheriff, who had only returned to Comanche the day after the mob rode through town, faced a series of bad choices. If he did nothing, he would alienate community leaders and violate his oath of office. But fighting the mob could be catastrophic. As he explained to the local paper, deputizing fifty or a hundred men to battle the mob "would be arraying neighbor against neighbor and be productive of feuds that would be handed down to the next generation." The only other option was to call in outside help. That was what he did, but it was futile. The nearest band of Texas Rangers was several hundred miles away. The call went out on July 27, but it was not until August 3, over a week later, that Captain S. A. McMurry with fewer than ten men arrived. By that time the blacks had already fled.[47]

While the community was waiting for the Rangers, the Law and Order people and the Mob fought a series of small skirmishes. As they had in the past, vigilantes sent threatening notes to people who they thought opposed them. One such note, sent to J. F. Manning, warned, "You think you are very smart try to play in with both sides. The other nite you was stanin in with the mob. We hear that you ar on the other side now. Go slo or you may pul on the tight end of a rope." The note was signed "Comitty." Manning, not one to be intimidated, pistol-whipped a man named Tom Stewart, whom he accused of making the threat.[48]

The Mob also denounced the Law and Order people as radical Republicans and "negro lovers." C. W. Carnes, who ran the meeting, was stopped by a mob member and warned that he and the others at the meeting might have to flee the county. For townspeople these kinds of attacks were outrageous. Among those at the Law and Order Meeting was "Uncle Jack" Nabers who had lost two sons to Mose Jones. Carnes, who had helped settle the county, was such a respected citizen that even being related to him was considered an honor. One of the headstones at the Downing cemetery gives the name of the deceased, his date of birth, and death, and then notes he was a "Nephew of C. W. Carnes."[49]

For blacks the choice was clear. On August 5—ten days after the lynching—*Town and Country* announced, "The negroes have all left town in obedience to the mandate of the mob. There were not more than forty or fifty of them. Several of them had lived here long enough to acquire homes of their own. Of course it need not be said that they earned every dollar's worth of property they had by honest labor. They sacrificed whatever little stuff they had for money enough to get away."[50]

They left behind a county in turmoil. McMurry and his Rangers arrived on August 3, and by August 23 headquarters wanted to know when he would be able to leave for his next assignment.[51]

McMurry's reply has been lost, but the state adjutant general's report for 1886 gives some sense of the trouble. "Captain McMurry and his company had to be taken from Wilbarger county for some weeks, this summer, and stationed in Comanche county to assist in giving peace and security to certain neighborhoods there, which had been kept in terror at times for a long period, by nameless and unknown miscreants who committed various outrages at night, killing sheep and other stock and beating and sometimes killing the owners and peaceable persons."[52]

W. H. King, Texas adjutant general, wrote again four days later asking McMurry whether, even if he could not leave Comanche County, he could at least detach some men to go to Hardeman County, where citizens were feuding. Again the reply is lost, but it appears that some of the Rangers remained in Comanche County as late as September. By all accounts they got nowhere. The adjutant general's report, which omits any mention of the racial cleansing, also does not say anyone was arrested. A Comanche County grand jury report released at the beginning of September describes a county gripped by fear.

> Owing to our inability to get witnesses, we have been forced to refer some matters of grave importance to the next Grand Jury. We have examined witness after witness relative to the spirit of lawlessness that has been pervading our county for the past six months and especially in regard to acts and threats of mob violence but we find ourselves almost powerless in ferreting out crime without the assistance of our fellow citizens. Its next to impossible to make a witness jeopardize his own life by testifying against a mob and a grand juror can do no more than any other citizen in an investigation of this character if he fails to get the necessary testimony to find a bill of indictment.[53]

In time the threats and fighting sputtered out. In DeLeon a sign posted over a well in the center of town warned, "Nigger—Don't let the sun set on your head in this town." From time to time traveling road shows would think about playing in Comanche County. They were warned not to bring any of their black stagehands. A black youth in a neighboring county supposedly bet his friends he could cross Comanche County on foot. He was never heard from again.[54]

————

By the turn of the century any vestige of the old dispute had disappeared. In 1907 the county published a newspaper-size brochure to encourage people to settle in Comanche County. It opened with an essay on what residents considered one of the county's main attractions. Comanche, the brochure assured readers, is "entirely and absolutely ALL WHITE; there is not a negro in the county, and the chances are there will not be any for many years to come." Two decades earlier the local newspaper had opposed the racial cleansing and reminded readers of how blacks had helped settle the land. Now, after self-imposed isolation, the brochure said, "Wherever the negroes are numerous, there crime abounds and all sorts of trouble."

The stories of white families raising black orphans and white widows depending on the help of black workers had been forgotten. In its place the brochure explained that, "By many who know the traits and capacities of the black race it is asserted that it is by nature not only signally inferior to the white race, but is also by nature a depraved and brutal race." The essay rattles on worrying about "baser passions" and "a whirlwind of bestiality" that can only be kept in check by "the gallows" or "maceration and laceration and torture." For a brochure trying to attract people to Comanche County, the message was clear: We only want white people who think the way we do.

Its racial problems "solved," Comanche County now faced what turned out to be an intractable problem: getting whites to stay. In the county's heyday of 1910 the population peaked at 27,000. But that same year boll weevils decimated the cotton crop. In the "dirty 30s" the topsoil blew away and with it went many of the farmers. By 1940, there were only 18,000 residents. Then came the droughts of the 1950s, leaving 11,800 people, of whom two were black.

By the time Evelyn Young and her children arrived, flood control programs had stabilized the water supply, the rise of agribusiness had stabilized the population, and the civil rights era . . . well, the civil rights era had left Comanche untouched.

When the other children would taunt Nicole, her mother would comfort her by saying, "The kids don't know that they are doing wrong. They think it's a way of playing with you because you are different and you are unique."[55]

In fact, Nicole was unique in ways her mother never imagined. A tomboy who excelled at sports, Nicole developed faster than her classmates. "I was bigger than the other girls. I was more muscular." It was an effortless kind of strength. In junior high school, Nicole's basketball coach thought those guarding Nicole were slacking off. "I decided I would [try guarding Nicole]," said Marcia Glasgow. Within seconds the coach, then five feet eight inches and 150 pounds, had a rude awakening. "She could push me around pretty well."[56]

But it wasn't only her size and power. All her coaches discovered that, while on the court, Nicole carefully watched opponents play, found their weak points, and ruthlessly attacked. "You might get something by her the first time," Glasgow explained, "but if you did it again, she would steal the ball."

Partly because she was a gifted athlete, the name calling stopped. But athletics also meant she could turn on her tormentors. "What I would do is find sneakier ways to actually get the anger out and that would be playing football against that person or beating them on a touchdown," Nicole said. Becky Raesz, her high school coach, noticed the telltale sign was Nicole's grin. "Every once in a while she would hear the N word," Raesz said. It was not uncommon for the fans to yell racial epithets. "She would give a little smirk and then somebody was going to either eat the basketball or it wasn't going to be theirs anymore."[57]

Nicole's success in sports also began to help her family. "When we first started going to some of the games just to let her watch," Nicole's mother said, "it was like people didn't want us there. When she was old enough to start playing, people would save seats for us."

But other towns were a different story. When Comanche played Early, Young said a fan for the opposing team shouted, "Somebody needs to check that nigger and see how old she really is."

"I stood up and I said that's my daughter so I know her age and so do they. He said some remark like 'f' you nigger or something to that effect. I turned around and I said, 'I'm sorry, but, if I let you, you would probably have a heart attack 'cause you wouldn't know how.'"

Young and the heckler were thrown out of the game. More important, it led to an understanding between mother and daughter. "Momma, don't pay them any attention," Nicole told her mother. "I got them zoned out. I don't hear them anyway."

Some things couldn't be zoned out.

During the O. J. Simpson trial, the family started getting death threats. The police chief said they pulled Nicole and her sister out of school and offered to move the family to a safe location. Young, with her characteristic bravado, told the police, "I'm not running. If they step foot on my property, then I'll call you afterwards to see who it is that I just had to deal with."

Nicole, however, remembers it as the worst time of her life. "That was the time I was really afraid. That was one time that I did not sleep at all. I thought I was going to die."

The threats came to nothing, and Nicole's basketball career made her unstoppable. In 1997—Nicole's junior year—the team made it to the state finals. Her senior year they won the state championship—the first time since 1954—and Nicole was chosen for the all-state team.

For Comanche County, the girls were celebrities. Their pictures were hung in a local store. People honked as they drove by. To celebrate, the community threw a parade. The little girl who had been jeered in grade school, heckled at games, and threatened by anonymous callers waved at cheering fans from atop a fire truck driven through the center of town.

Then the cheering stopped.

Nicole went off to college in Abilene in August 1998 and returned home that December.

"All of a sudden I was getting harassed by the [Comanche] police. Like they would pull me over as if I was speeding but I actually wasn't.

And then whenever they would look at my driver's license and it would say Comanche, they would be like, OK. Then everything is fine and they would let me go on."

Today mother and children have moved about twenty miles away to Brownwood, where they work for the Texas Youth Commission.

But why did they struggle on in Comanche for nineteen years?

"I stayed," said Nicole's mother, "because they didn't want me to."

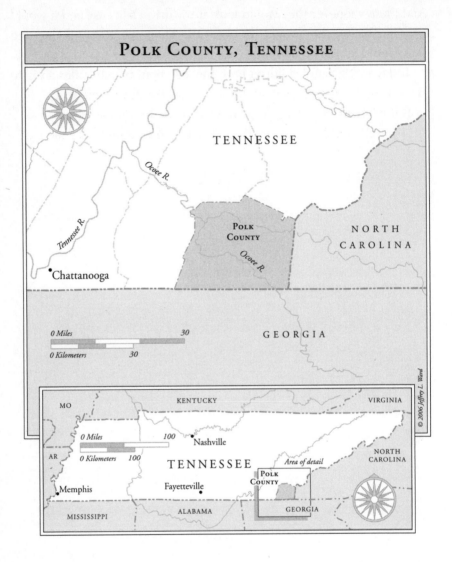

Polk County, Tennessee

TENNESSEE

Ocoee R.

Tennessee R.

•Chattanooga

POLK
COUNTY

Ocoee R.

NORTH
CAROLINA

GEORGIA

0 Miles   30

0 Kilometers   30

© 2006 Jeffrey L. Ward

MO

KENTUCKY

VIRGINIA

0 Miles   100

•Nashville

AR

0 Kilometers   100

NORTH
CAROLINA

TENNESSEE

Area of detail

POLK
COUNTY

•Memphis

Fayetteville•

MISSISSIPPI

ALABAMA

GEORGIA

CHAPTER 3

Forced Labor

Polk County, Tennessee
1894

As he waited for the fighting to start, Charles Livingston stood on a hillside near Ferguson Station, Tennessee. It was almost dusk on Friday, April 27, 1894, and below him approximately fifty white men armed with rifles and dynamite were marching up a dirt track from a company store called Mary Mine. To stop them, Livingston had gathered his own gunmen, who were blocking the path to the camp where Livingston housed his black laborers.[1]

Although he could not know it, Livingston was facing more than an armed mob. Powerful social forces that were building in the country had, like a dust devil, coalesced on this hillside. What happened here would mark a turning point. Before Polk County there had been only two major racial cleansings in the past thirty years. After this attack in 1894 there would be at least five in a single decade. Something had changed in the country, and unfortunately for Livingston, he was standing on the wrong side of history.

At first glance, Polk County—rural, remote, and thinly settled—seems an unlikely place for anything more momentous than a county fair. It sits on the Tennessee–North Carolina border fifty miles east of Chattanooga, and because it is bisected by a mountain range, it is, in a sense, two counties. At the turn of the century the western portion was devoted to farming while the eastern part of the county—where Livingston now stood—was developing into a major source of copper.

But in this remote and mountainous part of Tennessee, the copper mines relied on the railroads to haul the ore to smelters. That was why Livingston, a local contractor, was building a railroad spur that began at Ferguson Station—where it could intersect the railroad's main line—and went three miles up a steep incline to the mouth of the Polk County Mine. The spur Livingston was building was literally the mine's lifeblood.[2]

There are two versions of what happened at Ferguson Station. According to one, written in 1975 by a local historian, when Livingston first rounded up a work crew to build the spur, he hired both whites and blacks. But as time passed, the white workers noticed that the labor force was gradually changing. Livingston was adding only black workers. A newspaper account written at the time—and relying heavily on Livingston's version of events—says he brought in a black work crew after claiming he could not get whites to work. In either case, for Livingston the math was simple. He could pay black workers less, and the less money paid for labor, the more money he could put in his own pocket. The math was equally simple for the white workers. If they did nothing, the labor camp that the blacks built a short distance from Ferguson Station would continue to grow while the number of jobs for whites would shrink. That was why angry white men were struggling up the trail from Mary Mine. It was also why Livingston was waiting on a hillside as the light dimmed.[3]

It was a short-lived affair. Livingston and his few men faced fifty well-armed laborers. He might slow their advance, but he could not stop them. After a brief argument, he stepped aside.[4]

The white workers surged forward, shouted to the blacks to leave, and then began peppering the camp with rifle fire. It was over in minutes. The defenseless black workers tumbled out of their tents, raced down the hill, across the railroad tracks that ran parallel to the Ocoee river. The darkness swallowed them as they fled.[5]

This clash decisively settled the issue of black workers in Polk County. According to the 1890 census, 8,361 people lived in Polk

County, 566 of them black. Ten years later only 303 African-Americans remained, nestled in the relative safety of the western end of the county, protected by the mountain range from what awaited them if they ventured near the copper mines.[6]

The attack at Ferguson Station would appear to be a simple story of a labor dispute settled at the point of a gun. In fact, it was emblematic of the pressures building as the country underwent a series of wrenching changes. The economic changes were plain to see. In 1894 the United States was rapidly becoming an industrial power, and white men like those who gathered at Mary Mine were being pitted against blacks for a paycheck. It was no accident that men like Livingston were separating their white and black workers into different camps. Southern railroads were segregated before 1900, and after the turn of the century segregation took root everywhere in the South. And as it did, it encouraged a hothouse climate of paranoia and sadism.

Making matters worse, starting in 1890 southern states began a campaign to disenfranchise black voters that would, over the next two decades, triumph in every state of the old Confederacy. Tennessee disenfranchised its blacks around 1890 with predictable results. The black workers could be driven from Ferguson Station because, among other things, they were not citizens. As the light faded on that spring day in 1894, the world that Livingston could see from the hillside was one where whites believed that stateless blacks who were strangers to the community threatened public order and economic security. In that world racial cleansing was an acceptable solution.

In standard economic theory, the laws of supply and demand set the price of labor, and whether you are white or black is incidental. But in the rules of the southern economy, blacks were a captive labor force. Even if wages were low, black workers could not move outside the South to find better-paying jobs. In the former Confederacy, the government stepped into the market to make sure the cost of black labor was kept artificially low. In some cases state governments even set up programs that allowed white farmers and mine owners to rent black labor for pennies a day and literally work their captives to death. In such a system the only way for whites to compete was to drive their black competition away.

This strange economic system had its roots in the overriding question following the Civil War: Who was going to pick the cotton? With the Black Codes as the blueprint, the goal of every southern state government was to replace slavery with something that yielded the same result.[7]

By the 1890s every state in the former Confederacy had forged a new system of bondage. Instead of owning people, you owned their labor. An employment contract replaced shackles, and the Dred Scott decision morphed into "enticement laws." Refuse to work, and you were arrested as a "vagrant" and sent to work on a county work crew. Run away from your employer and, instead of slave catchers, the police would arrest you and ship you off to a chain gang.[8]

What made this new system of forced labor possible was an invisible but highly effective economic "fence" that surrounded the former Confederacy. While the most likely route out of the South for a black was a job in a northern factory, those jobs were not available. Northern factory owners, who depended on almost unrestricted immigration of whites from Europe, had no need of black southern field hands. Between 1870 and 1890 five million immigrants came to the United States. During that same period only 150,000 southern Negroes moved to the North. What Frederick Douglass observed in 1853 continued to be true. "Every hour sees the black man [in the North] elbowed out of employment by some newly arrived immigrant whose hunger and whose color are thought to give him a better title to the place." It was only when the flow of immigrants was interrupted by the First World War that the economic fence along the Mason-Dixon line collapsed. With northern jobs available, the "Great Migration" of blacks from the South began.[9]

But until the fence came down, most of America's blacks, though supposedly free, were trapped in the South for over half a century after the Civil War. The first census after the Civil War found that ninety-one percent of all blacks lived in the South. Forty years later, the numbers had barely changed: eighty-nine percent. Behind this fence, African-Americans faced a miserable existence. In 1917, just as the Great Migration was about to begin, a black lawyer explained what it was like to live in the South.

In my views the chief causes of Negro unrest and disturbance of mind are as follows: The destruction of his political privileges and curtailment of his civil rights; no protection of life, liberty and property under the law; insufficient wages to the laboring classes with which to buy the necessities of life; Jim Crow car, residential and labor segregation laws; no educational facilities worthy of the name for the education of Negro children in most of the Southern states.

Per-capita income in the South during this period was half that of the rest of the country, and black incomes were less than half than those of whites.[10]

Penned in by the Mason-Dixon line, black workers had to contend with a series of interlocking laws at the core of southern labor policy: enticement and contract enforcement. Enticement made it a crime for anyone to lure a worker from his current employer. In Georgia you violated the law if you enticed a worker "by offering higher wages or in any other way whatever." In Louisiana you could even run afoul of the enticement law if you helped someone to run away from his employer. The law made it illegal to "feed, harbor or secrete any person who leaves his or her employer."[11]

Before the Civil War, slave owners would advertise a reward for runaway slaves. The enticement statutes brought with them similar notices: "NOTICE—I forbid any one to hire or harbor Herman Miles, colored, during the year 1939. A. P. Dabbs, Route 1, Yanceyville."[12]

On the other hand, the contract-enforcement statutes chained the worker to his job. Normally, when there is a contract dispute, it is handled as a civil matter. Both sides go to court, and a judge or jury decides which party is at fault. The winning side usually gets a cash settlement. But the contract-enforcement statutes turned contract disputes into criminal proceedings. If a worker refused to do his job as called for in a contract or to refund an advance, that was taken as an attempt to defraud the employer. In other words, if you didn't work, you went to jail.

To make sure that blacks would sign these labor contracts, every southern state had vagrancy laws. Police regularly conducted vagrancy sweeps arresting any black who "could not account for himself." In Birmingham, Alabama, mill owners went to the city council in April 1918 complaining that there was a labor shortage. Their solution, which was adopted by the city council, was to pass a new anti-vagrancy statute. The new law said a defendant, who was found "wandering or strolling about, or remaining in idleness during any working day in any calendar week," had to prove he was not a vagrant. The factory owners soon solved their labor problems.[13]

The anti-vagrancy laws were also popular with the government because "vags" were a source of revenue. The Birmingham city fathers, for example, leased some of their convicted vagrants to work in coal mines. Others were put to work on the city streets. When Savannah was chosen as the site of a car race in 1910, the city promptly began a vagrant dragnet to find free convict labor to work on the city's racecourse.[14]

Such oppressive labor policies created a ready supply of cheap black labor in a job market that was carefully circumscribed. The only jobs available were the most menial. Advancement was limited by the fact that placing blacks in charge of whites was unthinkable. Some industries such as textiles were closed to blacks. Before the Civil War blacks had been field hands or servants, and after Emancipation field hands or servants they remained. In the 1910 census eighty-nine percent of the blacks living in the South worked either in agriculture or as domestics.[15]

It was left to men like R. A. "Peg-leg" Williams, a one-legged ex-Confederate soldier with an enormous walrus moustache, to rip one small tear in the net of these coercive labor laws. "Peg-leg" was an emigrant agent. He and his fellow agents, working for anyone who needed black workers, would scour southern states looking for recruits.

Williams, who had a flair for self-promotion, regaled reporters with his exploits, boasting that in one seven-year period he had moved over 80,000 blacks. When an agent like Williams arrived in town with the promise of a better job and a train ticket for anyone who was interested, pandemonium could result.[16]

In early March 1910, whites in Athens, Georgia were puzzled that blacks were packing their belongings and leaving town. Soon someone noticed that, whenever a trainload of blacks left, a one-eyed African-American named Dock Evans was always at the train station. After Evans was arrested "on suspicion" and searched, police found a telegram from Peg-leg Williams authorizing Evans to buy twenty-five train tickets. The day after Evans was arrested, a thousand blacks from area farms descended on the railroad. The station agent, rather than anger local farmers, refused to sell any tickets to the blacks. "That, of course, checked the movement and the darkies couldn't get away," the *Atlanta Journal* noted.[17]

Undeterred, the black laborers remained at the depot. According to an Atlanta paper, "During the day they hid out to keep their former employers from catching them and at night they returned again, but again failed to get off." Meanwhile farmers began to arrive, and, because breaking a labor contract was a criminal matter, "planters were . . . having negroes arrested who had jumped their contracts." On Monday, when the crowd had dwindled to 400, the sheriff deputized twenty men, marched to the depot and "read them the state law as to vagrancy and warned them they would be arrested as vagrants unless they as speedily as possible, dispersed." That ended all hope for what the newspaper called "the deluded darkies."[18]

Because men like Williams endangered a cheap and plentiful labor supply, several states passed laws that tried to tax the emigrant agent out of business. Georgia made an emigrant agent pay a tax of $500—the equivalent of $10,000 in 2000—for each county where he wanted to recruit. Williams took the state to court, arguing that the tax was unconstitutional because it indirectly restricted the right of people to move from one state to another. In 1900 the case went all the way to the U.S. Supreme Court, which upheld the Georgia statute, ruling the tax was simply a revenue measure and that laborers "were free to come and go at pleasure." Another exit had been blocked.[19]

The black men at the Athens depot were cheap labor. But they risked a far worse fate if they were caught trying to leave their white employers. If they were arrested, the government could turn them into virtually free labor for white farmers and mine owners. They would become convict labor. That was why, when police went through the Athens depot threatening to arrest everyone for either "jumping contract" or as vagrants, resistance collapsed. Once arrested, a black worker risked falling into the hands of the criminal surety system. If convicted of a petty crime, a prisoner could sign a criminal surety agreement in which he agreed to work for an employer if the employer paid his fines and court costs. The courtroom, in effect, became a hiring hall. Ray Stannard Baker, writing in 1908, described a typical case.

> I saw a Negro brought into court charged with stealing cotton.
> "Does anybody know this Negro," asked the judge.
> Two white men stepped up, and both said they did.
> The judge fined the Negro $20 and costs, and there was a real contest between the two white men as to who should pay it—and get the Negro. They argued for some minutes, but finally the judge said to the prisoner: "Who do you want to work for, George?"
> The Negro chose his employer and agreed to work four months to pay off his $20 fine and costs.[20]

Although a prisoner might spend far longer working off his sentence on a local farm than he would in jail, the local farm was the better bet. The alternative was to fall into the clutches of the murderous convict-leasing program, which every southern state used to dodge the cost of housing and feeding prisoners. As the name implies, an employer would lease convicts from the state prison, often for a rate that worked out to as little as 6.5 cents a day. The convicts would then serve out their sentence working in a mine or factory or on a railroad construction gang. Men who did not mine their quota of coal were beaten. Prisoners building railroads laid track during the day and were packed into cages mounted on flatbed cars at night. The death rate among convicts in the South was five to six times greater than that in the North. In South Carolina nearly half the convicts sent to build a railroad in 1877 died. One businessman summed up the attitude of the companies that leased the convicts: "One dies, get another."[21]

Behind the web of laws and regulations was a society that would use unimaginable brutality to enforce its control over the black underclass. The country got a first-hand look at what southern whites were doing when, in 1918, the National Association for the Advancement of Colored People (NAACP) sent Walter White, an African-American who could pass as white, to investigate racial violence in two Georgia counties. When White returned, he brought back a report that, although it focused on a murderous rampage by whites in Brooks and Lowndes counties, described the South's perverse system of forced labor.[22]

In normal circumstances, a boss who mistreats his employees soon finds that no one will work for him. Not so in the South at that time. When he couldn't pay people to work for him, Hampton Smith, a white farmer notorious for cruelty and dishonesty, simply dipped into the pool of black prisoners. That was how Sidney Johnson, a black convict, wound up working for Smith. In return for paying Johnson's $30 fine for gambling, Smith owned the man's labor. When Johnson didn't show up for work one day because he was sick, Smith made the mistake of beating his employee. A few days later, while Smith was sitting in his home, Johnson shot through the window, killing the farmer and wounding his wife.

With the murder as the centerpiece of the story, whites began embroidering a fantastic tale of rape and revolt. They said there was a conspiracy among several blacks to kill the farmer. In turn the newspapers claimed that, after they killed her husband, this gang assaulted Mrs. Smith until she passed out.[23]

What followed was an orgy of violence. On May 17, two blacks were grabbed at random by a mob and quite literally shot to pieces. It was estimated that 700 bullets were fired into them. The next day Hayes Turner, suspected of being part of the black conspiracy, was lynched. His body, left hanging for two days, became a grisly tourist attraction for local whites. Sidney Johnson was tracked to Valdosta and shot to death.[24]

When Turner's wife, Mary, threatened to find his killer and swear out arrest warrants, her "unwise remarks" became a death sentence. The day after her husband died, the mob grabbed Mary, eight months pregnant, hung her upside down from a tree, doused her with gasoline, set her on fire, then disemboweled her and tore out the fetus. The baby gave a feeble cry before a member of the mob stomped it to death. Although the exact death toll will never be known, the mob murdered at least eleven people.[25]

According to the NAACP report these terror tactics to cow the black workforce had an unintended consequence: Blacks who could started leaving. Unlike in counties where there were racial cleansings, blacks, who made up half the population of Brooks and Lowndes counties, were a substantial labor force. If they ran away, it would be an economic disaster. So what occurred next was the mirror image of a racial cleansing. Whites threatened blacks with death if they tried to leave.[26]

The message was clear. Blacks were a captive workforce and every white was a potential jailer. Any sign of revolt would be met with ruthless suppression.

Forced labor on the farm was a southern tradition. But what if, instead of farming, whites had to compete with blacks in factories and mines? By 1890 that was a question worth asking because the South was beginning to industrialize even in remote places like Polk County. Although copper seams were discovered in the county in 1843, there was no good way to get the ore to market. It wasn't until the Marietta and North Georgia Railroad Company built a line through Polk County in 1890 that mining became feasible. Suddenly there was a relatively cheap way to bring in fuel to refine the ore and then ship copper ingots to market. Industrialization had come to Polk County.

The same process was happening across the rest of the South. Between 1870 and 1880 railroads added only 3,000 miles of track in the South, but in the next decade that number tripled. With a way to ship things like coal and copper to market, mines opened. At the same time factories began to open. In 1880, ten thousand people worked in the mines. Twenty years later that number had increased fivefold. Wage earners in textiles grew from 16,700 in 1880 to over 97,000 in 1900.[27]

With industrialization, the old equations changed. The pool of cheap farm labor could be shifted to factories, where blacks would compete with whites. But for blacks to be a real economic threat to whites, they had to be turned into a skilled or at least semi-skilled labor force. And so a group of northern industrial philanthropists and southern white reformers met at Capon Springs, West Virginia, in 1898 to discuss how to reform the education of African-Americans in the South. This group would later pour millions of dollars as charitable donations into black education, form an alliance with black leaders, and have an enormous impact on what black schoolchildren in the South did and did not learn. These men had various motives, including egalitarian idealism, and a key member of the group, William H. Baldwin, Jr., a railroad magnate, was not shy about his. If blacks were given an "industrial education,"

Baldwin believed they could be "directed to produce infinite wealth for the South." At the same time these black workers could be used to undercut white labor demands. "The union of white labor, well organized," Baldwin predicted, "will raise the wages beyond a reasonable point, and then the battle will be fought and the Negro will be put in at a less wage and the labor union will either have to come down in wages, or Negro labor will be employed."[28]

As promised, blacks were used as strikebreakers at a time when that tactic was widely employed. In two thousand strikes between 1881 and 1894, management resorted to strikebreakers forty percent of the time. And blacks were particularly receptive to recruitment because they generally were not part of the labor movement. White-run unions would either bar blacks from joining or shunt them to segregated unions. With little stake in the fate of organized labor, blacks were available as, in the words of Booker T. Washington, a "race of strike breakers." Andrew Carnegie used black workers to crush the steel union during the Homestead strike of 1892, and they were used again in the coal strikes of 1898 and the meatpacking strikes of 1904. By 1905 Samuel Gompers, head of the American Federation of Labor, warned that "if the colored man continues to lend himself to the work of tearing down what the white man has built up, a race hatred far worse than any known will result."[29]

Businessmen found, however, that using black strikebreakers was also a tactic that could backfire. After a company in Freemont, Ohio hired blacks to break a strike in 1903, public sympathy swung to the strikers, and when three blacks were accused of killing a striker, the blacks were run off and the company was forced to settle. In 1909 the Georgia Railroad Company began replacing white firemen on its trains with blacks, whom it could pay less. The union appealed to the public: "Will the people of Georgia back their own men or will they back the Georgia railroad in trying to ram negro supremacy down the throats of its white firemen?" The answer was immediate. White mobs stormed trains, pulled off black firemen, and beat them. The railroad was forced to binding arbitration. And when a company tried using strikebreakers in East St. Louis in 1917, there was a race riot that left well over thirty people dead. No one knows the exact number because some bodies were either dumped in the Mississippi River or incinerated as mobs torched black homes.[30]

Before industrialization, blacks, relegated to work in the fields, could be dismissed as "inferiors that . . . should be under the rule of a master." But now they inspired fear and murderous rage. One man noted in a 1906 letter to the *Atlanta Georgian,* "Take a young Negro of little more than ordinary intelligence, even get hold of him in time, train him thoroughly as to books, and finish him up with a good industrial education, send him into the South with ever so good intentions both on the part of his benefactor and himself, send him to take my work away from me and I will kill him."[31]

The system of forced labor, however, does not account for the racial paranoia that would grip the country at the turn of the century. Slave-owning whites had always worried about rebellion, but this was something different. During slavery whites and blacks had always lived close to one another on the plantation. And after the Civil War, as Comanche County showed, it was not uncommon for blacks and whites to be neighbors and friends. But now whites began walling themselves off from their black neighbors. Segregation, like kudzu, covered southern society. And as it grew, paranoia flowered.

White beliefs became increasingly bizarre. "There is the 'blue gum nigger,'" explained the *Evansville* (Indiana) *Journal* in 1900, "whose bite is supposed to be poisonous. And the 'yellow nigger' as they are called. These are the two classes that invited the trouble if any is to come."[32]

Worse yet for whites, blacks had the vote, and these terrifying people with poisonous bites were poised to take over America. Vowing to fight what they called "Negro domination," whites began a campaign to disenfranchise blacks.[33]

The campaign to destroy the black vote had already succeeded in Tennessee by the time of the Ferguson Station attack. Although Tennessee was part of the Confederacy, during the war the state had been as divided as the nation. More than 51,000 Tennesseans joined the Union Army, and eastern Tennessee was a bastion of Union support. After the war there was a seesaw battle between Democrats and Republicans for state government as white Unionists in eastern Tennessee and black voters in urban areas joined forces to counter Democrats in middle and western Tennessee. But in the 1888 elections the Democrats gained a solid majority in the legislature that would allow them to rewrite the election rules. Through a variety of measures such as a poll tax and a ballot designed to confuse illiterate blacks, they prevented African-Americans in the state's major cities from voting for Republican candidates. At the next election in 1890, the Democrats won handily.[34]

The attack at Ferguson Station was not the only warning that more racial cleansings were brewing. Two months after the attack on the work camp, there was another, more deadly, sign of the approaching storm. It started as a scuffle on June 20, 1894 between two groups of men on the streets of Monett, Missouri. One group was white and the other black. What exactly happened is not clear except that Robert Greenwood, a white man who worked on the railroad, was shot and killed.[35]

A few days after Greenwood's death, police arrested a black man named Hulett Hayden in the nearby town of Neosho for the murder. The Barry County sheriff telegraphed the two officers holding Hayden, telling them to take their prisoner by train to the county jail in Cassville. As any railroad schedule would show, it was a bad idea. To get to Cassville, the police and their prisoner would first have to take an eastbound train to Monett, wait an hour at the Monett station, then board the train south to Cassville. When word got around Monett that the black suspected of killing Greenwood was waiting at the train station, Hayden's fate was sealed.

Although angry townspeople gathered at the station, the two deputies were able to get their prisoner on the train. But a half mile outside of Monett, the train stopped and a mob of fifty to a hundred men dragged Hayden out of the coach where he was being held and hung him from a telephone pole. Then, for good measure they drove all the blacks out of town.[36]

It could have ended there, but it didn't. The men from Monett who lynched Hayden and "cleansed" their own town would play a pivotal role in what was to happen next.

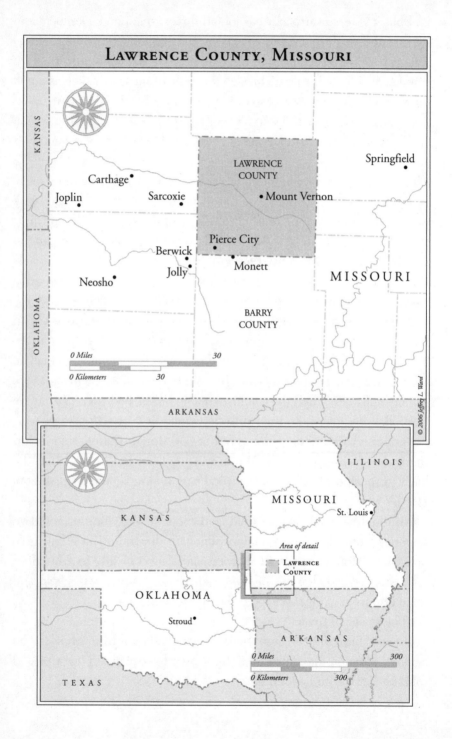

LAWRENCE COUNTY, MISSOURI

KANSAS

LAWRENCE
COUNTY

Springfield •

Carthage •

Joplin •

Sarcoxie •

• Mount Vernon

Pierce City •

Berwick •

• Monett

Jolly •

MISSOURI

Neosho •

BARRY
COUNTY

OKLAHOMA

0 Miles   30

0 Kilometers   30

ARKANSAS

© 2006 Jeffrey L. Ward

ILLINOIS

MISSOURI

St. Louis •

KANSAS

Area of detail

LAWRENCE
COUNTY

OKLAHOMA

Stroud •

ARKANSAS

0 Miles   300

0 Kilometers   300

TEXAS

CHAPTER 4

Disturbing Situations

Lawrence County, Missouri
1901

James Brown's wife was the first to tell him Pierce City, Missouri was gone. She had heard the reports on the morning radio at their home in St. Louis. A tornado had torn up Pierce City's tiny, decrepit downtown and tossed it into the air. Offices, stores, apartments, and government buildings came raining down on the surrounding fields and woods of Lawrence County.

Brown, who had been lying in bed half asleep, was suddenly wide awake. It was Monday, May 5, 2003, and the radio announcer repeated the news. Pierce City had been destroyed.

"Great. Good. I'm glad it's gone." Brown said. His wife smiled.[1]

———

When twenty-four-year-old Gisella Wild stepped out of the Methodist Church at the corner of Walnut and Washington around noon on August 18, 1901, she had less than thirty minutes to live. She and her brother had walked into town that morning along the railroad tracks that ran past their parent's farm west of town. She had gone to Sunday

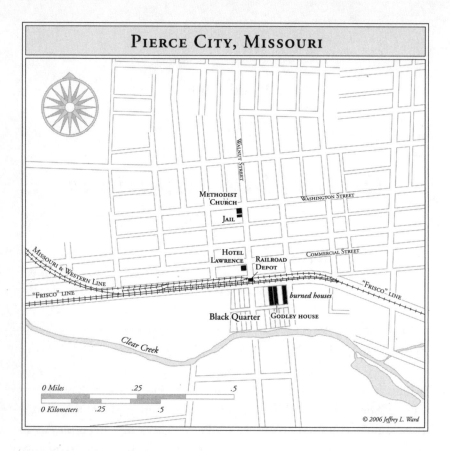

PIERCE CITY, MISSOURI

METHODIST CHURCH

WALNUT STREET

WASHINGTON STREET

JAIL

HOTEL LAWRENCE   RAILROAD DEPOT   COMMERCIAL STREET

MISSOURI & WESTERN LINE

"FRISCO" LINE

"FRISCO" LINE

burned houses

Black Quarter   GODLEY HOUSE

Clear Creek

0 Miles   .25   .5

0 Kilometers   .25   .5

© 2006 Jeffrey L. Ward

school and then to church while her brother, Carl, went downtown to see his friends. As she left the church to find Carl, Gisella was in a hurry. They had company at home, and, when Carl wouldn't leave immediately, she set off alone.[2]

About fifteen minutes after Gisella left, Carl headed home, a route that took him past the rail yards. Pierce City's fortunes rested on the railroads.[3] The Missouri and Western Line jogged into the northern end of the town and intersected tracks popularly known as the "Frisco line," which ran east and west and were owned by the St. Louis and San Francisco Railroad. Where rail lines intersected, there was a dollar to be made. Repair yards and hotels sprung up. Porters, brakemen, firemen, and engineers settled. Industries that needed access to the railroad were established. As Carl headed west walking along the Frisco track that passed near his home, he left behind a small knot of prosperity baking in the humid Missouri summer.[4]

About a half mile outside of town, a little railroad bridge spans a gully. It still stands today. It is hardly a bridge at all. Stone piers on either side of the gully anchor the framing that spans about a six-foot drop. The bridge did not have a superstructure or even handrails that Gisella could have clutched in the last few panicked moments of her life.[5]

No one knew whether she was thrown off the bridge or forced down the embankment. As Carl approached the bridge, the first things he probably saw were her fan and parasol lying on the tracks. As he ran forward, he found Gisella's fully clothed body in the culvert. There was a gash in her head, one finger was broken and her throat had been cut. Carl said her body was quivering. If she was still alive, the last thing she heard was Carl screaming.[6]

When word of the murder reached town, the fire bell started ringing. Police, family, neighbors, and the curious all walked out on the tracks or cut through the fields to see Gisella's body. Her bible and hat were found nearby.

As they gathered around the bridge, people began to talk about what they had seen in the moments leading up to the murder. Some boys who had been swimming nearby said they saw a black sitting on the bridge. Another boy said he saw two men on the bridge. William Ruark—his farm was adjacent to the culvert—said he saw a "copper-colored Negro" on the bridge. That was all that it took. In those first few minutes the course of the investigation was set: Gisella Wild was killed by one or more black men trying to rape her. A black man would have to be found.[7]

The Negro section of town was literally the wrong side of the tracks. It was a small strip of land only a few hundred yards wide that was bounded on the north by the tracks of the Frisco line and to the south by Clear Creek. Whites lived north of this area, across the tracks on a rise above the noise and dirt of the railroad and the business district. The blacks were not so lucky. The creek would flood the area periodically. Freight was unloaded by the depot. Day and night trains rumbled through.[8]

If most of Lawrence County's 280 blacks lived in Pierce City, it was not always by choice. In 1894, there had been a fight between whites and blacks in Monett, a small town a few miles east of Pierce City. When a white man, Robert Greenwood, was killed, townspeople lynched Hulett Hayden and drove all the other blacks out of Monett. Running the blacks off was hugely popular. Until the 1930s the letter-head on the town's official stationery bragged that Monett had "6,000 good citizens—all white."[9]

Blacks willing to accept some compromises could make a life in Pierce City, however. You could send your children to school, but only to the black school. You could celebrate your emancipation from slav-ery during June, but the town's Fourth of July parade gave the Ku Klux Klan a place of honor. White servants lived in the homes where they worked while black servants stayed in the Negro quarter. You could buy a plot in the city cemetery but only in the section reserved for the indi-gent. You could read the *Pierce City Empire,* a Republican newspaper, which covered black events because most blacks voted for the party of Lincoln. The Democratic paper was openly racist. You could vote, but it didn't mean much. Pierce City was dominated by the Democrats. One year, through a quirk, the Republicans nominated a black to run for city council. The Democratic candidate, rather than campaign as a Democrat, declared he was running on "The White Man's Ticket" and, of course, won.[10]

Perhaps because they were accustomed to these compromises, there did not seem to be a sense of panic among Pierce City's blacks on that hot Sunday afternoon as townspeople began searching for Gisella Wild's killer. Joe Lark, a black porter on the Frisco line who lived out-side of town, had finished work Sunday morning. Scheduled to work again that night on the nine P.M. train, he went to sleep about noon. He woke briefly when the fire bell sounded announcing the murder, but it wasn't until 5:30, when some friends dropped by, that he learned what had happened. Yet no one bothered him later that evening when he headed down to the depot. People had been coming into Pierce City from the surrounding countryside all afternoon, and there was a crowd at the train station. Lark chatted with a few people and then got on his train for the St. Louis run. He had no idea that within forty-eight hours he would become a wanted man.[11]

The Cobb family, which lived in the heart of the black quarter, seemed equally unconcerned. Two ministers from Carthage, who were going to hold a revival meeting in town, planned to arrive Monday morning and would be staying at the Cobb house. The Cobbs lived only a short distance from the depot where Joe Lark had cut through the crowds to get on his train. If the Cobbs were worried about any violence, they did not warn the ministers to stay away.[12]

While Gisella Wild's body was being carried home, the hunt for her killer began. Men who had arrived at the murder scene were organized into groups and sent in every direction. As the day wore on and more people arrived, Mayor Washington Cloud called a mass meeting to organize more posses. The mayor borrowed rifles from the National Guard armory for the volunteers, and Joseph Manlove, the county sheriff, arrived from Mount Vernon to help direct the search. Despite hundreds of men searching everywhere, the only thing they found was Gisella's handkerchief a quarter mile from the murder site.[13]

Monday morning began uneventfully. The two black ministers, Rev. S. S. Pitcher and Rev. L. M. Smith, arrived during the morning and, despite the excitement, began putting up their tent for that night's revival meeting. Officials apparently abandoned the idea of continuing the citizen dragnet because the National Guard rifles were collected and returned to the armory. Someone who thought that bloodhounds might help contacted the sheriff from neighboring Barton County, who had some dogs. But from all appearances the investigation was foundering. Sheriff Manlove went to the homes of two blacks, Will Godley and Eugene Barrett, because they had been "suspicioned." The plan had been to arrest them, but after talking to the pair, Manlove thought better of it. Although angry townspeople had gathered downtown and were now talking about lynching blacks, the sheriff inexplicably left Pierce City around noon and did not return.[14]

As the day wore on, the mood grew uglier. Warned that now was not a good time for blacks to gather, the two preachers canceled their revival meeting. During the afternoon, a posse returned and arrested Godley and Barrett. And by late afternoon a crowd of several hundred gathered at the jail demanding the prisoners. Mayor Cloud, who had ordered the saloons closed earlier in the day, talked the crowd into dispersing. But downtown there were ominous signs of fresh trouble. Each train that pulled into the depot carried reinforcements for the crowds filling the streets. Before the night was over, there would be a thousand armed men along the tracks that bordered the black quarter. Earlier in the day the local head of the National Guard told the mayor his unit was ready to help, but Cloud demurred, a decision that was now looking more and more questionable.[15]

At about six P.M. John Harlow, the Barton County sheriff, arrived with his bloodhounds. The dogs were taken to the murder site. They sniffed at Gisella's handkerchief and headed east toward town. They circled the house of Joe Lark, stopped briefly, and then went past the city cemetery before losing the scent by the Lawrence County line. For men looking for a black rapist, Lark was now a suspect.[16]

The case against Lark was airtight compared with those against Will Godley and Eugene Barrett, who were in the city jail. A headline in the Carthage, Missouri newspaper would later say that what happened to Godley was done "On General Principles." The headline got it about right. Aside from a criminal career, there was nothing linking Godley, thirty-two, to the murder. He had been convicted of raping a sixty-year-old woman in 1891 and had served seven and a half years of a ten-year sentence. After his release, he was arrested again in 1900 for the murder of a night watchman but later released. His fellow inmate, Barrett, was a seventeen-year-old who had recently been hired by the railroad. Barrett was such an unlikely suspect that even the mob that was now forming for a second run at the jail would eventually let him go.[17]

While there are contradictory accounts of what occurred in the last few hours before the mob stormed the city jail, every version mentions one pivotal moment. At around eight P.M. a passenger train with three extra cars pulled into the station and three hundred men from Monett poured out. "When they alighted from the train a volley was fired," said one account, "and they then demanded a negro." Monett, which had lynched their own black seven years earlier and driven every other black out of town, was here to help Pierce City. If there was any doubt about what would happen, the arrival of the Monett contingent dispelled it. The fire bell, used the day before to call people out to search for Gisella's killer, was now clanging wildly telling the world that a mob had formed.[18]

At some time between eight and nine P.M. the mob stormed the jail on Walnut Street just a few doors down from the church where Gisella had been the day before. No one stopped them. Six or eight men entered the jail with a sledge hammer and with a few blows sprung the lock on a grated iron door. They grabbed Godley and Barrett and put ropes around their necks. As they marched the prisoners out of the jail, the mob fired a volley into the air.[19]

The gunfire continued as the mob leaders ran the two men down Walnut Street a few hundred feet toward the train depot until they reached the intersection with Commercial Street. The Hotel Lawrence, a boxy three-story building, stood on the southwest corner of the intersection. An iron balcony that ran the length of the building jutted out over the sidewalk. Just a block south of the hotel were the train tracks, the depot, and, beyond the depot, the black quarter. The mob stopped by the hotel and the two prisoners were asked to tell what they knew about the murder. Neither man spoke.[20]

The mob marched the prisoners another block down Commercial Street, stopped again, and ordered them to confess. Barrett cracked. Hemmed in by the mob, a rope around his neck, the teenager said he knew who had killed Gisella Wild. What exactly he said is in dispute. One account said he named Joe Lark. Another version had Barrett blaming Will Favors, a porter on the Frisco line who supposedly was staying with Joe Lark. Some people thought Barrett said "Stark" instead of "Lark," and in the next few days police would look for a railroad porter named Stark. The one name he did not mention was Will Godley, a fact no one bothered to consider.[21]

Barrett was hustled away, but Godley's continued silence enraged the mob. He was forced over to a telephone pole, and they tried to hang him there. When they found the rope was too short, they marched him back to the Hotel Lawrence. As they stood under the glare of an electric street light, men in the crowd shouted "String him up." Someone snatched the rope tied around Godley's neck and climbed one of the posts that held up the hotel balcony. As several men grabbed him and boosted him up, the man on the balcony tied off his end of the rope to the balcony railing. Then they let go of Godley's body. As he started to strangle, the mob cheered.[22]

While Godley hung there, someone shouted, "Everybody towards the depot, get out of the way." The men on Commercial Street took aim, and then there was the cry "Now shoot boys." To one eyewitness it looked like the wind was picking at Godley's clothing as the bullets ripped through him. Under the impact of each volley, the body began to sway back and forth. When the firing stopped, a drunken man walked up and began hitting the corpse and cursing it.[23]

The body hung at the hotel entrance for a half hour until a businessman in shirt sleeves shouted to the mob, "Boys, the ladies in the hotel want the body cut down. Whaddya say?" To cries of "down, down, down" the rope was cut and Godley's body sprawled face up in the street. What had been the focus of their hatred now became the object of their curiosity. Someone tore away his shirt to see where the bullets had hit. A dozen or so women were escorted through the crowd to look at the corpse. A police judge tried to hold an inquest but was hooted down. Eventually the body was carried back to the jail and dumped there.[24]

Not everyone was interested in Will Godley's corpse. From the corner where the Hotel Lawrence stood you could look down Walnut Street to the black quarter. It was a tempting target. Some in the mob now crossed the tracks and headed for the home of Pete Hampton, a leader in the black community.

On the gentle rise above the downtown where whites lived, people stood on the sidewalk watching what was happening below. The whites had the luxury of seeing that night as a spectacle. "We could see all from our house," one woman later wrote to a friend. "We sat out on the walks all night and until 3 o'clock in the morning watching the breaking in of the jail, the hanging, and the burning of the buildings. I couldn't keep from laughing at time at the strange things people did but all in all 'twas a serious matter." For blacks, crouching by their windows and staring helplessly, the night was somehow to be endured. Hiding in your home had provided the illusion of sanctuary until now, but with whites advancing across the railroad tracks, that last illusion was gone.[25]

To resist was suicidal. But as they came to get him, Pete Hampton stepped to a window and fired. An attacker went down. He fired again, and another man went down. The mob fell back to Commercial Street.

The rioters were furious. Men poured out of Commercial Street, formed a rough skirmish line along the railroad tracks and began riddling the Negro quarter about fifty yards away with gunfire. Inside the small two-story Cobb home, there was pandemonium. As bullets ripped through the wood frame house, it was obvious the only safe place was the basement. But, as windows shattered and walls sprouted bullet holes, it was equally certain there was no way to get there through this firestorm. Some people hid under the beds. Maria Moss, a Cobb relative, used a trunk to shield herself. The two ministers lay on the floor terrified.[26]

Within minutes the gunfire died away. The mob had used up all its ammunition. Uncertain of what to do next, the rioters fell back to Commercial Street. As the mob milled about, a few men trotted up Walnut Street to the state armory next door to the city jail and seized the rifles and ammunition—by one estimate a thousand rounds—that had been loaned to the posses the day before. Unlike the shotguns, pistols, and assorted family weapons, these army rifles represented a new level of violence. At the time the Missouri National Guard was using Model 1888 "trapdoor" rifles, which were able to penetrate a 3.5-inch piece of seasoned oak at twenty-five feet. Their steel-jacketed bullets could easily pass through the wood-frame homes in the black quarter.[27]

While the mob rearmed, the people in the Cobb house used the lull to crawl to the basement. As she wiggled to the basement stairs, Maria

Moss noticed three bullet holes in her trunk. Outside the mob streamed back to the railroad tracks and resumed the barrage. But not content to just pot away, members of the mob ran up to the homes lining the railroad tracks and began setting them on fire. By the end of the night, they would raze five homes.[28]

Fifteen people hid in the Cobb basement: the two ministers and thirteen members of the Cobb and Moss families who shared the house. As they sat in the dark, bullets slammed into the house and the unmistakable odor of burning buildings drifted across the Negro quarter. Amazingly none of the fifteen had been injured in the first barrage. If their house was set on fire, however, they would all die horribly. The only escape was to the south. They would have to run through the Negro quarter, wade a stream called Clear Creek, and then race up a small hill and into the tree line. Once in the woods they would be safe. It was a distance of four hundred yards over open, fairly level ground. Every step of the way would be lit by the burning buildings. They crawled up the stairs, and one by one they burst out of the house and ran madly toward the creek. Behind them rifles cracked, and they could hear the zip of bullets. Pinky Cobb, the teenage daughter of James Cobb, made it as far as a well. Three bullets whistled past, she panicked, grabbed the well rope, and swung herself down. As Rev. Pitcher ran through the yards, a bullet hit a soapbox lying on the ground next to him. Some people stumbled into the creek and lay there, too frightened to go farther.[29]

Pinky, hiding inside the well, faced a new dilemma. If she let go of the well rope, she would drown. If she clambered out of the well, she might be shot. She chose gunfire. "When I got to the creek they were still shooting at me in the light of the burning buildings," she said. "I jumped into the creek and bent down low to miss the bullets. Finally I got across and escaped up the hill."[30]

By about three A.M. the mob had spent its fury. Some blacks, who were hiding in the woods, rested while others, like the two ministers, decided to get as far away from Pierce City as they could. Pitcher and Smith began walking home to Carthage. In the white section of town, people slept in their clothes, afraid they might be called out again. Most of the rioters drifted away, but a few remained to patrol. Out of the darkness, one of them called, "Speak quick—are you friend or foe and be damn quick about it!" Pierce City fell into a long, uneasy sleep.[31]

Morning brought fresh horrors. Two corpses were pulled out of one of the homes razed by the mob. They were so badly burned that there was no way to directly identify them. While bystanders debated, "an old colored woman," who was probably Pete Hampton's mother, solved the mystery. She said that during last night's gunfire she had entered the house and found her son's body at the base of the stairs and French Godley upstairs with a bullet in his head. These gruesome trophies— one corpse had its arms and legs burnt off—were taken to the jail and put on display next to Will Godley's corpse. Iola LeGrand, who worked at a bookstore, later wrote a friend, "The next morning we went to see roast negro, scared negro and a hanged negro."[32]

The "scared negro" was probably the few blacks who ventured out of the woods in the morning. It was too dangerous for the men, but black women poked among the ruins trying to salvage what they could. The ruins drew curious whites as well. The previous night's hunted and their hunters were together for one last time in Pierce City.

Some townspeople took pity. A white man pressed a dollar into the hand of an elderly black woman saying, "You may need this." Another found three silver dollars and gave them to a woman who stood sobbing amid the destruction. Not all whites were so kind. Blacks trying to gather their possessions had to compete with celebratory whites hunting for trophies. In the sacking of Pierce City, the conquerors carted off everything from a toy pistol to a railway porter's cap. And in a moment that symbolized the incomprehension and economic gulf between the races, a solicitous white man asked a black woman if her home was insured. "Lord a mercy, honey, these people don't know what insurance is."[33]

After collecting what they could, those who had not already fled on foot boarded trains. In one last indignity, blacks were not allowed to board at the depot, forced instead to wait in the dust by the tracks.

Some headed twenty-nine miles west to Joplin or farther still to Oklahoma. Others went east. Pinky Cobb and her family headed for Springfield, forty-three miles away. In either direction whites treated them as outcasts.

The *Daily Headlight* in Pittsburg, Kansas reported that "Without regard to sex the Pierce City negroes, as a class, were a low degraded set who would steal, murder and rob varying the program with raping and assaults upon white women." Some towns forced the Pierce City refugees to move on. Others, like Springfield, allowed them to stay but were wary. The *Springfield Leader-Democrat* blamed the lynching and expulsion on the blacks. "The quickest way to stop the outrages would be for the negroes to quit raping," the newspaper opined. It did, however, praise some blacks for trying to "demonstrate to the world that all coons do not look alike. The respectable negroes have determined that they will organize their forces and make character represent the race more conspicuously in the future than it has in the past."[34]

Pinky Cobb and her family, who had gone east to Springfield, briefly became celebrities. They were interviewed by Robertus Love, a star reporter for the *St. Louis Post-Dispatch,* who was writing a feature story on the Pierce City riot. Love posed Pinky and her family in front of the house where they were staying, and the picture ran as part of a full-page story.

The two footsore ministers arrived home in Carthage Tuesday night. They had first marched eight miles west to Berwick, then south to Jolly, and finally fifteen miles north to Sarcoxie, where they boarded a train home. "I am utterly worn out," said Rev. Pitcher, "with a night and day of walking amid hostile white people."[35]

Rev. Pitcher's sense of fear proved well founded. In the weeks after the Pierce City expulsion, whites in nearby towns began driving out their black residents. The newspaper in Neosho, about fifteen miles from Pierce City, reported that whites "requested" its blacks to leave and that twenty-two had. Neighboring Barry County became all white when its last remaining black resident sold his farm and left. The *Cassville Republican* said that, in the days following the Pierce City riot, blacks were boarding trains at every depot along the Frisco line to escape to either Joplin or Springfield. The *St. Louis Post-Dispatch* counted five towns along the Frisco line where "no negroes are permitted to live." Locals were calling the region a "white man's heaven." In 1900 the census counted 283 blacks in Lawrence County. Ten years later ninety-one remained.[36]

The example of Pierce City even crossed state lines. On August 27, a week after the Pierce City racial cleansing, the Carthage newspaper published a chilling, one-paragraph story from Stroud, Oklahoma, 168 miles to the west. After what the story described as "a heavy immigration of negroes within the past few days believed to come from Pierce City," a mob was "organized . . . for the purpose of ridding the town of its colored population."[37]

The racial cleansing in Stroud began at about nine P.M. when a mob of twenty-five attacked a shack where several black laborers lived. They drove the workers off, burned their possessions, and upended the hut. Next the rioters fell on two blacks walking along the street and chased them. The two hid behind a livery stable until the mob passed and then raced out of town. The mob moved on to a house where they suspected blacks were living. They broke in the door only to find the house unoccupied. Finally rioters attacked a woman living in a tent. They smashed what they could and set fire to the rest. At the end of the night the rioters posted a sign in town that said, "Nigger, don't let the sun go down on U." Stroud's Republican newspaper deplored the mob violence, but the Democratic paper was more upbeat. "While the mob unquestionably did things which cannot be approved," the *Stroud Messenger* explained, "it is the consensus of opinion that the amount of good done in ridding Stroud of a large number of 'worthless niggers,' far outweighs the amount of injustice done in the method used to expel them."[38]

While the refugees struggled to survive, Pierce City braced for an imagined counterattack. On Thursday evening the fire bells rang again. This time a swirl of rumors had conjured up a vast black army about to attack the town. "We were shocked by the peals of the bells and the cry that came through the streets, 'The negros are coming, coming in bunches over the cemetery hill,'" wrote Iola LeGrand. "Such scream-ing, fainting and crying. In less than 20 minutes after the alarm was given Co. E had been called and there was at least 500 armed men who guarded the town all night." A local newspaper observed the following day that Pierce City had "nigger tremens."[39]

Criticized by none other than Missouri native Mark Twain, the town went on the defensive. In September the *Pierce City Empire* published a version of the lynching and expulsion written by a citizens' committee that featured the town as victim. "There is no city in the great state of Missouri that has treated its negro population with higher consideration than Pierce City," the committee explained.

> Though it was widely suspicion [*sic*] that nearly all the crimes com-mitted in Pierce City, were perpetrated by negroes, it could not be fastened upon them because of the impossibility to get a negro to tes-tify against another negro. Dispite [sic] faithful effort almost always an alibi would be proven. The most law abiding and really good and ac-ceptable Negroes, have since acknowledged that these statements were true. One of them said, "That under the circumstance he could find no fault with the way people had done." For these and similar reasons the colored population were warned to leave Pierce City and never come back.[40]

But even though the blacks were gone, the gnawing fear remained. "I guess our troubles are at an end for awhile," wrote Iola LeGrand, "but one thing I assure you I shall never be found out in the country with a crowd of girls or out after dusk without my little revolver with me. I have the sweetest little 38."[41]

After all the suffering and bloodshed, Pierce City was no closer to knowing who had killed Gisella Wild. Joe Lark was arrested as he was returning home from his run to St. Louis and Will Favors was found in Oklahoma. Lark was tried and acquitted. Favors, with no evidence against him, was simply released. Eugene Barrett, who was repeatedly questioned in the month after the riot, was also released. Over time what had happened in Pierce City faded from memory. In 1970, as part of the town's celebration of its centennial, a local historian published a history of Pierce City and described the terror that had gripped the town in August 1901:

> The Frisco then moved its local junction of the Missouri and North Arkansas line over the Plymouth Junction. This then slowed down Pierce City revenue, which coupled with the recession left people with smaller pocketbooks. There were "hard times" for most everyone. So that after disturbing situations, the Negro population left Pierce City as well as most other small towns in border states; economics [*sic*] were not such as to offer much work for Negro families. Thus ended the period when households could find ready help for houses and gardens and handy-man work.[42]

———

James Brown had not always wished for Pierce City's destruction. An electrician who lives in St. Louis, he knew his family had once lived in Pierce City. But if he thought about Pierce City at all, it existed on the periphery of his world. That was until a chance encounter in the spring of 2000.[43]

It was one of those awkward moments. Brown and his wife were at a conference at the Lake of the Ozarks and were getting to know the people at their lunch table. The woman next to Brown said she was from Springfield, Missouri then corrected herself and said it was actually outside of Springfield.

Brown, his interest piqued, asked where exactly.

"Pierce City," she replied.

"Really. My family lived there over one hundred years ago."

The woman looked stricken. "Oh, I'm sorry. I'm so sorry."

Brown did not know what to say so he said nothing. When he was a boy, his father told him the family had been chased out of Pierce City. Brown, who can be single-minded, had pressed for details, but his father said he knew nothing more. It was not something discussed in the family. But the question he raised as a boy had unexpectedly returned in middle age. Why was this woman sorry? What had happened? Brown said it was at that moment that he decided to go to Pierce City.

James Brown's return to Pierce City could not have measured more accurately the distance his family had traveled over the last century. When they escaped, the black population had left with little more than their lives and a few possessions. Worse still, even among an outcast race, they were pariahs. It was a time of danger and desperation.

By contrast, James Brown returned during a leisurely excursion made on what started as an overcast day in the fall of 2001. Brown was driving his new, steel-gray Jeep Cherokee, accompanied by his wife and the Tollivers, a couple who had been visiting the Browns at their summer home near Branson, Missouri. They chatted, stopped to shop at antique stores and later to have lunch. And, while his wife and friends were willing to indulge him, no one in the car except Brown was particularly interested in visiting Pierce City. The bustling town of 1901 was now a seedy relic. When the railroad moved its operations to Monett, the town started to slide and the slide never stopped.

"Well, we're here," said Brown's wife dryly as they rode down the dilapidated main street. "I told you there was nothing here."

His first visit would prove to be, at best, inconclusive. Brown tried unsuccessfully to get information at two of the town's antique stores. Then he walked farther down the street to the little city hall that operates out of a storefront and doubles as the town's police station. Again the clerk at the counter said, sorry, but she didn't know about the town's past. He paid $10 for a booklet on the town's history on sale at the counter, and as he was leaving, the clerk suggested Brown talk to Murray Bishoff, the editor of the Monett paper. Bishoff, she said, was interested in the town's history. With his wife growing impatient, the Browns and their friends drove away.

The booklet, which made a vague reference to "disturbing situations," explained nothing. And Brown's first phone call to Bishoff was puzzling. Bishoff explained how the blacks had been driven out, but, no, he had never heard of any of Brown's family names. Bishoff, who is a classical music fan, said he was going to be in St. Louis for a concert in a couple of weeks. The two men decided to meet.

What Brown didn't know was that Bishoff was a man obsessed with the riot in Pierce City. In 1991, he had created a minor sensation when, after digging through old records, he had written a three-part series in the *Monett Times* on the lynching. It was the first time in nearly a century that a local newspaper had raised the topic.

"When I talked to people about this I ran into a lot of hostility about even bringing the subject up," Bishoff told me. "There was still some latent fear of blacks coming back and demanding their property back. We had never had anything sell out like that did. They were furious that I had brought this up because they wanted it forgotten. One of them said to me, 'We just started to get the economy going around here and then you had to bring this up again.'"[44]

Undeterred, Bishoff paid for a memorial to be placed in the city cemetery naming the three men murdered by the mob, and he made the marker's installation a front-page story in his newspaper. Even after his series ran, Bishoff continued to scour the county for anything that could shed light on what had happened. When the Wild family home was about to be torn down, he got permission to look through the building for any family records. And in his spare time he started work on an historical novel that revolved around the riot. It was natural then for Bishoff to use the St. Louis trip to run down a tip: Supposedly the *St. Louis Post-Dispatch* had published a full-page story on the lynching and expulsion a week after it occurred.

When Brown answered the door, Bishoff was holding the results of his latest research. He had left Lawrence County early, found the newspaper article on microfilm, and laboriously copied it. It had indeed been a full-page story and, because the copier was limited to copying an area the size of a piece of typing paper, Bishoff had to reproduce the page in sections. Sitting at Brown's dining room table, Bishoff began laying down the pieces of paper into a rough mosaic of the page.

Across the top of the newspaper the headline shouted, "NEGROES DRIVEN FROM SOUTHWEST MISSOURI TOWNS." Just below the headline were pictures of the hotel where Godley had been murdered and the bridge where Gisella Wild's body was found. A sub-headline declared, "Pierce City's Terrible Vengeance." As Bishoff arranged the next row, Brown stared in amazement. After being copied from microfilm, the newspaper photo was blotchy and indistinct, but the people lined up outside a house in Springfield on a bright summer's day could be easily made out. Standing at the left of the picture, her hands folded, was Arminta Cobb, Brown's great-grandmother. Seated next to her and staring directly at the camera was Arminta's daughter, Pinky Cobb. Next to them, some sitting, some standing, were the other members of the Cobb and Moss families. Brown's eyes moved from face to face, recognizing them from old photographs that had been handed down through the generations. Across the gulf of a century, the Pierce City refugees, his family, stared out at Brown.

Brown was stunned.

"I just got this a few minutes ago and here it is, your folks," Bishoff later recalled saying. He went on: "Maybe I should say that really helped my connection there because I had given him a link to his people and I just wasn't a stranger walking in. I felt a little odd here about being the source of this story about a lynching. God, this is such an ugly story from this small town far away where I'm at."

Brown's return to Pierce City, where his family had once been outcasts, closed a chapter. And his search for what had happened ended a taboo in his family: talking about the expulsion. But there was one last step he was able to take.

Three years before the expulsion, James Brown's great-grandfather, James Cobb Sr., had been buried in the Pierce City cemetery. The graveyard, like the town, was segregated, with blacks consigned to the paupers' section. If there ever was a marker on the grave, it was long gone.

James Brown and his brother, Charles, set out to find their great-grandfather. A local historian, Judy Reustle, helped locate the plot number, which cemetery officials then used to find the burial plot.

On June 2, the two brothers looked on as a backhoe clawed at the earth. It was an oddly muted event. After a hundred years all that remained was some discolored earth and the metal handles of the casket. These bits and pieces were put in what looked like a Styrofoam cooler to be reburied after a brief prayer in the Cobb family plot in Springfield.

As the brothers loaded their great-grandfather's remains in a car for the trip to Springfield, one thing had changed. This time it was their choice to leave Pierce City.

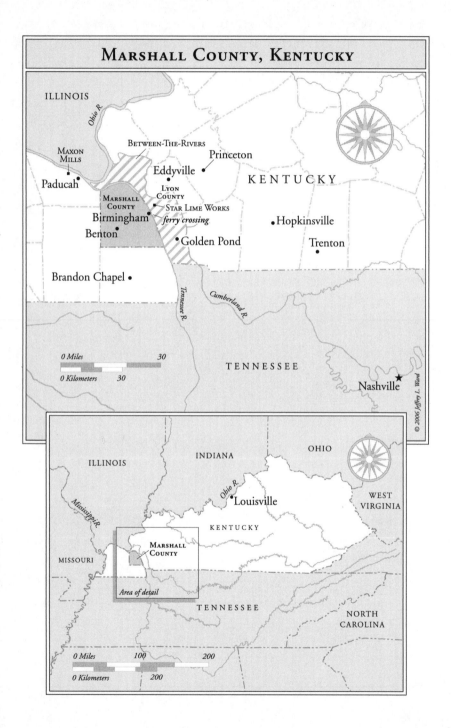

MARSHALL COUNTY, KENTUCKY

ILLINOIS

Ohio R.

MAXON
MILLS •

Paducah•

BETWEEN-THE-RIVERS

Princeton •

Eddyville •

K E N T U C K Y

MARSHALL
COUNTY

LYON
COUNTY

• Star Lime Works
ferry crossing

Birmingham•

• Hopkinsville

Benton•

• Golden Pond

Trenton •

Brandon Chapel •

Tennessee R.

Cumberland R.

0 Miles   30

0 Kilometers   30

T E N N E S S E E

Nashville ★

© 2006 Jeffrey L. Ward

ILLINOIS

INDIANA

OHIO

Mississippi R.

Ohio R.

• Louisville

WEST
VIRGINIA

K E N T U C K Y

MISSOURI

MARSHALL
COUNTY

Area of detail

TENNESSEE

NORTH
CAROLINA

0 Miles   100   200

0 Kilometers   200

CHAPTER 5

"Don't Kill Us All"

Marshall County, Kentucky
1908

Just after midnight on December 1, 1906, some 250 armed and hooded men attacked and briefly held the small town of Princeton, Kentucky. They overpowered the tiny police force and seized the telephone and telegraph offices, cutting contact with the outside world. They guarded the courthouse so no one could sound an alarm by tolling its bell, and patrolled the streets forcing everyone to stay indoors.[1]

With the town helpless, the Night Riders began their work. They set several fires inside the J. G. Orr tobacco warehouse and tossed in dynamite for good measure, destroying 250,000 pounds of tobacco. The raiders then moved across town to the Steger & Dollar warehouse, which stored another 200,000 pounds of tobacco. The raiders splashed the walls with kerosene and set the structure ablaze. The townspeople did not dare venture out to fight the fires. In any case, they would have failed. The invaders had taken over the town waterworks as well.

Then, as suddenly as they had come, the invaders vanished into the night.[2]

The Night Riders—farmers angry about the prices they were being offered for their tobacco crop—lived in a region of Kentucky known as the Black Patch, named for the type of dark tobacco grown and processed there. And in this battle between growers and buyers it was a name that stuck: The years-long struggle came to be called "The Black Patch War." But, because in the South all roads ultimately led to the issue of race, it was only a matter of time before the Black Patch War would mutate into a war on blacks.

The results would be tragic.

Three weeks before the Princeton raid, on Sunday, November 11, 1906, trains from across the South began arriving in Nashville with delegates for the second annual Southern Conference on Quarantine and Immigration. In the last two decades of the nineteenth century the number of people working in southern manufacturing had doubled, as had property values, and total wages had tripled. The old Confederacy's economic resurgence was being hyped as the "New South," and an imposing emblem of the boom greeted the delegates: the new Romanesque Revival Nashville train station, with its massive clock tower, sturdy arches, and interior faced in Tennessee marble. The delegates who hurried through the station's ornate lobby seemed a world away from the old hard-scrabble life of rural Kentucky. They were on their way to a find out how to attract immigrant labor to this New South.[3]

When the conference opened on Monday morning, however, it quickly became apparent that New South Nashville and backwater Princeton were in the grip of the same invisible forces. The convention delegates would try to talk about immigration, but the pressure to change the subject overwhelmed them. That same unrelenting pressure would bend the Night Riders' cause into a murderous rampage.[4]

The purpose of the Nashville convention was straightforward. As industrialization took hold in the South, businessmen looked at the immigrants pouring into northern ports and wondered how they could tap into this seemingly bottomless labor pool. Attracting immigrants to the South, they believed, was the path to prosperity.[5]

Tennessee's governor, John Cox, opened the convention at the state capitol by declaring grandly, "We are met here in conference that the

industrial and commercial conditions of the South may be improved."
But then a strange thing happened. Within minutes he drifted on to the
subject of race. "The National government has conferred upon the
Negro civil and political rights not warranted by the standards of his
manhood and his relations to society." It was the blacks who were holding back the South, Cox warned.[6]

Governor D. C. Heyward of South Carolina also began with a bold
vision: "It is to immigration we must look for our future development."
Then within a few sentences he too wandered off. "The white race is
the predominant race and the Negro must understand once and for all
that the bounds of the social and political questions will be determined
by the white man alone and by the white man's code." Most of the rest
of Heyward's speech was about race, and when he did finally circle back
to the subject of immigration, it was only to argue that it would solve
the race problem. "We must bring into the South not hundreds, not
thousands, but hundreds of thousands of desirable white immigrants,
make this land literally a white man's country."[7]

Like a dog with a bone, the delegates, gnawed endlessly on the question of race. One claimed that the only solution was to deport all blacks.
Still another disagreed, arguing that blacks were in America to stay. Yet
another proposed that authorities arrest African-American vagrants and
ship them off to dig the Panama Canal. It was as if immigration were
only a pretext for a meeting about Negroes.[8]

For all the talk about race and immigration, there was a riddle at the
heart of the convention. At this conference, like many others held in
the South, employers and politicians portrayed the region as starved for
workers and painted a rosy picture of the lucrative opportunities for immigrants. But if jobs were going begging, why were wages so low?

There was, in fact, no labor shortage. When labor is scarce, wages rise.
But at the turn of the century, southern workers, and southern blacks in
particular, were among the most poorly paid in the nation. In 1899 an
agricultural worker in the South earned fifty-six cents for the same job
that paid a dollar in the rest of the county. Ten years later the southern
field hand's share had dwindled to fifty-three cents. In another two
decades black workers would stream north to work in factories and then
there would indeed be a labor shortage in the South. That labor shortage

would not be solved by immigration, however. Instead, southern farmers invested in machinery and became more productive. But until that happened, the South was a place of many workers and few jobs.[9]

No doubt the delegates at the conference would benefit by increasing the supply of workers—employers always do. But outside the conference hall, where people struggled every day to eke out a living, the calculations were much different. Attempts to attract immigrants were hardly the problem. If you sold your labor, it was in your interests to restrict supply not increase it. With wages already depressed, the South was unlikely to entice immigrants. For most workers, the real goal was to shrink the existing labor pool in order to raise wages. And that brought you immediately to the issue of race. Black labor was plentiful and cheap, but it was also politically powerless and socially vulnerable. If white workers were able to organize a paramilitary force, they had the means to drive off black workers, shrink the labor pool, and demand better pay.

Here the Nashville convention had an oddly prophetic moment. "When a mob for any reason takes the law into its own hands," Governor Heyward told his audience, "a blow is struck at the very roots of our civilization." The line caught the eye of an editorial writer at the *Louisville Courier-Journal*. The next day the newspaper said Heyward "spoke many impressive words with reference to the Negro problem" but criticized the governor for not prosecuting white men who lynched blacks. "While the Negro must learn to favor enforcement of the law against his own race, the white man should set him a good example by showing his devotion to the law."

The editorial had it almost right. As events unfolded after the Princeton raid, the example that needed to be set was for the whites. And as the governor predicted, the raid was about more than a few tobacco warehouses in ruins. It meant that anyone with a cause and a few gunmen became the law in western Kentucky. In Princeton the gunmen had been farmers and the cause was tobacco. A year later the gunmen were iron workers and the cause was removing people like John Scruggs, an elderly black man living in Birmingham, Kentucky, and his infant grandson. Although they had no way of knowing it, the old man and the child stood at the very end of the trajectory described by the Nashville convention. They would have to die.[10]

The Princeton raid wasn't the first attack against the tobacco interests in Kentucky. A warehouse was destroyed in Trenton in December 1905, and in November 1906 two more were attacked in Eddyville and Kelsey. But these had been furtive affairs. A few men had stolen into town in the dead of night, set fires or planted dynamite, then run away. The attack on Princeton was entirely different. As a reporter wrote at the time, "The mob worked carefully showing that it had been well planned beforehand and each knew what he was expected to do."[11]

For as long as anyone could remember farmers had sold their crop at auction where agents from the tobacco companies would bid against one another. But as with many other industries, by the turn of the century, the tobacco companies had organized themselves into a trust that allowed them to dictate the price of tobacco. As a result, farmers had only a single buyer for their crops. The agent set the price, and the seller either accepted it or starved.

With the trust steadily driving down the price of tobacco, desperate farmers in Kentucky and parts of Tennessee organized into what they called the Planters' Protective Association. The members of the association agreed to hold back their crop until the trust paid what they considered a fair price. But some farmers refused to join the boycott. As long as the trust could get enough tobacco from non-association farmers, the boycotting farmers were doomed.[12]

The pressure on farmers who violated the boycott mounted quickly. Efforts at persuasion gave way to social ostracism. When that failed, some farmers turned to vandalism. Farmers who were not in the association found their tobacco seedlings "scrapped" and, after the harvest, their barns burned. Men were beaten and shot. Still, the trust was able to buy tobacco at advantageous prices.

Desperate, the secret paramilitary arm of the association, called the Night Riders, hit on an ingenious plan. Instead of attacking individual farmers, they would destroy the tobacco warehouses of the trust. In one blow the trust would lose a huge store of tobacco along with all the money it had paid for the crop.[13]

To make absolutely sure the tobacco companies were the ones hurt, the Night Riders sent an anonymous letter before the Princeton raid warning the companies that insured the warehouses. "We do not want to damage parties who are not concerned in buying [tobacco]," the letter said in part. "This is to notify you to cancel insurance immediately." The Night Riders needn't have worried. Following the raid, the State Board of Fire Insurance Underwriters said the policies were void because they did not cover "riot and invasion."[14]

The Princeton raid inspired similar attacks in Hopkinsville and Eddyville. The Night Riders also targeted tobacco buyers and recalcitrant farmers. Anyone who opposed the Night Riders lived in fear of a late-night visit, a beating, and an order to leave the county.

Because the battle with the tobacco trust was central to the region's economy, the Night Riders enjoyed the support not only of farmers but also of townspeople whose financial fortunes rose and fell with the price of tobacco. In some counties the sheriff, the prosecutor, and even the judge were in league with the Night Riders. In those counties where a judge or prosecutor tried to uphold the law, jurors often refused to convict or even indict. Governor Augustus Wilson tried calling up the state militia, but even as troops patrolled the Black Patch, the raids continued. The rule of law had collapsed in Western Kentucky.

Where men like Governor Wilson saw the Black Patch War as a threat to civilized society, Emelius Champion, a country doctor, saw an opportunity.

There is no record to show that Dr. Champion owned a tobacco farm or even cared about the price of tobacco. In fact, he lived in a strip of land in western Kentucky called "Between the Rivers"—because it was between the Tennessee and Cumberland rivers—dominated by the iron industry. But as the violence spiraled out of control, Champion decided to form a band of Night Riders. They would use the same tactics as the Night Riders in the tobacco war, but they would work for much different ends.[15]

To find recruits, Champion toured the smelters that dotted Between the Rivers. Years later, Boyd Hudson, one of the men who worked at a smelter, described Champion's recruiting pitch. "There was a bunch of us young guys, you know, and older ones too, met down there on that hillside. There was a big rock and we sat down there on the big rock. So, we joined the organization, didn't cost us anything. . . . They says you don't have to do anything." Champion ran the meeting.[16]

Hudson recalled Champion telling his followers to check "if some-body wasn't working or wasn't treating their family right." Anyone who stepped out of line got a visit from the Night Riders. The interview notes of a prosecutor give some idea of what Champion was doing. One of his victims told officials, "Night Riders visited me five weeks ago. . . . Dr. Champion said there was a hell of a tale out on me and that girl . . . took me 100 yard from house . . . took vote on whipping me. Told me I had better marry the girl."[17]

Champion knew something about not treating a family right. In 1892 his wife, Amanda, sued the doctor for a divorce. Their thirteen-year-old son testified in a deposition, "My father has treated mother very badly which has been kept up ever since they moved to this county. He would abuse her when he was about the house and would threaten to strike and beat her and on one occasion [I] saw him strike her with a stick." Asked whom he would rather live with, he said his mother. The doctor did not contest the divorce.[18]

But errant husbands and boyfriends were not Champion's only, or even his major, concern. His obsession—an obsession that bound him and his followers together—was blacks. For his followers, there may have been an economic issue. Whites and blacks competed for jobs smelting iron, and whites would benefit if the blacks were chased away. Champion, however, had no such worries. By any measure he was a racist, and the small black community in nearby Birmingham, Kentucky was a tempting target.[19]

Birmingham never amounted to much. Laid out in 1853 as a grid of lots along the banks of the Tennessee River, it remained a tiny country town for all of its life. In 1908, just before the raid, the town consisted of a mill, some stores, and homes for a few hundred people. Its most distinctive feature was the ferry that linked Birmingham and Between the Rivers on the far bank. The river itself was the boundary between Lyon County, where Champion lived, and Marshall County on the Birmingham bank.

Champion planned to ferry his recruits from Lyon County across the river for the attack on Birmingham. But it would help if they could be met by another band of Night Riders recruited from Birmingham itself. Not only would the Birmingham men have an intimate knowledge of their town, but recruiting some locals would reduce the chance that white townspeople, caught by surprise, would resist the attack. Champion set about pitting neighbor against neighbor.

Otis Blick was one such recruit. Just before the raid, two men stopped the twenty-four-year-old Blick at the public well and told him they were recruiting for the Night Riders. They hurried him off to the barbershop, where they held an impromptu induction. In a ceremony akin to those of the Ku Klux Klan, the men told Blick to kneel and take an oath that he would never reveal the secrets of the organization. One of those secrets was the password. One member says, "Silent brigade." The other member replies, "I see you have been there," which is followed by the countersign, "Yes, on my bended knee." Otis Blick was now one of Dr. Champion's Night Riders.[20]

The first inkling that there might be trouble in Marshall County came on the night of January 20, 1908. Mary Whitefield told investigators she first heard the dog barking and then "Someone hollowed 'Hello' and came up to the door and kicked the door open. Three men came in the house. One man got a shotgun and one got a pistol. They broke the lamp chimney." Mary and her husband, Steve, were black. They had made the mistake of renting a house that had previously been used by whites.[21]

The Night Riders, who were wearing hoods, hustled Steve Whitefield outside, told him "I was not wanted to live there," and then whipped him. Despite the hoods, the Whitefields were able to identify two of the men as Marvin Farley and Tom Childs.[22]

The man who rented the house to the Whitefields later told investigators that, shortly after New Year's, he had gotten notes "warning me not to have Steve Whitefield as a tenant." The reason was very straightforward: "Farley's folks had lived in the house the year before and did not want me to rent the house to the Negroes and wanted to rent it. So had Tom Childs."[23]

Perhaps as a threat or a show of bravado, Farley appeared at the Whitefield home the day after the attack, ostensibly to buy a hog. Although Farley had worn a mask during the attack, Whitefield later told investigators he recognized Farley as one of the men who had beaten him. Predator and prey were now customer and clerk. As Farley played out his role, he surveyed his handiwork. "He said he didn't know the door had been knocked down," Steve Whitefield recalled. The Whitefields moved.[24]

After the Whitefield whipping, notices appeared all around Birmingham warning blacks to leave. Some were tacked to telephone poles, others to fences, and at least one was stuck in the mail. At the same time people in Birmingham began talking about what was about to happen to the blacks. One white resident recalled a man named Joe Washburn arguing that "they could be run out." When investigators later talked to Washburn, he was circumspect. "I had heard talk at that time about running Negroes out of Birmingham," but he could not remember who told him. Others recalled hearing another resident, Tom McCain, talk about what was to come. "He said some of these nights they would swoop down on the Negroes in Birmingham. There would be weeping and wailing of teeth."[25]

In fact, by early March 1908, Champion's plans to raid Birmingham were well along. What was probably the final planning meeting took place during the week of March 1 at a barn in the village of Brandon Chapel, only a short distance from Champion's home. It was a convenient place to meet and, because it was on the road that ran directly to the Birmingham Ferry, the perfect assembly point for a raid.

As men stationed outside the barn tended the horses, Champion and his followers finalized their plan. The Princeton raid had set the standard. The men were organized into squads. Each wore a hood and a single white sash, and the leader of each squad had two sashes crossed on his chest. The squads moved in columns of two; each had a specific assignment. One squad cut all the telephone lines into a town. Another patrolled the streets to keep residents inside. Other squads were ordered to round up blacks.[26]

On Monday evening, March 9, 1908, Alex Stafford came to Brandon Chapel, a small town near where Champion lived, to court nineteen-year-old Orphea Rodgers, the daughter of Joe Rodgers. As the two passed the time sitting in the breezeway of the Rodgers home, Stafford heard the constant shuffle of people moving about in the darkness. It puzzled him, but he apparently said nothing. Instead, as it grew late, he said good night, mounted his horse and headed home. The road that passes the Rodgers place ascends a steep hill. At the top of the hill Stafford saw a terrifying sight: Dozens of hooded men with pistols, rifles, and shotguns lined the road near the Rodgers barn.

If he was to make his way home, Stafford had no choice but to ride through these Night Riders as they were forming up. Years later he would tell his family how, as he picked his way through the crowd, here and there from beneath a hood, a man would say, "Hello, Alex" or "Evening, Alex." Alex Stafford's friends and neighbors were about to raid Birmingham.[27]

From the Rodgers barn, Champion and his Night Riders rode past the Star Lime Works to the Birmingham Ferry. Once across the river, they joined a band of Marshall County Night Riders who had been waiting at a nearby mill. Estimates vary, but, between the two groups, some 150 men were about to descend on the small town of Birmingham.[28]

The plan for the raid was simple. After the phone lines were cut at midnight, several squads of Night Riders were assigned to attack black homes. A squad would first fire a volley into the home to scare its occupants and then order them outside. Anyone who resisted would be shot. Once the blacks were collected, an unlucky few would be marched down to the river, where Champion would take over.

At least one black resident of Birmingham sensed that there would be a raid that night. After a day spent selling eggs in Benton, a farmer named Walter Clone ran into a white neighbor when he got back to Birmingham that evening. The neighbor, who was himself a Night Rider, warned Clone to stay indoors because that night "hell would be to pay."[29]

Around midnight, Clone heard gunshots. He stepped outside, yelled at his dogs to stop barking, then retreated into his house. A few minutes later, he went out again. This time, he squatted at a nearby house and tried to make out what was happening. In the darkness, he heard one of the Night Riders say, "Walter Clone lives here. He's a good Negro. He's got a bad boy but he is not there." The men moved off, and Clone survived the night unharmed.[30]

The Scruggs family was not so lucky. Brooks Gaines, who lived nearby, heard gunfire and screaming at the Scruggs home.[31]

"The children were saying, 'Don't kill us all! Don't shoot us!'" Gaines would later testify. It did them no good. Dr. Champion personally led the squad that attacked the six people in the Scruggs home. When they were done, everyone in the Scruggs house had been wounded, including the elderly John Scruggs and his two-year-old grandson.[32]

Having witnessed what had happened at the Scruggs house, Gaines grabbed his own son and hid him in a gully that ran through a field. "If I get killed," Gaines told his son, "go to Paducah." After making sure his son was safe, he headed back into town. He had apparently heard a battle raging at the house of Lee Baker.[33]

From a hiding place about thirty yards from the Baker house, Gaines watched a furious gunfight. In Lee Baker, the Night Riders had met their match. Although he was surrounded by twenty Night Riders, the forty-three-year-old farmer, firing from inside the house, had already driven off one charge. One of the leaders of the Night Riders, complained, "We will have to have help to get this damn Negro." A Night Rider grabbed an ax and began smashing at Baker's door while another went in search of kerosene. As Baker continued firing, Otis Blick cried, "I am shot." A round had pierced the hood he was wearing and lodged in his shoulder. As three or four men carried Blick off, the Night Riders shouted to Baker that they were going to burn him out. With that, Baker surrendered.[34]

How the Night Riders selected those to be sent down to the river is not clear. Nat Frizzell, a schoolteacher, was picked along with Baker. The Night Riders grabbed Alex Terry but not his wife. Mark Skinner, a fifty-three-year-old laborer who lived a few doors down from Alex Terry on Pierce Street, was chosen. But Wyatt Muse, who lived with his wife and six children between Skinner and Terry, was not. A few women were ordered to the river: Annie and Julia Bishop went along with Claude Bishop. The Night Riders even picked one white man, Arthur Griffin. In all about a dozen people went down to the river.

After the raid, Griffin told investigators that he thought he had been singled out because one of the raiders "had it in for me." The Night Riders dressed his three children and took them to their mother's house and then marched Griffin down to the river. What awaited him there was so scary that he later admitted he almost soiled himself. The other captives sat on a log, guarded by scores of hooded men with guns. Two of the Night Riders were holding whips. Griffin found a place to relieve himself.[35]

The first person to be tortured was Lee Baker, who had wounded Blick. The vigilantes laid Lee Baker out on the ground, where two men whipped him in tandem. But the Night Riders weren't satisfied: Convinced that Baker was not suffering enough, they made him bend over a log with his back arched, so that the whips could cut into him more easily. As they laid into Baker, one of the whips broke. Dr. Champion said they should use a "good, healthy ox whip."[36]

By most accounts, Lee Baker was whipped in tandem by two men for fifteen minutes. It is impossible to understand what this means without understanding the physics of a whip. The handle of a whip is attached to a thick leather braid. The braid is tapered—the end is no larger in diameter than a piece of string. When a person flicks the handle, the energy from that action ripples down the whip. Because of the tapering, that coil of energy acts on a smaller and smaller leather mass. Just as a car would speed up if it continually grew lighter, the coil moving down the braided leather accelerates as the whip's mass grows smaller. By the time it reaches the end of the whip, the coil is moving at 750 miles an hour, faster than the speed of sound. It is at that moment that it slams into human flesh.[37]

The first few blows rip away the skin. As the beating continues, the fatty tissue below the skin is torn away. The longer the beating goes on, the more flesh is lacerated until finally the whip bites into muscles and the blood vessels that feed them. One former slave described the effects of a whipping with a spare eloquence. "One slave girl got a whipping for sometimes singing about that John Brown. They tied her to a tree and the lashing bloodied up the tree all around."[38]

According to eyewitnesses, of the dozen people the Night Riders marched down to the riverbank, five were whipped. While one was being beaten, the others were forced to sit on a log and watch. For the onlookers, watching would have been a form of torture in its own right. It would also function to intensify the pain of subsequent victims, who could now visualize the torture being inflicted on their own bodies.

It is not clear how long the torture went on. Terry's wife estimated her husband was gone for an hour. Others thought it was closer to thirty minutes. But after whipping Lee Baker, the Night Riders forced Nat Frizzell to bend over a log and submit to a beating. He was followed by Annie

Bishop, Alex Terry, and Claude Bishop. The Night Riders spared Griffin, the white man, who was let off with a warning to treat his wife better.[39]

When his men had finished torturing the captives, Champion gave a little speech. He said that "there were thousands of Night Riders in the United States and their actions would be watched and in the course of thirty, sixty or ninety days a return visit would be paid. He also ordered them to leave Birmingham and remain away." With that Dr. Champion and his band rode off.[40]

Dr. Robert Overby, who lived in Benton, said he was called to Birmingham between around one A.M. He tried to save John Scruggs by amputating his leg. But both Scruggs and his grandson died. He also bandaged the wounds of those who had been whipped. He would later describe the beatings as "unmerciful." On the other side of the river, Otis Blick was taken to Champion, who probed for bullets and dressed the wounds.[41]

In the following days, Birmingham must have seemed schizophrenic. Blacks were forced to confront their attackers, who were in many cases their own neighbors. The man behind the counter at the grocery store was the same person who shot out your windows. A passerby could have helped drag off your neighbors in the dead of night. Alex Terry, one of the victims of the whippings, ran into one of the Night Riders on the street. "He looked at me and laughed and turned his head," Terry reported. Another Night Rider came to Terry's house "wanting to buy wild geese I had. His father with him wanted to buy my property. . . . [He] said looks like my house was tore up pretty bad."[42]

By Tuesday afternoon, newspapers throughout the Black Patch were carrying front-page stories about the raid. Wednesday morning the *Louisville Courier-Journal* published a front-page story headlined "Negroes Shot and Whipped." After describing what had happened in Birmingham, the paper noted that "Tobacco stemmeries [warehouses] have been warned to discharge negro hands and have complied and many landlords have turned them out. The same policy has been pursued in Lyon County in the vicinity of Kuttawa and along the Cumberland." Champion's campaign to rid the region of blacks was picking up speed.[43]

In the weeks after the Birmingham raid, newspapers reported raids throughout western Kentucky. On March 24, twenty Night Riders fired into the house of a black in Lyon County and ordered him to leave. The next night gunmen shot into the home of a white farmer in Lyon County and demanded he fire his black workers. Two days later Night Riders struck again in Golden Pond, a community in Between the Rivers. They walked into the local hotel and shot to death a black man who lived there. Around the same time black farmers in Maxon Mills started getting letters ordering them to leave. In Marshall County notices were posted in Benton, the county seat, ordering all blacks out. By March 28, one newspaper reported, "Only six negroes remain in Benton since the notices to leave the town have been posted. The negroes are thoroughly intimidated and it is the general opinion that every colored person in Benton will leave by Saturday night."[44]

Champion had warned blacks in Birmingham that he would be back. Just before the end of the month, the steamer *Kentucky*, which had churned its way up the Tennessee River from Birmingham, docked in Paducah. On deck with whatever they could carry were about a hundred blacks. Nat Frizzell and Lee Baker would eventually move a few miles up river to Metropolis, Indiana. Brooks Gaines settled in Paducah. Others moved to the river town of Brookport.[45]

Dr. Champion had won.

Judge William Reed was not a man to be taken lightly. Born in Graves County, Kentucky, in 1848, educated at Princeton University, he had long been a prominent attorney in western Kentucky before he became a judge. Portly with a carefully clipped mustache and a penetrating gaze, he looked every inch the pillar of the community that he was. And after the Birmingham raid it was becoming very clear to Judge Reed that the community he loved was under attack.[46]

The raid had clearly rattled Paducah, where Judge Reed lived. Whether it was true or not, in the weeks after the Birmingham raid Paducah residents believed they had seen Night Riders on the city's outskirts. One local attorney, fearing attack was imminent, wrote the governor begging for help. "Paducah is absolutely terror stricken. We have absolutely no protection here beyond our small police force and the guards hired by the tobacco men." Worse yet the Night Riders or their spies could be anywhere. "I have not trusted this letter to a stenographer," the lawyer explained, "but written it on the typewriter myself. It has been shown only to a few trusted men."[47]

Judge Reed himself had learned details of the Birmingham raid from fellow Judge William L. Crumbaugh of Lyon County. The elderly Crumbaugh, with a craggy face, hooked nose, and full beard, was the rustic counterpoint to the younger and more urbane Judge Reed. Because the two judges opposed vigilantes, they shared a signal honor: The Night Riders had threatened to kill them both. Whatever else the threats may have done, they did not scare either man. Instead Judge Crumbaugh spent most nights for over a year lying in ambush outside his home waiting for his killers to appear. It was, in fact, one of the few ways Crumbaugh could fight back. Because grand juries of his fellow citizens in Lyon County would not indict, much less convict, Night Riders, Crumbaugh was reduced to collecting information that he passed along in a steady stream of letters to Governor Wilson.[48]

When Judge Crumbaugh appeared in Judge Reed's office on March 18, he brought a somewhat inaccurate but chilling account of the Birmingham raid from one of his informants. "When the miscreants came, the old man [John Scruggs] went out as ordered, both hands raised, his wife with a three-year-old baby in her arms. All were shot to death. The two men [members of the Scruggs family] went out the back way thinking to escape but a large crowd of riders stood in their way. They fired both guns at the men and in the confusion both men escaped."[49]

Faced with a vigilante movement on his doorstep, Judge Reed convened a grand jury in Marshall County in mid-March to bring indictments for the Birmingham raid. In his instructions to that grand jury, the judge was so emphatic that one newspaper described his speech as "one of the most forceful appeals for a rigid investigation of the outrages that was ever heard in the Benton Court room." But if he hoped to indict, much less convict, the approximately 150 men in the raid, he was about to be disappointed.

The Night Riders responded to Judge Reed by trying to intimidate the grand jury. On the night of March 30, a band of men rode into the yard of Joseph Minter, the grand jury foreman, and ordered him to come outside. Minter was staying in Benton while the grand jury was in session, and all his wife and children could do was huddle in the darkened house and hope the men would go away. The Night Riders banged on the door, "uttered dreadful oaths," and then "fired off their revolvers in the air and rode away."[50]

Henry James, a black farmer who lived nearby, was not as lucky. That same night the Night Riders descended on his house and ordered him to leave. By morning James and his family were seen in Mayfield, a town sixteen miles away in neighboring Graves County, their wagon loaded with whatever they could haul away.[51]

The Marshall County grand jury issued subpoenas for eight of the Birmingham blacks to testify. Because all had fled the county, the subpoenas had to be sent to Paducah, where most of the Birmingham refugees now lived. For those who had been tortured by the river, it meant returning to a nightmare.

Among those summoned was Brooks Gaines, seventy, who had witnessed the attack on Lee Baker's home and had seen Otis Blick shot. On Wednesday afternoon, April 2 Gaines dutifully took his seat before the grand jury in Benton to tell his story. It would have been an unremarkable moment except for one thing. As they questioned him, it dawned on the grand jury that this elderly man, who had lost everything, had walked the twenty-two miles from Paducah to Benton to sit in that witness chair. Given the distance and his age, it might have taken him two days. Every step was, as Gaines knew too well, through a dangerous countryside. The grand jurors and the court officers passed the hat so he wouldn't have to walk back.[52]

Despite the bravery of men like Brooks Gaines and the insistence of Judge Reed, the Marshall County grand jury was clearly not eager to take on the Night Riders. Although some 150 men had been involved in the Birmingham raid, when it handed down its indictments on April 2, the grand jurors named only eleven.[53]

Even those few indictments seemed like an empty gesture. When eight of the eleven men were arrested, a newspaper account showed that the Night Riders were confident their fellow citizens would never convict them.

> Like coming in from a pleasant outing, with accused men and officers alike jollying and joking each other, Sheriff Pete Eley and Deputy

Sheriff Will Eley arrived in town late this afternoon with eight of the 11 alleged Night Riders who have been indicted, as their prisoners. The sight that greeted citizens of Benton, in the place of shackled and chained "bad men," was a merry, laughing crowd of horsemen that appeared more like so many prosperous Kentucky planters on their way for a county fair than they did sheriff's men in charge of alleged members of the bold torch-operating Night Riders.[54]

Unable to get what he wanted in Marshall County, Judge Reed tried to outflank the Night Riders by convening a grand jury in Paducah, which was across the line in McCracken County. Reed left little doubt about what he wanted when on April 9, 1908 he empaneled this new grand jury: "If this grand jury or any number of you shall fail to do your duty, then crime must go unpunished."[55]

But even after all but demanding more indictments, Judge Reed fared even worse. When it adjourned on April 15, the McCracken County grand jury failed to indict a single Night Rider.[56]

That left Judge Reed with only the men who had been indicted in Benton. Those few cases were hardly the massive blow he had hoped to deal the Night Riders when he convened two grand juries. But when he opened court in Benton on Monday, June 15, he may have felt these trials would at least send a message. Unfortunately, the first few trials were not the message Judge Reed would have hoped for.

Burnett Phelps was the first to be tried. His case started on Monday, went to the jury on Thursday, and by Friday they were hopelessly deadlocked. As for Sam Collie, who had led the attack on Lee Baker's house, his jury started deliberating on Friday and pronounced Collie not guilty the following day. Champion's trial was scheduled next. It seemed obvious that a Marshall County jury would acquit him as well.[57]

On Tuesday, June 23, just before Champion's trial was to start, Reed told the court, "I will summon a venire from McCracken County," the next county over, and then adjourned for lunch. His written order was only slightly more forthcoming. "The court being of the opinion that an unbiased jury can not be obtained in Marshall County, the sheriff was directed to summon 50 men from McCracken County to appear in this court tomorrow morning from which a jury is to be selected." The prosecution had not requested a different jury, and the defense must have been furious. Reed was unmoved.[58]

When the trial began the following day, with the McCracken jury, Nat Frizzell was the first witness. He identified Champion as the man who ordered his whipping. Next came Anderson Scruggs, who said he saw Champion lead the assault on his family's home. J. A. Smith, another of the Birmingham refugees, also identified Champion as the man who led the raid. Smith was followed by Brooks Gaines and Arthur Griffin. Then the prosecution brought in its star witness: Otis Blick.[59]

After he confessed to his role in the Birmingham raid, Blick had been guarded by the Kentucky National Guard at a camp in neighboring Calloway County. When he was moved to Benton, he was given a uniform and told to live with a small contingent of troops sent there by the governor to protect the Night Rider trials. There had been one attempt on Blick's life. When that failed, Blick's father told him they could get $1,000 if the son would change his story. The bribe attempt failed as well.[60]

Before the Champion trial, Blick had testified in the Burnett Phelps trial, and he would tell the same story again and again both in court and to reporters. He described his induction into the Night Riders, named the men who took part in the raid, told how the Night Riders met at a mill before the raid and of the assault on Lee Baker's house, where he was shot. It was the story of the shooting that led to the high point of his testimony.[61]

After the Birmingham raid, Blick had stashed his hood in a hollow tree stump. When he agreed to testify for the prosecution, the commonwealth attorney took him to the stump to retrieve his mask. In court it made a wonderful piece of theater. Blick showed the jury the scar from his bullet wound and then put on the hood to demonstrate how the bullet hole in the mask lined up with his wound. The sight of a hooded man in court was jarring.[62]

To counter Blick's testimony, the defense in the Phelps trial brought in Blick's father, who said that because of a case of sunstroke as a boy, his son's "mind had wandered at times." Under cross-examination, the father acknowledged he never had his son examined by a doctor or treated for sunstroke. He also admitted trying to bribe Otis.[63]

For its part, the defense paraded more than forty witnesses through the courtroom, all claiming the doctor had either been at home or making house calls.

On Friday at four P.M. the case was given to the jury. When by midnight there still had been no verdict, people assumed they were deadlocked. They were not far from wrong. Two of the jurors wanted to acquit the doctor while six wanted him sentenced to fifteen years. The remaining four thought the doctor was guilty and should serve five to ten years. Saturday morning they reached a compromise.[64]

At 10:30 A.M. they filed back into court. Champion was guilty. But for a raid that had resulted in the murders of an old man and a child, the torture of at least five people, and the destruction of a community, he would serve only one year. Whatever Judge Reed thought of the sentence, he had won his battle with the vigilantes. Louise Stafford, the daughter of a Night Rider, said the specter of being called before a grand jury and the possibility of going to prison, "scared the pee out of" the Riders. When Dr. Champion went off to prison, his band of vigilantes disintegrated.[65]

But neither Reed nor his fellow judge, Crumbaugh, would realize just how complete their victory was until the following year. After his release from prison in 1909, Champion, who was facing charges in Calloway County for sending threatening letters, became a turncoat. Judge Crumbaugh, always trolling for information, brokered a deal with the doctor: In return for $5 a day plus expenses, Champion would inform on his fellow Night Riders. On October 6, 1909, Crumbaugh wrote the governor that Champion had spent four days meeting with the Night Riders and exulted, "I do not believe there is the slightest suspicion about our man."[66]

Champion was more interested in a pardon from the governor than in money. Suspicious of Crumbaugh, Champion wrote the governor on October 3, 1909 to make sure he would not have to face trial in Calloway County. "Judge Crumbaugh has employed me to do some Secret Service work," the doctor wrote. "He claims he has [an] understanding with you. He has agreed to pay me $5.00 per day and expenses. He claims he [has] written you. I told him what I could do on certain conditions provide[d] you would pardon me of those indictments at Smithland and restore my citizenship rights."[67]

When the governor wrote back that he could not promise a pardon but would consider "faithful and honest services to Commonwealth," Champion exploded. In a rambling five-page, handwritten letter, Champion accused the governor of handing out pardons as favors and noted that Otis Blick, his fellow Night Rider, had gotten a pardon even though "he is one of the worst characters in the county." Champion boasted that he did not need a pardon because "I can beat the case" then quickly added "but it cost me money to do it." He told the governor he should get a pardon because he was innocent and accused someone else of writing the letters. Then he threatened the governor. "Unless you pardon me and restore me at once I cannot go any further with this business. My trial is set for the 10th day of this month. If you see fit to do this I will go to work any time you think best. All I ask is you to protect me at the proper time."[68]

The governor was aghast. He wrote to Judge Crumbaugh that Champion's letter "is so wrong in its statements that I do not think I ought to have any correspondence with him." With that, Champion's career as an informer ended.[69]

———

Birmingham no longer exists. The name still lingers on some maps, but don't look for the place where John Scruggs and his grandson were killed or Lee Baker was beaten. In the 1940s, the Army Corps of Engineers began damming the Cumberland and Tennessee rivers to form two artificial lakes. When it did, Birmingham was buried beneath the waters. Between the Rivers is gone too. When the waters rose, the government changed its name to Land Between the Lakes and converted it to a recreation area. Mines and smelters disappeared. Towns were closed and their residents relocated.

And the blacks who were chased away have not come back. At the turn of the century, 348 blacks lived in Marshall County. Ten years later there were 135. The blacks who did stay were landowners, but even they could not hang on. By 1920, there were sixty-four blacks. People in Marshall County today say they can remember only one black in the entire county in the late 1950s—a middle-aged man known only as "Jip" who shined shoes at a barbershop in Benton. By the 1960s, he was gone.[70]

It was not that blacks didn't want to live in Marshall County, it was that they were not welcome. Judge William Cunningham, who is now the circuit court judge for Marshall County, grew up there and knows its history as well anyone.[71]

Cunningham is a natural storyteller. Like a man playing a pinball machine, he uses body English to tell his story. He hunches forward and moves closer to signal he is about to take the listener into his confidence.

"Here's an experience," the judge begins. It was the 1960s, and he had returned home to Benton, the seat of Marshall County, after graduating from college. "My brother-in-law and I went down to Hutchen's BBQ. We were down at Hutchen's eating and Richard, who is a lawyer, told me there had been a black couple move into Marshall County."

The judge pauses. His voice changes key slightly to indicate he is now a character in the story, and he says as if he is musing, "Well that's interesting."

Then the judge becomes the narrator again. "Joe Tom Halton, the county sheriff, happened to just walk by. He had seen me. How are you doing, blah blah, blah."

The judge leans even closer and acts out both roles in the conversation.

"Joe Tom, I heard that a black family moved into the county."

"Well, they are not here anymore."

"They're not. What happened?"

"Ahhh, they're trouble makers."

"Well, did somebody bother them?"

"No, nobody bothered them. I think somebody burned a cross on their lawn or something. But nobody harassed them."

The judge laughs at the outrageousness of the sheriff's statement and ends the story with the moral: "So that was the attitude."

Things have changed since then. Once an ardent segregationist, the judge now embraces Martin Luther King, Jr. as one of his heroes. His son married a black woman, and the judge keeps a picture of his daughter-in-law and grandchild perched in the cluttered study of his home.

But that is inside his house. Outside, the legacy of Dr. Emelius Champion lives on.

BOONE COUNTY, ARKANSAS

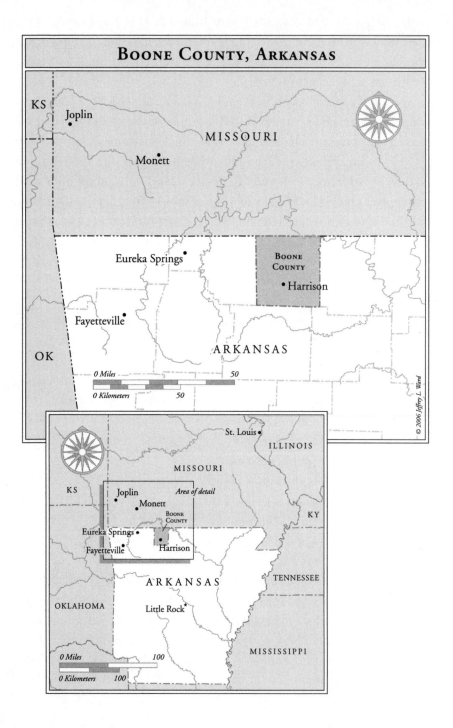

KS

Joplin

MISSOURI

Monett

Eureka Springs

BOONE COUNTY

Harrison

Fayetteville

OK

ARKANSAS

0 Miles   50

0 Kilometers   50

© 2006 Jeffrey L. Ward

St. Louis

ILLINOIS

MISSOURI

KS

Joplin   Area of detail

Monett

BOONE COUNTY

KY

Eureka Springs

Fayetteville   Harrison

ARKANSAS

TENNESSEE

OKLAHOMA

Little Rock

MISSISSIPPI

0 Miles   100

0 Kilometers   100

CHAPTER 6

All-White Diversity

Boone County, Arkansas
1905 and 1909

If young Charles Stinnett had not decided to rob the spinster Emma Lovett, there might still be a black community in Boone County, Arkansas. It would probably be a very small black community, in part because the county is what people politely call "out of the way." But it would have been very small for another reason as well: When Charles Stinnett showed up at Emma Lovett's house in 1909, most of the blacks had already been run out. In the history of racial cleansings, Boone County is unique: It hosted two in just four years—in 1905 and 1909.

Today local civic leaders describe Boone County as a warm, welcoming community unfairly tarnished by a racist past. Others are less sanguine. One resident recently described Boone County as a place "known all over the world as a haven for racists and bigots." Whichever view people subscribe to, the county remains very white. For much of the twentieth century, Boone County has had fewer than ten black inhabitants, and during one thirty-year stretch beginning in 1930, the census takers could not find a single African-American. The most recent census lists thirty-nine blacks in a county of 34,000 people. And while the story of how the county shed its black population is sketchy, one thing is clear: Its demographics were eventually settled by a bungled robbery.[1]

Charles Stinnett and his parents were one of the few black families to stay after the cleansing of 1905. Because so little is known about this first expulsion, it is hard to judge whether their staying put was courageous or foolhardy.

The 1905 cleansing was centered in Harrison, the county seat. Unfortunately, copies of the local newspaper from that time no longer exist. What little we know comes from personal recollections and from newspapers outside of Harrison.[2]

The most detailed extant account, headlined "Drive Negroes from Harrison," appeared in the *Arkansas Gazette* on October 6, 1905. The lead is straightforward. "With the thrashing and deportation of several negroes during the past few days, a movement has begun here which it is believed will result in the driving out of most of the negroes from this city." The article describes how a mob broke into the city jail, took some blacks outside of town, whipped them, and then "ordered them to leave." A porter at a local barbershop, Tom Armstrong, was "treated in the same manner" the next night. But the paper never really explains what precipitated the raid. It only says that the mob formed after a "negro named Dan" broke into a doctor's house to keep warm and was subsequently arrested. Even allowing for the rampant racism of the time, a harmless black trying to stay warm does not seem like the stuff of mass hysteria. The article also does not really explain why the black community was so terrified, saying only that "It has been rumored that other negroes are to be given the same treatment." But the level of violence and threats described in the story don't seem to match the terror that the blacks obviously felt.[3]

In the last line of the story, however, lies a clue to the origins of the cleansing: "The completion of the railroad work at Omaha and other points on the Missouri Pacific has left many negroes out of work, and many of them have come to Harrison." In 1899 the St. Louis and North

Arkansas Railroad had announced it was going to build a line from Seligman, Missouri that would pass through Boone County and terminate in Helena, a town 185 miles to the south.

The train was the superhighway of those days; where tracks were laid, people felt prosperity was sure to follow. Farmers donated their land as a right of way, and, as an incentive, towns raised cash to finance the railroad companies. Harrison collected more than $40,000 for the new railroad. What no one seemed to ask was if there was anything worth shipping between Helena and Harrison. The answer appears to have been not much. The line, which pushed though Boone County in 1901, went bankrupt on July 1, 1905. What the bankruptcy left behind was an impoverished community and unemployed men. Among those idled workers, which the *Arkansas Gazette* alluded to, were "many negroes" who had now drifted to Harrison.[4]

In an economically depressed town with a sizeable group of unemployed blacks, whites could improve their chances of economic survival by tossing the blacks out. It was certainly not unheard of. A year later five men in Arkansas County were fined $500 each and sent to prison for trying to drive off black laborers. At their sentencing the judge noted, "There seems to be on the part of a few men in the state a disposition to prevent these men from working because in this instance they happen to be Negroes." Which was precisely the same thing that happened in Harrison. After describing the whippings and the expulsion of Harrison's blacks, an editorial in the *Rogers Democrat,* a newspaper in a neighboring town, noted, "The affair has the disapproval of the better elements of the town, who say the trouble has been fomented by a few white day laborers who fear the negroes will displace them."[5]

What is not touched on in any of these stories is the sense of entitlement that whites felt. White workingmen, facing economic competition from black neighbors, felt it was perfectly acceptable to terrorize blacks into leaving. In part this can be understood by the circumstances. Some of those being driven out were people who had drifted in from other places and were, at best, not members of the community. But how to explain why Tom Armstrong, the porter at the barbershop, was attacked the night after the mob broke into the city jail? He and his family were long-time residents of Harrison, he held a job, yet he was as expendable as any drifter.[6]

The answer was that in turn-of-the-century America, race trumped all other considerations. A humble black porter, no matter how respectable, was still a black. His treatment reflected not only the mood in Harrison but the spirit of the country. When the North and South sought a political reconciliation during the 1880s and 1890s, blacks were an inconvenient presence. If their rights had to be ignored to achieve national unity, then so be it. When the South pressed for segregation, the North acquiesced. When America's imperialist adventures of the 1890s won it colonies of brown-skinned peoples, the country lamented that it was the "white man's burden." Men like Tom Armstrong might live here, but they did not belong here.[7]

Arkansas was very diligent about making those distinctions. The state legislature first passed a "separate coach" bill in 1890 that segregated the railroads and then followed that with a series of restrictive voting bills designed to disenfranchise blacks. Having marginalized the black vote, white politicians were free to demonize African-Americans without fear of political retaliation.

In 1904, when Governor Jeff Davis was running for re-election, he declared, "Every time you educate a nigger, you spoil a good field hand." His solution, he told white voters, was to segregate the school tax. Under the Davis plan, taxes raised from white voters would go only to white schools and blacks would be left to finance their schools as best they could. "We have come, in my judgement, to a parting of the ways," Davis declared. "The South for nearly half a century has done her best to try to make something out of the negro and we have totally failed."[8]

As a matter of policy, the idea of segregating the school tax went nowhere. It was voted down in the state legislature because illiterate black workers only created headaches for potential employers. But the Davis rhetoric was a measure of how little blacks counted in public life. He could ridicule and abuse them and still win re-election because blacks did not belong to the electorate. By the same token, the citizens of Boone County could embrace the idea of driving out their black population because, stripped of the vote, blacks were no longer part of the community. And in the perverse equation of disenfranchisement, local officials like the sheriff apparently calculated that they had no obligation to prevent white voters from terrorizing black non-voters.

Perhaps because they saw themselves as civic boosters, the newspapers only hinted at the extent of the terror. It was left to local residents writing personal histories years after the cleansing to describe what actually took place. "A mob moved through the dark streets and alleys of the town," wrote Ralph Rea, a local white who described the expulsion in his account of Boone County's history. He said the mob went "house to house in the colored section . . . sometimes threatening, sometimes using the lash, always issuing the order that hereafter 'no nigger had better let the sun go down on 'em.'"

Another account, by local historian Loren Watkins, paints a similar picture of the 1905 expulsion. Quoting an eyewitness, Watkins writes that a heavily armed mob went from house to house ordering blacks to leave, setting some houses on fire and shooting out the windows of others. The Watkins account helps us understand why blacks were so terrified. He describes how the white mob tied eight to ten blacks to trees and, using bull whips, tortured the victims. Others were bound together and tossed in a creek, presumably to drown.[9]

There is no way to tell how accurate the Rea and Watkins descriptions are. Watkins acknowledges that he did not actually see the 1905 expulsion, and Rea mixes up events of 1905 and 1909. But in addition to what he was told, Watkins describes his own encounter with one of the victims of the mob, which supports his account in chilling detail. Watkins and his father were working on their farm after the 1905 attacks when "a large negro man by the name of Clark, bare headed and bare footed, face scratched and legs below the knees bleeding, stopped by where we were working and stated he had been whipped, beaten and ordered out of town by a mob the night before, along with all the other negroes in town." Clark told Watkins and his father that he had gotten separated from the other blacks who were fleeing and spent the night in the woods. He also said that the mob had set fire to some black homes and sacked others.[10]

Whatever took place in Harrison, it seems clear that the mob violence went well beyond the "thrashings" described in the newspaper. It is certainly clear why most blacks fled in 1905. For the few blacks like the Stinnett family who remained after 1905, living in Harrison must have been like camping on the slopes of a volcano. No matter how quiet the day, the vigil never ends.

The volcano erupted for Boone County's blacks with a cry for help on Sunday morning, January 17, 1909. Sixty-two-year-old Emma Lovett, who had hidden in her barn throughout the long cold night, was now at her neighbor's door with a horrifying story. The day before, she had been chopping firewood when Charles Stinnett stopped and offered to help. After Stinnett brought a load of wood in the house, Miss Lovett said that they had warmed themselves by the fire. When she opened the door for Stinnett to leave, according to a newspaper account, "He grabbed her and threw her on the bed, covered her head with a quilt and accomplished his heinous purpose." She said that, after the attack, he drew a knife and threatened to kill her if she ever breathed a word to anyone. Fearing he would return, Miss Lovett said she hid in her barn all night, only daring to get help at daybreak.[11]

What followed exemplifies the term "speedy justice." Stinnett was arrested on Sunday, indicted on Monday, convicted on Friday, and sentenced to death on Saturday. Through it all, he insisted that he had never raped Miss Lovett. Instead, he claimed that he had gone to the Lovett house planning to rob the elderly woman and that he had only pulled a knife to reinforce his demand for money. It was a distinction lost on nearly everyone on the all-white jury. One juror wanted to convict Stinnett of a lesser charge, but after four hours he caved.

After the trial, police moved Stinnett out of the county. He would be executed in March. But immediately after his conviction, Boone County's few remaining blacks fled. As with the story of the 1905 expulsion that described "thrashings," the newspaper accounts say only that blacks "have left." The version handed down in the Cotton family is not so bloodless. Interviewed in the 1990s, Hugh Cotton, an eighty-three-year-old resident of Harrison, said,

> Granddad used to have an abstract office [having to do with titles of land ownership] and a saloon on the south side of the square and Nig-ger George done all the cleanin', washing the shot glasses and sweepin' and all. And then when they had the trouble, they run 'em out. They hung one and gave the rest of 'em 24 hours to—all ten, eleven, twelve [of them]—to leave. Then they got hot and heavy after Nigger George because him and one old lady was still in Harrison. They threatened to lynch him, so Granddad put him in the buggy one night at midnight and took him to Eureka Springs.[12]

By January 28, 1909 it was over. The *Arkansas Gazette* reported, "All the negroes have left the town except old 'Uncle Dick Fancher,' who has been here for many years and is well behaved." In fact, the story was not exactly accurate. Fancher left, and it was an old woman called "Aunt Vine" who was the only black to remain. A decade later she was dead.[13]

As if putting an exclamation point on their racism, the Harrison Chamber of Commerce crowed in a 1920s promotional pamphlet that the county had "no mosquitoes and no Negroes."[14]

———

The Reverend Wayne Kelly never holds a meeting. Instead he likes to say he "visits" with people. His stories, recounted in the silver-edged drawl of his native Texas, brim with memories of prayer meetings and good fellowship. And when he ends a conversation with "God bless you," you are not the least bit surprised. So when he is asked about the state of race relations in Harrison, Arkansas, where he is the pastor of the New Hearts Church, he replies without even a trace of irony.[15]

"You can't really say that we have a race problem in Harrison," he explains, "because there is no diversity of race really."

He is absolutely right. There are a few blacks working for the Federal Express freight facility, the town's largest employer, but they

commute from outside the county. If pressed, civic leaders will rec-
ollect a black man working in town at North Arkansas College or a
woman as a food service worker for the public schools. But beyond
that, nothing. Which is not to say, the same civic leaders quickly add,
that blacks are not welcome. Rev. Kelly sums up the prevailing wisdom on racism in Boone County. "Bottom line is we did have our
problems and there were racists in our community and probably still
are racists in our community. But it's not the majority." The problem
is more one of image, Rev. Kelly explains. Other towns have racial
problems, but when anything happens in Harrison "it makes the national news."

D. Jeff Christenson, publisher of the local newspaper, goes even further. "From all my experience in living in this community for thirty
years, I have never witnessed any acts of racism. The fact is, I believe
this community goes out of its way to do just the opposite." The problem, he says, is that "there is a concerted effort to make our community
look bad." [16]

Which may be why Halloween 2002 came as such a fright.

That day, a junior high football team from Fayetteville sixty miles
away came to play the Harrison team. When the day was over, Ken
Ball, the Fayetteville coach, was so angry he fired off a letter to his
local newspaper, the *Northwest Arkansas Times*. In it, Ball described
his team's day there as a series of racist encounters; after the game,
the Harrison players refused to shake hands with the black Fayetteville players. "These actions go beyond poor sportsmanship," Ball
wrote. "My players never want to return to Harrison to play. The
Northwest Arkansas Athletic Association should drop Harrison from
its conference."[17]

When the letter was published, the people of Harrison were scandalized. Although he still refuses to reprint the Ball letter in his newspaper, the *Harrison Daily Times*, Christenson denounced it in his
column along with another letter about race problems in Harrison. He
described the allegations as "hogwash." Rev. Kelly is a bit more diplomatic. He said he investigated some of Ball's accusations, and "The stories didn't line up so well."

There was, however, at least one person in Harrison who was more curious than outraged. George Holcomb remembers sitting in the newsroom of the *Harrison Daily Times* when he heard about the letter and suddenly getting very interested. Which was, in its own way, odd because up to that point in his fifty-five years of life, George Holcomb had not taken much of anything very seriously. A mediocre student, he ambled through college. Then for twenty-nine years he worked as an interviewer for the Social Security Administration not because he liked the work—he hated his job—but because it paid well. He spent most of his career working and living in Harrison. When he retired in 2002, he used the first few months of his newfound freedom remodeling a bathroom. When that ended, he, well, drifted.[18]

"Finally when my wife came home early from work one day and found me sitting on the sofa eating chocolate ice cream out of the tub and watching Oprah," Holcomb said, "she just started reading me the want ads."

One of the ads was for a reporter. Even though his entire experience in journalism consisted of getting kicked off his high school newspaper ("I kept missing the deadlines"), the editor of the *Daily Times* sensed promise in this deceptively youthful-looking retiree with spiky white hair and large glasses. It also helped that Holcomb was willing to work for $8 an hour. In any case, that was how Holcomb came to be sitting in the newsroom of the local paper wondering about the Ball letter.

On November 1, 2002—the day after Ball and his junior high football team left Harrison in disgust—Holcomb started his new job. About a week later, when Ball published his letter in the Fayetteville newspaper, Holcomb recalls the reaction in the newsroom. "Everybody was talking about this infamous letter. Everybody had an opinion on it including people who hadn't read it." While the general feeling was that the letter was a slur on the good name of Harrison, Holcomb knew better. As an interviewer for the government, he had spent most of his working life talking to people in Boone County, and one thing that stuck out was their casual disdain of blacks. Race relations in the county, Holcomb says, have "always been abysmal. It's always been a place where everybody felt perfectly free to talk whatever kind of racist shit they wanted because nobody was going to question them."

Holcomb, who moved to Harrison in 1976, had grown up outside of Wichita, Kansas. The Kansas of his youth was not an island of tolerance, but Holcomb said his parents made it clear that racism was not permitted. "I remember making a trip one time," Holcomb said, "where we stopped at a segregated cafe in Oklahoma and the waitress told us we were sitting in the wrong section and my mother said you either serve us here or don't serve us."

Holcomb decided that the letter provided a perfect opportunity for him to write about the problem of race in Boone County. The ensuing months, which he spent researching and writing the story, proved to be a turning point for him. The man who rarely took anything seriously found that what he was doing was important. He recalls that when he went to Fayetteville to interview the people who had been verbally attacked, "I thought I have to do this right. [The people of Boone County] need to understand what these people are saying."

"I think I had lived with years of frustration of peoples' sort of casual acceptance of racist attitudes," Holcomb said, "People I really liked, there was no way I could talk to about the topic. And this was an opportunity to talk to them, to try to explain something to them about who we are and where we are in the world. I really, really, really didn't want to get it wrong."

He didn't.

He started by going to Fayetteville, where he interviewed a number of people including some of the football team and their adult chaperones. They painted a compelling picture of the racism they had encountered. He also talked with Jacqueline Froelich, a TV reporter who had co-authored a history review article on the Boone County expulsion, and Ron Brewer, one of the state's celebrated black athletes. Froelich provided the historical context while Brewer, who played professional basketball and is considered a "demigod" in the state, talked about his own problems with racists in Harrison.

When he returned from Fayetteville, Holcomb started interviewing everyone in Harrison from a Ku Klux Klan leader to local businessmen. As he collected his interviews, he began crafting a series of stories. Rather than deal with the distractions of a newsroom, he would work at home starting around midnight and continuing until three or four in the morning. As the stories took shape, he would send drafts to a group of friends to get their reaction. The first few attempts were not promising. Holcomb said that Froelich, after reading his first draft on the history of the cleansing, said the story "gave no evidence that I had ever written anything." Undeterred, Holcomb wrote several more drafts and sent them off. For Holcomb, with almost no experience, the days spent on the series were "my journalism school."

The story that he documented was not pretty. Long-time residents talked about "the old days" when there were informal agreements among local stores not to serve blacks. During World War II black soldiers who were passing through were confined to the bus depot. Vigilantes ran off a dozen Mexican workers who came to town in 1946. The KKK leader praised the town for its "traditional values and traditional people." In one story Holcomb described in detail what had happened to the Fayetteville junior high football team and how blacks remained leery of spending any time in Harrison. To its credit, the *Harrison Daily Times*, which had denounced the idea that the people of Harrison were racist, printed every word.[19]

Holcomb assumed that once the series ran, he would be run out of town. His ever-practical wife, Marsha, convinced that angry townspeople would deface their house with swastikas, experimented with ways to add additional graffiti that would make them look like flowers. What they never expected was that the community would take his series to heart.

Holcomb said his first inkling of the reaction was a phone call from a parishioner at Rev. Kelly's church, the day after the first story ran. Holcomb had written about one of the descendants of the expulsion, who was currently living in a beat-up trailer outside of Batesville. The parishioner wanted to know how he could help the person.

For some Holcomb's stories represented an opportunity for cathar-
sis. One woman confessed in an email to the editor that "when I was in
my late teens, in the late 1940s, I worked at the Lyric Theater as a
cashier. One evening a young black man wearing a U.S. Air Force uniform came down the sidewalk and approached the box office. I knew I
would be fired if I sold him a ticket so I buzzed the manager, Doyle
Branscum. He came out and 'took care' of the situation." The woman
was seventy-four, but she said the incident still "shames and embar-
rasses me to this day."[20]

The most tangible result of Holcomb's stories was the formation of
what was called the Task Force on Race Relations. Headed by Rev.
Kelly, it included ministers, business people, the mayor, and the head of
the chamber of commerce. But where Holcomb saw a broad stain of
racism, the task force saw an image problem.

Rev. Kelly said that people reacted to the series with, "We're tired of
having all this stuff said about us. We don't even know why they're saying it and what's the cause. That was the task force job. What is the
skeleton in our closet and what do we need to do about it to get rid of
this negative image that is about our town." To counter the "negative
image," the task force organized a series of events.

"Prior to the National Day of Prayer," Rev. Kelly explained, "we had
a prayer summit and had about fifteen pastors go away for a day of
prayer at a little resort." At the prayer summit, they laid plans for a
spectacle on the courthouse lawn in the center of Harrison for the National Day of Prayer in May 2003.

The spectacle started with the ministers washing each others' feet.
They didn't actually wash feet, Rev. Kelly explained. "We took a rag
and wiped the shoes." After this symbolic moment, Rev. Kelly said, "I
basically issued a challenge that, if God would save Sodom and Go-
morrah if just ten righteous men would repent, I asked the question
if there are ten righteous men here that would repent for driving the
blacks out of Harrison and get on their knees and ask for forgiveness
and follow me in prayer. There was about 300 people there and I
mean instantaneously every single person in the crowd went to their
knees."

Members of the community then signed an open letter. "We had 800 signatures," Rev. Kelly said, "on the letter saying we recognize these events [the expulsion] and we as a community say we will not tolerate this kind of stuff."

The task force organized a trip to Helena, a town about 185 miles to the south, where townspeople helped repair a predominantly black church. In turn, Rev. Kelly said the black church members came to Harrison, and an ice cream social was held on the courthouse lawn. And Rev. Kelly noted with satisfaction, "We never had a problem."

The town voted to celebrate Martin Luther King, Jr.'s birthday, and a dinner was thrown to honor some black sports figures. And through it all the task force continued to meet and plan events. There is, however, one thing the task force has not been able to do: It has not found a single black to be a member.

When first asked about his all-white Task Force on Race Relations, Rev. Kelly pointed out how few blacks there are in the county.

"In terms of being an active part of the task force, there's really not a lot of people to choose from," Rev. Kelly said. "We are talking one in a thousand are black. A certain percentage of those people were not reputable people. So the percentage gets even smaller."

But he adds that the task force sought out what few blacks there were in the community. "As far as blacks, we went and talked with them and asked for their input and opinions."

Just whom exactly did they talk to?

It turns out the "them" was actually the janitor at the local community college.

Did the delegation from the task force ask him to join?

"I don't know him," Kelly said. "I know we approached him. I cannot remember his response."

What did Kelly say to the man?

Kelly admits he never met the man, and the "we" who approached the janitor was another member of the task force. After a few more questions, Kelly also explains that no one from the task force "formally" talked to the janitor. "We just did it through relationships." In other words, when Kelly said that the task force asked for input from the black community, what he actually meant was that one of the task force members knew a black man. But from that "encounter" it was clear that the task force could not find any blacks to serve.

"They didn't really want to be a part of the task force," Rev. Kelly said, "but they were consulted."

Even if you joined the task force, there was no guarantee you would be allowed to stay. Scott Hoffman, a local musician who has his own recording studio, started showing up at task force meetings in 2004. But he soon locked horns with Rev. Kelly over the group's mission. Hoffman wanted to encourage diversity in Boone County by including not only blacks but also gays and Hispanics. After the task force held a retreat in October 2004, the group asked Rev. Kelly to tell Hoffman they had decided on a "change of direction."

"The homosexual agenda was also a point of emphasis I was asked to clarify to you," Rev. Kelly wrote in an email to Hoffman. "The Task Force is divided on this issue but is united in the understanding that the main focus right now is black and white and that getting specific about homosexuals is not necessary. We feel our vision statement is adequate as a group to convey the message of warm and accepting. To address the homosexual agenda as you would propose would most likely cause an end to the task force as we know it."[21]

Since that email Hoffman says he hasn't been getting any mailings from the task force.

Others fared a little better. Reed Petty, a Mormon bishop, is allowed to serve on the task force but is not welcome in the county's ministerial alliance. Rev. Kelly, who helped start the alliance, explains the problem this way: The Church of Jesus Christ of Latter-Day Saints, he says, is a "cult." How Islam might fare—there are no mosques in Harrison—is anybody's guess. Rev. Kelly calls that religion "oppressive."

Gays, Mormons, and Muslims aside, Rev. Kelly is pleased with the progress the task force has made.

"Bringing the past to light, letting them see it," Kelly said, "has made people more aware, more conscious, more conscious of the things they say. Some of the education stuff was very enlightening to people. So there's a greater awareness and a greater sensitivity and more openness and warmness in the community that I can see. I can see a physical change in peoples, organizations, relationships, the churches, the things that we do together as a community. It's better. I'd say we've changed."

Holcomb is less optimistic.

"What has really changed? Not very fucking much."

Forsyth County, Georgia

WHITFIELD
COUNTY

SC

GEORGIA

DAWSON
COUNTY

HALL
COUNTY

•Gainesville

CHEROKEE
COUNTY

Cumming

FORSYTH
COUNTY

•Oscarville

Marietta

•Buford

JACKSON
COUNTY

COBB
COUNTY

GWINNETT
COUNTY

Atlanta

FULTON
COUNTY

0 Miles   40

0 Kilometers   40

© 2006 Jeffrey L. Ward

Area of detail

FORSYTH
COUNTY

★Atlanta

SOUTH
CAROLINA

GEORGIA

ALABAMA

Atlantic Ocean

0 Miles   100

0 Kilometers   100

FLORIDA

CHAPTER 7

The Burning Cow

Forsyth County, Georgia
1912

When the rock hit her windshield with a sound like a pistol shot, Lillie Nash started to pray. "Lord have mercy," she cried. "Help me Jesus! Don't let this man attack me! Help me Jesus!"[1]

Lillie, a middle-aged African-American, didn't lose control of her car. She might have even sped up a bit. But as she gripped the steering wheel in Forsyth County, Georgia on a fall day in 1985, she was almost certain she was going to die.

If she had had a choice, Lillie would never have driven through Forsyth County. In her family the county's name was as much a warning as it was a place. But when her only child, Balinda, called from the state university in Athens saying she was going to be put out of her dorm, Lillie bounded out like a coiled spring. By taking the shortcut through Forsyth County—an act of incredible bravado for this careful and precise elementary school teacher—she cut fifteen precious minutes off the trip. Bravado turned to fear, however, as she crossed the county line.

Lillie remembered as a child hiding quietly in a corner and listening as her mother, father, aunts, and uncles talked about the family's life in

Forsyth County. It had changed all of them, but none more so than Joe Naylor, the family patriarch. He had fled in the night with his wife and children and whatever he could throw into his wagon. After Forsyth County, he tried to put his life back together. He spent weeks on the road working odd jobs, but nothing ever seemed to go right. As life leaned hard, the family recalled how "Joe Pa" turned mean. He vowed he would never be pushed around again. But the memory of Forsyth County taunted him. He had not fought back, and for that he would never be the same.

Lillie looked around to see who had thrown the rock that cracked her car windshield. She laughed with relief when she realized that a man plowing his field had accidentally spun up the rock from the wheel of his tractor. But she was still shaking because she knew she was break- ing a taboo. Seventy years after people like Joe Naylor had grabbed what few belongings they could and slipped away, Forsyth County re- mained a dangerous place for a black person. As she drove through the county, she did not see another black face. The county was all white. Since October 1912, this had been white man's country.

––––––

In 1912, sixty-one blacks were lynched in the United States. Georgia lynched ten that year, including one in Forsyth County. Although blacks had lived in Georgia for generations, first as slaves, later free, they did not belong there. The state constitution of 1877 made that abundantly clear. It mandated a $1 poll tax to discourage black voters. Even if a black voter did pay the tax, his vote counted for little. In Georgia, where the Democrats dominated state politics, the real decisions were made in the primaries, and only whites could vote in them.

In the 1906 governor's race, Hoke Smith rode into office on a cam- paign that was "anti-corporation and anti-nigger." Atlanta was whipped into a frenzy partly by Smith's racist campaign and partly by the city's newspapers, which created a fictitious black crime wave. The most in- nocuous encounters were trumpeted as "insults" by black men against white women. A newspaper "extra" on September 22, 1906 with the headline "THIRD ASSAULT" was what finally sparked a riot. Egged on by a curbside orator who held the newspaper aloft and shouted,

"Are white men going to stand for this?" a mob began hunting blacks. Exact numbers are hard to come by but when the Atlanta Race Riot of 1906 had run its course, mobs had killed at least twenty-one blacks.[2]

Even in quieter times, whites could attack blacks without any provocation. When the Byrd-Matthews Lumber Company hired four blacks and 150 whites to cut timber in White County, thirty miles from Forsyth County, in August 1912, some white men shot up the tent where the blacks were living, wounding two. The blacks fled, and their tent was burned. Company officials, who suspected their white employees, were furious. But no one would talk, and no one was ever punished for the crime.[3]

A week later, the Forsyth County sheriff arrested five blacks after Ellen Grice, a twenty-two-year-old white woman, said she had been raped. The evidence against the men was flimsy, and all charges were later dropped. But on the day of the arrests, a crowd formed in the town square at Cumming, the Forsyth County seat, and attacked a black minister who they believed had said something insulting about Grice. Although the police rescued the minister, it was clear that events were spinning out of control. There was talk of storming the jail and lynching the prisoners. Rumors flew that blacks were "threatening to dynamite the town in the event any Negroes were lynched."

As things grew more ominous, the mayor telephoned the state and pleaded for troops. The governor mobilized a contingent of the militia from nearby Gainesville, the prisoners were moved to Cobb County, and order was quickly restored.[4]

But any hope that blacks in Forsyth County could live in peace evaporated after what happened to Mae Crow, a pretty eighteen-year-old white girl living outside the small town of Oscarville. Mae had been on her way to visit her aunt on Sunday, the day after the riot, when she disappeared. It wasn't until the following morning that searchers found her in a gully, covered with brush and leaves, barely alive and apparently a victim of rape. Whoever attacked her had beaten her so badly that she had lost an eye. Her skull had been crushed.

Mae was carried home. Sometime that morning, she regained consciousness long enough to name Ernest Knox, a black teenager, as her attacker. She died a few weeks later.[5]

Knox admitted raping her and, after bashing her head in with a rock, leaving her for dead, but then with great fanfare the sheriff arrested four more blacks. The prosecution would allege that after Knox attacked Crow, he left and returned with three men and a woman, and the men took turns raping Mae. Whites were incensed, especially after the alleged rape of Ellen Grice.[6]

On Monday, September 9, Knox was arrested and taken to the Gainesville jail in Hall County. When a lynch mob gathered, the Hall County sheriff hustled Knox to the lockup in Fulton County, fifty miles away. On Tuesday morning, the Forsyth County sheriff arrested Oscar Daniel, Rob Edwards, Ed Collins, and Trussie Daniel, who had allegedly been part of the second round of assaults. Despite the obvious danger, the sheriff locked them up in the jail at Cumming. Within a matter of hours, a lynch mob broke into the jail, shot and killed Rob Edwards, tied his corpse to a wagon, and dragged it around the courthouse. When they tired of mutilating the corpse, they hoisted the body on a telephone pole in the center of town, as if mounting a trophy to celebrate their handiwork.[7]

For some reason, the mob ignored the three other prisoners, who were taken, the day after the lynching, to the Fulton County jail in Atlanta, where they joined Ernest Knox. On September 30, a grand jury indicted him for murder and Oscar Daniel for rape. Trussie Daniel and Ed Collins were held as witnesses.[8]

It may have been that the lynching of at least one of the accused had temporarily satisfied the mob's taste for revenge. Or, believing the rumors of a possible black rebellion, whites may have thought better of launching an assault on Forsyth's black community of more than a thousand. For whatever reason, the rest of September passed without any record of attacks on blacks. But the calm was deceptive. There was an aching hatred of blacks in Forsyth County, and all that was needed was one defining moment to focus this rage.

On Wednesday, October 2, the accused were herded from the Fulton jail to begin their journey to Cumming for trial the next day. State and local officials knew there would have to be extraordinary security, and the governor called out four companies of the state militia. Rifles at the ready, the troops surrounded the prisoners, who were marched down the center of the city streets to the train station.

The group left Atlanta at 11:45 A.M. Wednesday and, because there was no train service to Cumming, disembarked fourteen miles away in Buford. From there, the soldiers marched their prisoners down country lanes and dirt roads until they arrived that evening in Cumming, where the soldiers and their prisoners bivouacked in a field south of town. The town itself was in a state of lockdown; the governor had declared martial law for the duration of the trial. The troops who had marched the prisoners from Fulton quickly established a "dead zone" around the courthouse that no one could cross without a pass. Even with a pass, anyone entering the courthouse had to be searched.[9]

Court proceedings started at 8:30 A.M. on Thursday. By four P.M., the jury convicted Ernest Knox and by 9:30, Oscar Daniel. Between them the two juries deliberated a total of sixty-two minutes before announcing their verdicts. The only surprise came when Daniel's sister, Trussie, decided to testify against her fellow defendants. She told the jury she had held a kerosene lantern as her brother raped the unconscious Mae Crow. On Friday, October 4, the judge told both men they would hang, and the condemned were packed off to the Fulton jail to await execution, scheduled for three weeks later.[10]

Once the trial ended, the campaign to rid the county of blacks began. If there was a single leader, he never revealed himself. The men who banded together to attack their neighbors never assigned themselves a name. The night the trial ended, a black church in neighboring Dawson County was torched. Only 152 blacks lived in Dawson County; by the time the reign of terror ended, two months later, they had all been driven out. The exodus began the weekend after the trial. One white man said he saw "six or eight families pass [my] father's house on Sunday, leaving their homes and crops, going to cities and towns where they can be protected."[11]

Other attacks in Forsyth County soon followed: Five black churches were burned, and a black home was dynamited. Whites were ordered to fire their black employees, and blacks were told to leave immediately or die. At one black home, when no one answered, the white raiders found another way to deliver their warning. They tied the family's cow to a stake in the yard, piled wood and brush around it, and burned the animal alive. To heighten the terror, raiders would demand instant obedience. "They had to leave with just what they had," one descendant of those driven out recalled. "They didn't have time to take anything."[12]

"They came around and knocked on every door," said a member of the family of Spencer Thornton, once one of the biggest black landowners in the county. "[They] said, 'Nigger, you got to move. Niggers now out of Forsyth County. Take everything you got and leave or don't take anything but move.'"[13]

If a family did not move fast enough, they risked destruction. According to one newspaper, "At least five hundred bullets were shot into some of the doors and walls of Negro houses one night last week, on account of the inmates not leaving out promptly as directed."[14]

Those living in the countryside were the most vulnerable. It appears they were the first to flee, and when they ran, it was usually under the cover of darkness. Annette Battle, a grandchild of Kathleen and George Black, said that her grandmother "would never want to go back there because they was run away in the night." Cleveland Bowen remembers his family's flight the same way. "We just picked up and left one night." Bobbie Bell's father was among those who fled. "They gave them twenty-four hours to get out," she said, "and he said his father packed his things on a wagon and they sneaked out that night and came to Atlanta."[15]

As word spread of what was happening in Forsyth County, it encouraged whites in other counties to act. By mid-October the campaign to drive out blacks had surged across northern Georgia. In Gainesville, twenty miles northwest of Cumming, a crowd of whites chased black bricklayers off a downtown construction site. In Cobb County notices were posted outside the town of Marietta: "Hurry up Niggers and leve this town if you don't leve you will wish you hadder got out." In Hall County, at the same time that white property owners were warned to get rid of black tenants, bands of whites began attacking black homes.[16]

Not all the raids were successful. Five men who tried to shoot up a black tenant's house in Hall County were driven off by a shotgun-wielding landlord. Three of the attackers were later arrested. In an editorial, the *Gainesville News* deplored the attacks: "The law-abiding white man and the law-abiding Negro have no trouble. The Negro with any sense does not have to be told his place—he already knows it and will keep it. The sentiment of the people is clear on the question and law and order must, and will, prevail." Nevertheless, the attacks continued.

In Forsyth County, where the violence had begun, it dawned on local officials by mid-October that this was more than random attacks on a few blacks. The thousand blacks who were being threatened accounted for nearly ten percent of the county's population. Blacks shopped in the stores, borrowed money, and built homes. Blacks owned or rented 109 of the county's farms and paid over $30,000 in local taxes. The women did the wash for well-to-do whites, and some men, like "Joe Pa" Naylor, worked in the few factories in town. Some had lived in Forsyth County for generations and, in a holdover from slavery, used (as did nearly all former slaves in other places) the last names of their former masters— some of the most respected people in the county—as their own.[17]

The terror was also touching white homes. Farmers who employed blacks were warned that their homes and barns would be burned if they did not send their Negro laborers packing. In town, those who rented to blacks were told to evict their tenants. Businesses were told to fire their black workers. These were not idle threats. In nearby Cobb County a store owner got a letter warning him to fire his Negro help. When he ignored it, the store went up in flames.

On the evening of October 16, C. L. Harris, the mayor of Cumming, held a public meeting of what newspapers called "the best citizens of the town and county," to respond to the violence. After noting that there "exists in the County of Forsyth an effort on the part of some unknown persons to drive the colored people from the county," the local leaders pledged to protect the blacks. They requested help from federal Judge William T. Newman and Governor Joseph M. Brown. Because blacks had received threatening letters through the U.S. mail, they argued, the federal government should step in. The appeal to the governor was based in part on the fact that there were to be "two capi-tal executions in the County."

Along with the resolutions, the mayor sent a cover letter to the gov-ernor that described what had happened. "Quite a number of churches have been burned and inhabited houses shot in to by unknown persons. We would be glad for you to take such steps as you may deem necessary to aid us in restoring order."[18]

The governor was unimpressed. On October 21, he replied that "this is a matter for the judge, sheriff and other local authorities to handle." While he hoped that the "good people of Forsyth County will co-operate in giving protection to all," Brown reminded the mayor that "the governor has no authority to take any steps to give protection until the local authorities advise him that they are unable to enforce the laws."[19]

On October 22, Dr. Ansel Strickland, who had a practice in Cum-ming, learned that his black washer woman was leaving. When he asked her why, "she replied that the white people did not give the Negro proper protection in this country as she was a widow." No one had threatened her personally, she said, but Negro men and boys were no longer safe. The doctor was outraged . . . at his laundress. "I told her in so many words that if I had to sell my daughter's virtue to Negro boys in order to retain her as a wash woman she could get." She left.[20]

Strickland volunteered his land for the October 25th executions of Ernest Knox and Oscar Daniel. The field behind his house was the per-fect place for a hanging. Because it was close enough to downtown Cumming, most residents of the town could walk to the spectacle. For those driving in from the countryside, there was plenty of room to park a buggy and allow the horses to graze.

It also had another advantage. The field where they set up the gal-lows was bounded on one side by a ridge, which functioned as a kind of natural amphitheater, with an unobstructed view of the execution site. But that was also the site's chief drawback. According to Georgia state law, the condemned were entitled to a private execution. So workmen built a wood fence to block the view, but the night before the execution, it was burned down.[21]

When the Atlanta newspapers later criticized the county for making the execution public, Strickland defended the way the hanging was conducted. He only drew the line at actually attending the event. "I did not witness it simply because I did not want to," he explained in a letter to the editor. He was one of the few not to attend. In a county of nearly 12,000 people, the crowd in Strickland's field numbered between 5,000 and 8,000.[22]

As they drove or walked to the field, spectators were met by two companies of the state militia led by one very angry major. The governor had once again called out the army to enforce martial law in Cumming, and Major I. T. Catron led the contingent sent to Forsyth County. It had taken the major, his two prisoners, and a hundred soldiers eight hours to travel the thirty-five miles from Atlanta to Cumming. The soldiers arrived sometime after midnight and locked the condemned men in the courthouse.

The next morning, Catron discovered the arrangements for the execution had gone seriously awry. Instead of being in some out-of-the-way place, the gallows had been set up in Strickland's natural amphitheater. The fence built to shield the hanging from public view had been burned down. And when the major offered to have his men rebuild the fence, sheriff William W. Reid declined their help.[23]

Catron had hoped the execution would be held early Friday morning before a crowd could gather, but the sheriff had told the doctors who would officially pronounce the prisoners dead not to arrive until noon. As people streamed down the road to Strickland's field to what was now going to be a very public hanging, Catron toyed with the idea of arresting the sheriff for inciting a riot. But he didn't because, as he later explained, "[The sheriff] was playing for political advantage and would have welcomed an opportunity to openly espouse the side of a mob."[24]

Outmaneuvered by the sheriff, Catron set up his troops in a picket line to keep the crowd 200 yards from the gallows and hoped for the best. At some time between 10:30 and 11:30 A.M., Ernest Knox and Oscar Daniel were marched to the field under a chilly gray sky. They mounted the gallows, where they were given a chance to make a last statement. The newspapers reported that Knox admitted his guilt and Daniel did not. The sheriff cut a rope with a hatchet, the trap door under the condemned sprang open, the two men dropped, and the crowd cheered.[25]

After Knox and Daniel were cut down and the crowd began to disperse, a photographer, who had been taking pictures of the hanging, saw an opportunity for one last shot. He set his camera up on the gallows and took a shot of what was left of the crowd. It is the only picture of that day known to have survived. In the background is Sawnee Mountain. Buggies are parked along one side of Tolbert Street, and the horses are tethered across the road by some small trees. In the center of the picture a small crowd of white men are standing in a circle talking while, closer to the gallows, other white men are lined up, their hands in the pockets, looking up at the photographer.

It would be an unremarkable picture were it not for the figures at the bottom of the frame. In the lower right-hand corner, lounging around a wagon with a mule grazing nearby, are three black men. In the left-hand corner a single black is captured in mid-stride. Soon they would have to move out of the county. But on that fall day they apparently felt it was safe to attend the execution of fellow blacks. While the men around the wagon stand apart from the whites, they have been there long enough to unhitch their mule and they appear to be in no rush to leave. The black, who is by himself, seems to be strolling unconcerned out of the picture.[26]

Eight days earlier, whites had protested the violence against blacks. In a few months no blacks would be left in Cumming. Between those two points, these four anonymous men are caught for an instant somewhere along that continuum.

It would appear, from their presence at the execution, that the terror emptying the countryside had not reached Cumming. Yet as they looked around at the thousands of people gathered on that hillside to applaud an execution, they must have sensed something. Perhaps what was about to befall them was incomprehensible. If not blacks, who would clean clothes, gather crops, and haul water? Routine is understandable, and what happened yesterday is assumed for tomorrow. Maybe that is what makes the picture so chilling. We know what these men do not seem to grasp. As their world is about to collapse, they linger by the gallows.

Blacks owned more than 1,900 acres of land in Forsyth County, and the best that black landowners, hounded out of the county, could hope for was a quick sale. Otherwise their property would be left behind for the taking.

The first to sell was Garrett Cook, who received $200 for his twenty-six-acre parcel on October 11, 1912. Eight days later A. G. Brown, who owned sixty-eight acres outside of town as well as a lot in town, sold everything to two men named Edmundson and Pirkle, owners of a general store in Cumming, for $885. Even black churches went on the block, and Pirkle bought the grounds of the Methodist Episcopal Church for $40.[27]

Each such sale is carefully recorded in oversize books, tattered and dirty from decades of use and stored in the basement of the Forsyth County Courthouse. Each sale tells a tale of black people who struggled to build a life and were crushed by the terror. On page 104 of one book, William Davis buys a lot in Cumming for $100 on November 1, 1901. Eighty pages later, he is using his land as collateral to borrow a few hundred dollars for "lumber and nails and other materials . . . to improve the lot in Cumming." He apparently did a good job. When he was driven out, he sold the property and house he had built on it for $1,750. Under the circumstances he might have seemed fortunate, but six years later his one-time home was resold for $2,500.[28]

In another case, one of the county's largest black landowners, an illiterate black farmer named Joe Kellogg, outfoxed his white persecutors. Instead of selling, Kellogg mortgaged his 200 acres in mid-October, giving himself a financial cushion while he waited outside the county for the violence to end. The whites who lent him money now had an interest in preserving his property, and though Kellogg was never able to return to Forsyth County, he hung onto his land until 1914, when he sold it.[29]

A deed filed in 1890 by Clem Long, an elderly black farmer, gave ten acres to Nannie Carter, forty-five, "in consideration of the natural love and affection he bears the said Nannie Carter as well as for service and work performed." Nannie and her husband, John, owned the land "so long as [Nannie Carter] remains or lives on the property." In 1912, unable to stay because they were black, they lost their gift.[30]

In all, twenty-four African-American landowners and seven churches or black-run organizations sold their property when they were driven out. The timing of these sales gives a sense of the panic people felt. Eleven black landowners sold between October and the end of 1912 and another four by the summer of 1913. Some of them took a financial beating. The worst case was Alex Hunter, who, just three months before the expulsion, bought a farm for $1,500. Faced with death or leaving, he sold it in December 1912 for $550.[31]

Even if he sold at a loss, Hunter might have considered himself lucky. The majority of black landowners were helpless to prevent their white neighbors from stealing their land and their homes. With county officials unwilling or unable to fight the vigilantes and the state government evading any responsibility, black landowners who could not sell had to abandon their property. Once they left, there was little chance they would ever return. As one descendant put it, "They never went back to claim [their land] because they were afraid. They would just hang you to the nearest tree." That could mean only one thing: There was land for the taking, and in this free-for-all, the tax clerk kept score.[32]

The Forsyth County tax roll was divided by race. Before the expulsion, a clerk carefully inscribed the name of the fifty-eight black landowners in Forsyth County (churches did not appear on the tax roll) along with a list of the parcels they owned. After the expulsion, the whites would troop to the courthouse to claim their neighbor's land. Although some parcels had been sold and were now listed under the new owner, the majority had not. For thirty-four of the black landowners, there is no record that they sold their land. It made no difference. Whites, money in hand, would pay the tax on land they did not own and the clerk would note the transaction. In the three years after the expulsion, nearly two-thirds of the black-owned farmland that had not been sold was appropriated this way. By 1915, the number of black landowners paying their tax had shrunk to four names.[33]

A black woman, Martha Bailey, bought forty acres along the Dawson-Forsyth county line in 1905 for $300. There is no record she ever sold the land. In 1913, the tax clerk carefully noted that William A. Godfrey, a white man, was now paying the taxes. In 1916, Bailey's former next-door neighbor, H. G. Mathis, claimed ownership of the land and sold it for $185. The land would change hands several more times over the next sixty years. It seems that no one was troubled by the gap in ownership until 1985, when the Williams Brothers Lumber Company, which was now the owner, wanted to sell the Bailey property. Apparently realizing that no one could prove Mathis actually owned the land he had sold in 1916, lawyers fell back on the legal claim of adverse possession, whereby if someone occupies a piece of land "openly and notoriously" for some period of time, that person is considered the rightful owner. Filed with the lumber company deed are three affidavits by people living near the plot, stating that the Williams Brother Lumber Company "continuously used and occupied" the forty acres for the previous thirty years. The lumber company argued successfully that, because it had used the land, it was now the owner. The sale went through, and today the property, like so much of Forsyth County, has been turned into a housing development, Dunroven Estates.[34]

What is unusual about Martha Bailey's land is that anyone even tried to straighten out the tangled ownership. In most cases, people who bought land in Forsyth County after the expulsion simply ignored the gap in ownership. D. H. Webb, who was one of the trustees of the black Sunday school in Cumming, bought a lot just west of the Cumming town line in 1911 for $190. Again there is no record that he ever sold it. But in 1951 it turns up in the sale of three parcels of land by Webb's one-time neighbor, R. E. Kirby. The two other Kirby parcels border the Webb land.[35]

Morgan Strickland bought a forty-acre tract in 1910, but, in 1954, M. O. Terry had no problem selling Strickland's land and pocketing the proceeds. At the time he sold the land, Terry said that he had bought it in 1947. The deed he gave the new owner even provided the book and page number of the prior deed. There was only one problem. The deed from 1947 that Terry says shows his ownership is for an entirely different piece of land. No matter. The sale went through.[36]

For those driven out, the expulsion was devastating. Kathleen Anderson was eight years old when the terror struck her family. She did not live in Forsyth County, but her grandparents had a small farm there. "They were in slavery times," she recalled in a 1987 oral history. "They were just happy to have—being in slavery and not having anything and then having a home—they were just tickled to death. . . . My daddy used to carry us up there most Saturday nights. We spent the night with our grandparents or some of it. He would put us in the wagon and take us over there—sleep at the foot of the bed."[37]

As a child, Anderson got her first inkling of what had happened when her grandmother suddenly appeared in the house. "I just remember her coming in crying, you know, and Mama hugged her and all. And then they made us children go in and she sit down and talk to us. . . . They sent us children in the other room and they sat down and talked. She kept saying she was so hurt. They had never owned nothing before. I don't think she ever got over what happened."[38]

Anderson said her grandmother escaped with only the clothes on her back. "She had to just jump and leave and they couldn't move nothing. It just hurt her so bad. [She] just had a dress and my mother could sew and she made her some dresses. My mother made her two dresses."[39]

Along with the financial loss came a sense of shame. People no longer wanted by a community felt they were in some way to blame for their expulsion. Bobbie Bell recalled her father's pain. "He was ashamed of the fact that he was from there. He would tell people he was from Chicago."[40]

The cleansing didn't end at the borders of Forsyth County. By mid-December, the terror was threatening to consume all of northern Georgia. On December 16, the *Atlanta Journal* reported that "a prominent Jackson County citizen who, for obvious reasons requested that his name not be divulged," traveled to Atlanta to plead with the governor for help. Although thirty miles east of Cumming, Jackson County had been struck by "a band of unknown men who operate under cover of darkness." These men were "posting notices . . . which warn all negroes to leave under severe penalties." The warnings were apparently successful; the visitor from Jackson County reportedly told the governor that blacks "are becoming terror-stricken and are leaving there in large numbers." The "anti-negro movement" had also spread to Hall, Gwinnett, Whitfield, and Dawson counties. Before it ended, the terror would engulf a swath of land in northern Georgia larger than the state of Delaware.[41]

By January, the violence reached Cobb County as well. The editor of the Marietta newspaper at first tried to ignore the threats against blacks, believing it was "the work of mischievous boys." But when a local judge asked the grand jury to investigate this "serious menace," the editor acknowledged the problem. At the end of January he reported that "considerable excitement has been caused in some quarters of the county during the past two weeks by posting of notices warning negroes to leave."[42]

The reticence of some local newspapers in reporting on the expulsions was matched by Governor Brown's reluctance to do anything about them. When some Jackson County citizens asked for state help, the governor told them the same thing he had told the delegation from Forsyth County: The county authorities should handle the problem. He did suggest, however, that "if private detectives were employed better results might be obtained than through the mere offering of a reward."[43]

With the governor unwilling to use his office, the terror continued to burn through the northern counties. At the end of December, the fire jumped to the pages of the *New York Times*. Under a headline "Georgia in Terror of Night Riders," the *Times* reported that "an organized effort is being made to drive every negro out of North Georgia counties. . . . Hundreds of negroes have fled from the state while those who are remaining live in a state of constant dread."[44]

And then it was over. By January 1913 stories of threats, burnings, and expulsions simply dropped out of the newspapers. At some point the attacks must have stopped, but the newspapers do not say how or why this happened. But when they did, the demography of northern Georgia had changed dramatically. In the decade before the racial cleansing, the counties of Forsyth, Hall, Jackson, Gwinnett, and Cobb had all gained black population. In the decade after the cleansing, the black populations dropped in those counties as well as Dawson and Whit-field. The most extreme swings were in Forsyth and Dawson. The black population in Forsyth dropped by ninety-seven percent, and in neigh-boring Dawson County not a single black remained of the 152 who had been there in 1910. Jackson County saw its black population reduced by nineteen percent and Cherokee by twenty-three percent. By con-trast, Fulton County—which encompasses Atlanta—saw its black pop-ulation grow by more than 12,000 between 1910 and 1920—a twenty-one percent increase.[45]

If there was any doubt about why this was happening, Ophelia Blake, Frank Smith, and Alex Graham would have been able to explain these demographic trends with ease. In February 1913, these three blacks decided it was safe to move back to Cumming. At three in the morning on February 19, 1913 a series of explosions shook the town. Someone had planted dynamite under their homes. They all survived, but the message was clear: This was white man's country.[46]

———

"Go home, Nigger! Go home, Nigger!"[47]

It began as a few impromptu shouts from the crowd.

"Go home, Nigger. . . . Go home, Nigger. . . . Go home, Nigger!"

As more joined in and their voices fell into lockstep, a ragged chant was born.

GO HOME, NIGGER!

GO HOME, NIGGER!

Skinny, bearded men wearing baseball caps, men waving Confeder-ate battle flags, thirty-something women in sweatshirts and jeans, and, here and there, a few children tossed the chant back and forth. They had been waiting for this moment for the better part of the morning, their enthusiasm buoyed by stirring speeches.

"Rug-headed, fat-lipped, kinky-looking, gorilla-smelling niggers," was how one of their leaders described them. "Let 'em know we don't want 'em up here. You can't have law and order and niggers too. I say one's gotta go. Let it be the niggers. I say let's give 'em a good, Forsyth County welcome."

It was 1987, and Forsyth County's brotherhood march had begun.

The march had been Charles Blackburn's idea. Originally from California, Blackburn, a white man, had moved to Forsyth County in 1982 and opened a private, nontraditional school. He wanted the Martin Luther King, Jr. Day march to show that "times and minds had changed in Forsyth County." It was a spectacular miscalculation. Within five minutes of the march being advertised on the radio, Blackburn began getting threatening phone calls. As the anonymous callers made very, very clear, times had not changed.

With death threats multiplying, Blackburn beat a hasty retreat by canceling the march. But believing he could stop the march turned out to be Blackburn's second mistake. When Dean Carter, a white man who lived in nearby Gainesville, heard news of the cancellation, he picked up the idea. He too received an avalanche of death threats, but Carter, by nature pugnacious, was undeterred.[48]

The march would begin on Bethel View Road near the off-ramp of GA 400, continue for a few miles though the Forsyth County countryside, and end at Blackburn's school. The march terminus had no significance other than it was the site of Blackburn's school. Transportation was planned, a parade permit obtained, people volunteered, and on January 17—a cold, overcast day—the battle was joined.[49]

Around nine in the morning, the racists arrived, some in Klan outfits and others in camouflage, and rallied near the Exit 13 off-ramp of GA 400. Meanwhile, the marchers were on their way up from Atlanta, also on GA 400. Until the four-lane highway was built in the 1970s, Forsyth County had been isolated from the changes taking place in the booming state capital. In 1912, it had taken all day to transport Ernest Knox and Oscar Daniel from Fulton prison to Cumming. Now, it was a forty-five-minute commute. But some things had not changed. The 1980 census showed only one black in Forsyth County.[50]

The police had a plan for controlling the demonstration. Before the marchers arrived, the white separatists would move into a field behind an old barbed-wire fence. The fence, which ran parallel to the road, stood about thirty feet from the pavement down a gentle slope. Those behind the fence would be directly across from—but safely out of the way of—the starting point of the march. A bus with the hundred or so marchers, most of whom were coming from Atlanta, would park along the shoulder of Bethel View Road. The marchers would disembark and begin their walk north toward Cumming.[51]

At first the plan seemed to be working, but as the marchers got off the bus, everything began to unravel. Instead of stationing themselves along the fence, the police clustered on the road. Inflamed by the sight of blacks and whites getting off the bus, the white protesters pressed forward as they chanted "Go home, nigger!" With no one to bar their way, they scrambled over the rusted fence and, waving Confederate flags, advanced up the slope.

The police force, only thirty strong, formed a loose skirmish line along the pavement to hold the protesters back. Only a two-lane road now separated the white separatists and their prey. The marchers arranged themselves in a column of twos and began a ragged chorus of "We Shall Overcome" as they stepped off down Bethel View Road and straight into what was, in effect, a gauntlet. While the front ranks of the whites lining the road jeered the marchers, those in the rear began flinging rocks, bottles, and clods of earth. Their missiles arched over the throng of protesters; some hit the marchers, others smashed on the pavement. To shield the marchers, the bus driver pulled his vehicle into the road and moved alongside. It offered some protection, but the line of marchers was longer than the bus and, in any case, as they moved down the road, the separatists ran ahead, outflanking the column. Six helmeted police rushed to the head of the march to ward off the attacks, but it was clear that it would be only a matter of minutes before the white protesters would overrun the column.

The police and the march organizers made a quick decision, and the marchers got back on the bus. The white protesters were exultant; they had won. The bus moved a few miles to where the march was supposed to end and, in a face-saving gesture, the marchers disembarked to walk the short distance to the finish line. If the gesture was intended to show that the brotherhood march had triumphed over racism, it persuaded no one.

As television stations around the country began broadcasting pictures of racists besieging the marchers, people were gripped by a sense of shock and anger. That evening, an event originally planned as a benefit for Atlanta's Martin Luther King, Jr. Center for Nonviolent Social Change became an upscale mass meeting with people in tuxedos and evening dresses giving impassioned speeches. Governor Joe Frank Harris told the 1,800 people in the Atlanta hotel ballroom that he was "embarrassed." Former Atlanta Mayor Maynard Jackson said the Klan should be outlawed. Fulton County Commission Chairman Michael Lomax said it was important to "show the hate mongers that decent people outnumber indecent people." And the grande dame of the civil rights movement, Coretta Scott King, called the attack "inconceivable at this time in our nation's history."[52]

The sense of shock was understandable, because for the previous two decades the press had promoted the idea that race relations in Forsyth County were improving. When people in Forsyth County attacked or threatened blacks, the *Atlanta Constitution* balanced the stories with quotes from local officials who claimed that the county's virulent racism was a thing of the past. In 1968, for example, a group of black campers was chased away from Lake Lanier, one of the county's recreational areas. As part of its coverage, the *Atlanta Constitution* ran a story headlined "Cumming Deplores Racial Harrassment [*sic*]." Among others it quoted the local bank president as saying, "I feel sure that this sort of thing does not represent the sentiments or feelings of the majority of people of our county."

In 1977, the *Atlanta Journal* ran a front-page story titled "Lily-White Forsyth Looks Ahead—Racial Change Is Blowing in the Wind," in which civic leaders claimed it was just by chance that the county was all white. "Several local officials and residents contacted recently admit the characterization [as racist] was at one time at least partly deserved. But they say that now things are different. They say their county's unusually white complexion is no longer a preoccupation—it is simply a happenstance." In the story, a black man mentioned "a whole new attitude" in Forsyth County. Black people, he said, "should not have anything to worry about." But blacks in Forsyth County still had plenty to worry about. Three years later, a white man, none other than a distant relative of Mae Crow, shot a black man as he left a party in Forsyth. As Melvin Crowe later said, "Somebody has got to keep the niggers out of Forsyth County."[53]

Even after the attack on the marchers, the newspapers still clung to the idea that racism in the county was a limited problem. "There are 35,000 people in Forsyth County," one columnist explained, "but the bottom 400 showcased the whole county to the world." The same theme was sounded in an editorial the day after the march. The *Journal-Constitution* described the march as "a triumph of the misguided few over the indifferent—or was it simply the unaware?—many."[54]

The newspaper could believe what it wished. The sight of racists attacking the marchers demanded an answer. Within a week of the first march, an alliance of local civil rights organizations arranged a new brotherhood march. This time there were more than 20,000 marchers from not only Georgia but as far away as California, and they outnumbered the opposition twenty to one. There was also an overwhelming police presence.

After this second march, a Biracial Commission was formed, half community leaders from Forsyth County and half civil rights activists from Atlanta. For what was probably the first time in seventy-five years, people began to ask publicly what had happened to the black-owned land in Forsyth County after the racial cleansing. The question was of more than historical interest now because land in Forsyth County had become very valuable. Once remote and rural, by the 1980s Forsyth County was becoming a bedroom community for Atlanta. Farmland was being chopped up for housing developments, and real estate prices were soaring. At the turn of the century farmland was typically sold in forty-acre parcels for a few hundred dollars. By the turn of the new millennium, it was worth millions.[55]

The civil rights groups that had sponsored the second march formed a Legal Redress Committee to explore obtaining reparations for the blacks who had lost their land after the 1912 cleansing. At the same time, the Georgia attorney general began his own study of the issue. And the question of reparations was also added to the agenda of the Biracial Commission.

Attorney General Michael Bowers originally promised to search public records to find if any blacks owned land and, if so, discover what happened to it. His report, however, hedged the central question of the expulsion. He noted census figures showing the sudden drop in the black population, then added that during this time there were "various black and white migrations." Was Bowers saying the racial cleansing was a "migration"? Well, no, not exactly. "No study was found which may be said to explain the Forsyth County data entirely in such terms." Bowers allowed that during this period there were "episodes of racial violence." In fact, he discovered that "both academic and contemporary accounts specifically report efforts by white persons to cause the black populace to leave Forsyth County." But no one should jump to the conclusion that blacks were driven out because "both kinds of sources also report efforts by other white residents of Forsyth County to halt such campaigns." Since he did not determine whether or not blacks had been driven out, Bowers also did not feel obliged to keep his promise to trace the ownership of black-owned land to see if any of it had been seized by whites. What Bowers did say with absolute confidence was that "this overview is not intended to adopt or to reach factual conclusions regarding changes in the population and the ownership and occupancy of real property in Forsyth County."[56]

The *Atlanta Journal-Constitution* was the next to weigh in on the reparations question. In a front-page article in June 1987, the reporter, Mike Christensen, called the Forsyth County racial cleansing a "legend." Christensen found that some blacks—he did not say how many—remained after the racial cleansing. Because not every black had left, he declared that "Forsyth County's racial history, as it gradually unfolds from courthouse documents and state records, is not quite living up to its 75-year-old reputation."[57]

Christensen cited research by one Donna Parrish, identified as a genealogist from Forsyth County, which he said demonstrated that blacks who were driven out were paid for their land. "There is evidence in county records," he wrote, "that many black landowners who left Forsyth were later able to sell their property, sometimes after a lapse of several decades and sometimes at a profit."[58]

In fact, by Parrish's own admission, her research was "far from complete." She researched only about half of the sixty-five blacks who owned land. In at least one case—the land purchased by Martha Bailey—Parrish found the deed of purchase but either did not notice or failed to mention that Bailey did not sell her land. Parrish also does not explain what happened to Bailey's land after the expulsion.[59]

Alex Hunter was also on Parrish's list of black landowners. But while Parrish noted that he sold his property in December 1912 for $550, she did not mention that a few months earlier he had bought it for $1,500. Nevertheless, she concluded that "blacks did not necessarily take a loss" and that "black property was not just seized."[60]

The newspaper published a rebuttal to Christensen's article from two members of the Forsyth County Legal Redress Committee, who noted that all but thirty of the 1,098 black residents had been driven off in 1912 and that Parrish's research was suspect. All this made no difference to the paper. After printing the rebuttal, it dropped the issue, noting in a December 1987 editorial that it was not interested in "the mud of a distant and different past."[61]

"There's little point in dwelling on what happened in the past," the editors wrote. "[E]verybody knows there was ugliness and brutality and horror, sometimes not so long ago. But none of that can be changed no matter how much debate goes on or how much money some descendants get paid."[62]

Meanwhile, the Legal Redress Committee continued its work. The committee was made up of four volunteers: Brian Spears, a local civil rights attorney; Vincent Fort, a history professor at Morris Brown College; Pat Gilliard, a paralegal working for the American Civil Liberties Union (ACLU); and Amanda Kemp, a college intern. They began their work in February 1987, shortly after the second march. Spears would research what legal remedies were available for the descendants of those who had lost their land while Fort was supposed to document what took place in 1912. Gilliard would go to Forsyth County and trace the ownership of the black-owned land.

It was not a happy collaboration. When Spears delivered the committee's final report to the coalition of civil rights groups in October 1987, he noted his frustration with Fort. "Unfortunately we were unable to gain the cooperation of one of the Committee members who had conducted a number of the descendant interviews, Mr. Vincent Fort. Time spent in unsuccessfully seeking his material resulted in delay in the production of this Report." There were other problems as well. Gilliard's sole trip to the Forsyth County Courthouse had yielded little. The starting point for tracking black-owned lands is the tax rolls, which in 1912 were broken down by race and listed each parcel and owner. But no one at the courthouse could find the old tax rolls.[63]

According to the committee's report, a clerk said there were no records "of any tax levies of black land." In the "Record Department" the paralegal was unable to find "any tax books of black landowners." And the report quoted the tax commissioner as saying "a courthouse fire damaged or destroyed the majority of tax digests."[64]

There was no way for Gilliard to know it, but the 1912 tax roll did exist. Don Shadburn, a courtly gentleman who was the county historian, had a copy in his files. But he later recalled, "I didn't make any effort to locate my copy . . . at the time. I didn't see a need to." Without the tax roll, the volunteers on the committee were stymied: The Legal Redress Committee report recommended that an abstracting company be hired to do the title searches.[65]

The failure of the Legal Redress Committee left the Biracial Commission as the last, best hope for an accurate account of the expulsion and subsequent appropriation of black-owned land. The first step was to find out what the facts were. On April 1, a representative from the state attorney general's office met with the commission and promised a "factual investigation into the ownership, a real property ownership, of black persons in Forsyth County." At the same meeting, the commission invited Donna Parrish, a source of the "legend" story, to speak. As later events would show, it turned out to be a pivotal moment.[66]

Describing herself as a historian, she told the commission members that she had become interested in the land ownership issue after the brotherhood march because both whites and blacks were calling her to find out about Forsyth County property. "It seemed like a lot of the white people called and they said, 'Am I living on black land,' so I decided I would just find out what happened."[67]

What happened, Parrish found, would be welcome news for the whites of Forsyth County. Forsyth County members of the Biracial Commission had been complaining about calls they were getting from whites. "Unless we give our citizens some assurance," said one white commission member, "that we're not meeting behind closed doors here with a bunch of evidence, that we're just figuring a way to take their land back, we're in serious hot water. They'll run us out of town on a rail."[68]

Parrish told the commission that she concluded that no one was forced to sell their land and nothing was stolen. "Those people [black landowners] weren't being coerced by force to sign any type of deed," she explained. "It does not look like their rights were denied to everybody as far as dealing with property."[69]

With the investigation by the civil rights groups stymied and the attorney general's report a masterpiece of equivocation, Parrish's research became accepted wisdom—at least for the Forsyth contingent on the Biracial Commission. The final report, published in December 1987, was a measure of how completely the commission had failed. Unable to agree on much, the civil rights leaders from Atlanta issued one set of findings and the Forsyth whites issued another. The Forsyth members, citing Parrish's research, said, "the charge of unlawfully taken land resulting from the events of 1912 is an allegation without sufficient foundation in law or fact."[70]

The Forsyth report congratulated the majority of the county's residents for not being racists, argued against affirmative action, and accused blacks of blaming "minority problems" on racism. "The black community must face the proposition that many of its problems are based in socio-economic and cultural matters."[71]

But the Forsyth members were not quite finished. They calculated that the march had cost the government and local merchants $370,551.16. They claimed that civil rights groups should pay at least part of that amount.[72]

In its report the Atlanta contingent of the commission shot back that the marchers were exercising their constitutional rights and had there not been a counter-demonstration, "the larger March would not have occurred." If Forsyth County wanted to be reimbursed, it should talk to the counter-demonstrators. There remained one last irony. The black members of the commission, unhappy that the land issue still had not been addressed, asked the governor to appoint a new panel to investigate compensation for land and property lost by the blacks.[73]

Governor Joe Frank Harris's response sounded eerily like that of Governor Joe Brown seventy-five years earlier when Brown had been asked to protect blacks from a racial cleansing. "The governor can't mandate all of the kinds of changes that need to be made in Forsyth County," a spokesman for Harris said. "Most of them must come from the local and county government."[74]

———

On almost any weekday evening, the cars streaming out of Atlanta are backed up on GA 400 as commuters try to make their way home to Forsyth County. The population, about 44,000 in 1990, had climbed to 131,000 in 2004.

As farmland sprouted McMansions over the last two decades, it seemed as if the old attitudes were, if not washed away, at least submerged. Although in 1993 a near riot broke out when a newly opened Winn-Dixie store in Cumming brought in black cashiers from a store in another county, today it is not unusual to see blacks eating in Forsyth County restaurants and shopping in stores. When the 2000 census found 684 blacks living in the county—an increase from twenty-seven in 1990—the *Atlanta Journal-Constitution* applauded the developments with a front-page story headlined "Past Racial Tension Ebbs."[75]

But appearances can be deceiving. The newspaper story did not mention there were still far fewer blacks in Forsyth County than immediately before the racial cleansing. That was probably because the story did not mention the racial cleansing at all. And, as it has done before, the newspaper found Forsyth County residents who would say racism was a thing of the past. The *Atlanta Journal-Constitution* had this take on the 1987 brotherhood march and counter-demonstration: "Locals tell newcomers that those events were created by outsiders and did not represent the true Forsyth County."[76]

There are other indications as well that Forsyth County has not thrown off its racist past. In 2002 the Forsyth County Historical Society published a book called *Forsyth County: History Stories.* In this new version of history, the book sums up the 1912 racial cleansing as a "multiplicity of misdeeds." The rationale for the expulsion is simple. Following racial unrest in Atlanta and Gainesville, "it is little wonder then that the citizens of Forsyth County . . . would react strongly to the egregious deeds of certain African Americans." The author spends several pages describing the rape and murder of Mae Crow, the lynching of Rob Edwards, and trial and execution of Ernest Knox and Oscar Daniel. The racial cleansing of more than a thousand people is dispatched in one brief paragraph. But not before the reader is assured that the property of the blacks was respected: "Decades old rumors to the contrary, each and every parcel of land was sold, with the proceeds going to the African American owners. All of these individuals may not have received 'fair market value' for their property but deed records in the Forsyth County courthouse indicate that the land was sold and deeds recorded in a legal manner."[77]

The 1987 attack on the brotherhood march by racists hurling rocks and screaming "Go home, nigger!" becomes in this history "marchers who were unfavorably met by members of the Ku Klux Klan." The Biracial Commission, which was unable to agree on anything, is described as "a valiant attempt to end animosity between the two races." And the history ends with blacks visiting Forsyth County to pray at the unmarked graves of their ancestors.[78]

But perhaps the best measure of the racial climate is what Forsyth County teaches its young. Linda Ledbetter, a history teacher at Forsyth County Central High School, says that if students ask her about the racial cleansing, she pretends ignorance. When they ask about the signs that warned blacks not to let the sun set on them in Forsyth County, Ledbetter says, "I'm like, 'I don't know. I wasn't here. I didn't see the signs.'"[79]

In fact, she does know what happened.

My grandmother was thirteen when they had the hanging. She told us all about it. She thought it would be a lot of fun because she would get to meet a lot of new people. She said it was horrible because one of them didn't die real quick. She said one of the men just broke his neck. The other man didn't break his neck and he just struggled. It was horrible. Very, very, very horrible.

Her grandmother also told her about the warning signs, and the cross burnings.

But when she takes fifteen or twenty minutes in her one-semester course to teach students about the county's history, she never mentions the racial cleansing. "I generally don't go into the rape and all," Ledbetter says, "because I don't want to foster any bad racial issue and anytime anything in our history has been brought up it's to cause trouble. Like the race marches and all . . . just created turmoil and trouble."

For Ledbetter, the problem with talking about race is not that it exposes the racial prejudices of Forsyth County's white citizens but that there are too many unfriendly blacks around. "The more you discuss race here with Atlanta like it is, so totally black and so totally against whites, you just create problems."

In 2000, Linda Ledbetter was named Forsyth County Central High School's Teacher of the Year. She is also a Forsyth County Commissioner.

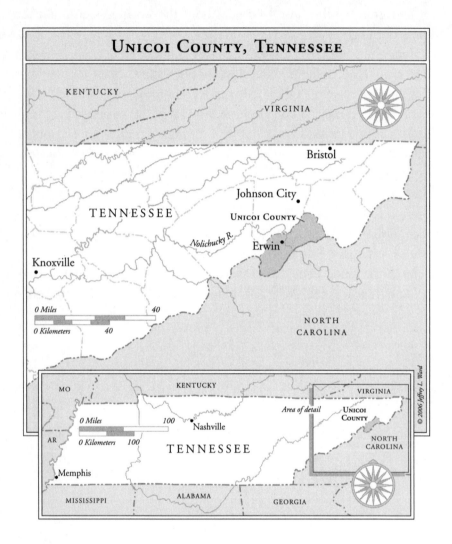

UNICOI COUNTY, TENNESSEE

KENTUCKY

VIRGINIA

Bristol

Johnson City

TENNESSEE

UNICOI COUNTY

Nolichucky R.

Erwin

Knoxville

0 Miles   40

0 Kilometers   40

NORTH
CAROLINA

MO

KENTUCKY

VIRGINIA

0 Miles   100

Nashville

Area of detail

UNICOI
COUNTY

0 Kilometers   100

AR

TENNESSEE

NORTH
CAROLINA

Memphis

MISSISSIPPI   ALABAMA   GEORGIA

© 2006 Jeffrey L. Ward

CHAPTER 8

Something in the Air

Unicoi County, Tennessee
1918

Tom Devert was already dead when they set his body on fire. In life, Devert had been a laborer in Erwin, Tennessee. In death, he became an object lesson.

On May 19, 1918, a balmy Sunday, a mob dragged Devert's body into town, where they built a funeral pyre of railroad ties. Then the mob rounded up every black in town—some sixty men, women, and children—and made them watch as they burned the corpse.

For the blacks forced to view this grisly spectacle, it would be their last memory of Erwin. After the flames devoured Tom Devert, the sixty blacks in town and eighty working at a quarry were told to leave Unicoi County within twenty-four hours.[1]

As an object lesson, Devert's immolation was a signal success. Two years later there were only four blacks in Unicoi County. Decades after, the county remained a dreaded place for blacks.

Mary Alexander, now a college professor in neighboring Johnson City, remembers what would happen when her family had to drive through Unicoi County in the 1950s. "Erwin was taboo for black folk.

153

Just going through Erwin was a problem." As they crossed the county line, her parents' apprehension would grow, and they would warn the children to be quiet because "we are almost to Erwin." The car would race over the Nolichucky River, where whites had shot Devert, skirt the railroad yard that was Erwin's life blood, and disappear down the macadam roads to the relative safety of North Carolina.[2]

But May 19, 1918, was more than a triumph for racial cleansing. It was also a missed opportunity for the nation's pre-eminent civil rights organization, the National Association for the Advancement of Colored People. The events in Erwin presented the issue of racial cleansing in the starkest terms imaginable, but the NAACP, which should have risen in anger, simply missed it. It was a failure that would have uniquely bitter consequences. Over the years, whites and blacks would unwittingly join together in a fellowship of silence. Racial cleansings would become America's family secret.

There is an irony in the NAACP's silence on the expulsions in Unicoi and elsewhere, for the NAACP itself was born out of a racial cleansing.

In its official history, the NAACP says a 1908 "race riot" in Springfield, Illinois was what led to the organization's founding. Two blacks had been arrested in separate incidents over a two-month period for alleged sexual assaults on white women. On Friday, August 14, when the sheriff prevented a white mob from lynching the pair, it turned its anger on the black community.

Whites looted a hardware store for weapons and then moved on to the black section of town. William Walling, a radical white journalist, covered the story. "The mob," Walling began his article, "set about to drive the Negroes from town." A black barber who fired on the mob was killed and his body was hung from a tree. The mob then started burning black homes and businesses.

The rioting spread to nearby communities. In Buffalo, fifteen miles from Springfield, residents posted a sign that read, "ALL NIGGERS ARE WARNED OUT OF TOWN BY MONDAY, 12 m. SHARP." The governor mobilized the state militia to protect the black community and restore order, but whites continued their campaign, "organizing a political and business boycott to drive the remaining Negroes out."[3]

Walling was shocked less by the cleansing than by the fact that it had occurred in the North, in the hometown of Abraham Lincoln. He predicted that, unless something was done, the race war would be transferred to the North, and he ended his article with a question about African-Americans. "Yet who realizes the seriousness of the situation, and what large and powerful body of citizens is ready to come to their aid?"[4]

The answer came quickly from a social worker, Mary White Ovington, who read Walling's article in a New York weekly and asked him and Henry Moskowitz, also a social worker, to meet at her New York apartment. From that meeting of three white citizens would grow a "large and powerful body," indeed, the NAACP.[5]

One of the first major steps the NAACP took in its early years was to bring W. E. B. Du Bois to New York to run the organization's magazine, *The Crisis*. The brilliant but prickly Du Bois had earned both a B.A. and a Master's degree from Harvard, went to the University of Berlin to work on his doctorate, and completed it back at Harvard. His academic achievements, centering on philosophy and history, remarkable by any standard, are even more so in the context of his era: Between 1875 and 1900, only seven blacks earned a doctorate in America. Under Du Bois, *The Crisis* became a vibrant mix of social comment, short stories, poems, reports on the state of race relations, and articles on successful blacks. The magazine, which published emerging black authors like Langston Hughes, is credited with fueling the Harlem Renaissance in the 1920s. It was a bravura performance that, nevertheless, sometimes fell short. It fell short in 1912 in the case of Forsyth County, and again in 1918 with Unicoi.[6]

Du Bois knew what was happening in Forsyth County in 1912. The newspapers in Atlanta, where he had taught for several years and still had contacts, reported on the rape, the lynching, the trials, the executions, and the expulsion. And while Du Bois was working at *The Crisis* in New York City, he could have read in the *New York Times* that "an organized effort is being made to drive every negro out of North Georgia counties."[7]

Instead, as the stories tumbled out of Georgia, Du Bois treated them as if he were posting them on a bulletin board with all the other racial incidents of the day. When Rob Edwards, who was arrested in the rape and murder of Mae Crow, was lynched in Cumming, the story made its way into the October 1912 issue in the same way other lynchings did, in a section called "Along the Color Line." Lynchings were so common that Du Bois simply printed the name of the victim, location, and reason given for the lynching.

The following month, Du Bois noted that the governor of Georgia had declared martial law to protect several blacks on trial for criminal assault in Forsyth County. Du Bois added that two had been sentenced to hang, referring to Knox and Daniel.[8]

There was no mention of the racial cleansing in the November and December issues of *The Crisis,* although almost immediately after the sentencing, whites had begun the campaign to drive out all but a few dozen of the more than a thousand blacks in Forsyth County. On October 13, the *Atlanta Constitution* ran a story headlined "Negroes Flee from Forsyth," which reported that Forsyth County whites were "determined to drive the negroes, good, bad and indifferent, from the county." Five days later the newspaper reported the mass meeting in Cumming that led to a request for help from the governor in preventing the expulsion.[9]

By the end of December, the racial cleansing that had begun in Forsyth was spreading to other counties in northern Georgia, but it wasn't until February 1913 that *The Crisis* revisited the subject:

> The unexplained movement which led to the killing of seven or eight Negroes in North Georgia several months ago has resulted in an attempt to drive out Negroes entirely. One prominent white citizen, appealing to the governor says:
>
> "If something is not done to check this movement the labor situation in Jackson county will become quite acute, for the Negroes, including some of the most trustworthy and law-abiding, are becoming terror stricken and are leaving there in large numbers. Our wives and daughters will soon be put to the necessity of doing the cooking and washing and performing other menial labor. In addition, the farmers will suffer greatly, for they will be deprived of field hands."[10]

The next mention of the expulsion appears in the March issue, which reprinted two stories from the *Atlanta Constitution* about how farmers and businessmen in Cobb County were being warned to discharge black employees and evict black tenants and how a white-owned store was burned after the owner ignored threats to get rid of black employees.[11]

In April there was one last mention of the Forsyth County racial cleansing: "the reign of terror in North Georgia continues. The homes of three Negroes were recently dynamited."[12]

A racial cleansing had come and gone, more than a thousand people had been forced to flee, and at least two counties were now exclusively white. But Du Bois and the NAACP did not seem to understand what had just occurred. Other racial cleansings had established the idea that blacks bore a collective guilt and would be punished as a group. But Forsyth County had taken it to a new level. Even innocent people who lived several counties away were now targets. Du Bois, *The Crisis,* and the NAACP should have been moved to eloquence and action. They were not, and those who were victimized were left with no one to speak for them.

But Du Bois and the NAACP would soon have another chance to speak out on behalf of the victims of racial cleansing. They would have Unicoi County.

Erwin, Tennessee, was born of a mistake by the U.S. Post Office. It had started life in 1832 as Unaka. Eight years later, the town's name was changed to Longmire and later to Vanderbilt. When D. J. N. Ervin donated fifteen acres of land for the Unicoi County seat in 1879, grateful residents renamed the town again. It was now Ervin. Alas, the post office mistook the "v" for a "w" and recorded the name as Erwin. After four name changes in forty-seven years, no one seemed able or willing to correct the error, and so Erwin it has remained.

The town sits in a long narrow valley that runs northeast to southwest. The Nolichucky River loops down through the town, travels southwest along the valley floor, and then, a few miles south of town, goes east toward the North Carolina border.[13]

As the river goes, so go the train tracks. They travel down from Johnson City, pick up the river in Erwin, and follow alongside it to North Carolina. The trains still run through Erwin, but its heyday as a repair yard and general office for the Clinchfield Railroad is long gone. The railroad started laying track through the county in 1886, and by the turn of the century it was the area's major employer. That made the general manager of the Clinchfield, a man with the Dickensian name of L. H. Phetteplace, one of the most important people in town.

Born in 1871, Phetteplace had started out as a telegraph operator on the Norfolk and Western Railway and worked his way up to trainmaster. When his boss at the N&W was hired by the Clinchfield line, Phetteplace went with him and in 1913 replaced him as general manager. It was a solid, respectable career. Pudgy and round-faced with wire-rimmed glasses, Phetteplace was a conventional-looking man with a conventional view of the world. When a reporter asked him why he was a success, he credited devotion to work and understanding his responsibilities.[14]

The one brief glimpse we have of Tom Devert prior to his murder occurred when he was working in construction on a store Phetteplace was building in Erwin. Devert and another black, Jake Hill, were mixing mortar for the brick masons when two black women walked by. To impress them, Hill suddenly rushed to where the brick masons were working, grabbed a trowel, and shouted to Devert for more mortar. When the surprised masons looked over the side of the building, they heard one woman, who was Hill's girlfriend, say to her friend, "See, I told you he was a brick-lier."[15]

The only other things we know about Devert are that at the time of his death he had lived in Erwin for six or seven years; he was about forty years old; whites considered him to be "of good character"; and he was considered trustworthy enough that some stores in Erwin had extended him credit.

Only two newspapers, the *Johnson City Staff* and the *Bristol Herald Courier,* covered the story in any depth. According to them, fifteen-year-old Georgia Lee Collins and her younger brother were walking home when Devert pounced on them in a secluded spot. The brother ran off, and Devert started choking his victim "into insensibility." Here, the accounts diverge slightly: In the *Herald* version, the girl screams before Devert starts choking her, while in the *Staff* account she screams as he grips his hands around her throat. In either case, Collins's screams attracted four unnamed men to the scene. Devert dropped the girl's body, then picked her up again and tried to escape by crossing the river. He swam with one hand while clutching Collins's hair with the other. According to the Johnson City account, one of the pursuers took out a .44 caliber pistol and shot

Devert, who died instantly from a shot through the head. At this point Georgia either drowned (Johnson City) or was already dead (Bristol).[16]

The author of the Bristol account makes no attempt to explain Devert's motives. Presumably, he considered it unnecessary: Readers could be expected to understand that burly black brutes lust uncontrollably after innocent white girls. The Johnson City reporter was less sure of the story line. The reporter had apparently heard that Devert had a good reputation and that such an attack was completely out of character. How then to account for this seemingly irrational act? "He is thought to have been either drunk or under the effects of a drug," the reporter speculates.

As written, neither account makes much sense. It is possible that both children started screaming when Devert appeared. But if the four men were to find the "secluded spot," Georgia would presumably have had to have screamed for some period of time. That she would be screaming while being choked "into insensibility" is physically impossible. Once the four men burst upon Devert and Georgia, the two groups would presumably have been relatively close to one another. Yet Devert had time to drop her, then pick her up, and run off. By the time Devert was shot, the two groups were now several hundred feet apart. How Devert could have gained so much ground while carrying Collins is not explained.

The four unnamed men were the only eyewitnesses to the shooting, and their version would have been the basis for both a police report and the newspaper stories. If these men had foiled a rape and killed Collins's assailant, they should have been applauded as heroes. Yet the four are never named. True, the girl had died—but that was Devert's fault. These were unusually modest heroes.

Several decades later, another version of what happened appeared in a local history of Unicoi County. The author, William Helton, had heard the anecdote about the two women passing by as Tom Devert worked, from Wade Kegley, one of the white brick masons working with Devert that day. In his interview with Helton, Kegley said that the day Devert was killed he himself had been in town at a baccalaureate service when he heard "yelling and the shooting of firearms" coming from the railroad yards. Kegley said there was an "altercation between some white men and a black. They were between the railroad shops and the river, and as the man tried to escape his pursuers, he grabbed a teen-age girl and took her as hostage out into the river. But he was shot dead and the girl drowned."[17]

This dovetails with a story Starlet Jean Williams was told by her grandparents, who were driven out of Unicoi County after Devert's body was burned: "Tom Devert and some fellow white workers had been drinking and gambling all day. Devert supposedly won their money and would not return his winnings. The white men began to chase him. He grabbed the girl as a shield."

There is no way to know if this latter account is more accurate than the 1918 version, but it is more plausible. In this account, Devert has a reasonable motive for grabbing Collins. The distance between Devert and his four gambling companions also is more logical. Instead of coming upon him in the secluded spot, they are chasing him through the rail yards next to the river. He is far enough ahead to grab a hostage but not so far that he is out of pistol range. This version accounts for why four men were by the river. They and Devert were gambling. Finally, this version may explain the continued anonymity of Devert's pursuers. They would have not had wanted the world to know that an innocent girl died because they had been gambling and lost money to a black man who ran off when they demanded it back. So they concocted their story to shift all the focus onto Devert.

It was a story that the white townspeople were all too willing to believe.

The shots that killed Devert apparently attracted townspeople to the river where they would have seen the bodies of Devert and Georgia Lee Collins. The girl's brother, who had run to town to raise the alarm, was also calling people to the river. "The sodden body [of Devert] was dragged back to town the entire distance of a mile and a half," the Johnson City paper explained. "The crowd growing in size until it reached a mob." It was this mob that rousted the entire black population of Erwin and forced them to line up in front of a funeral pyre that the mob was building. "The negroes, among whom there were men, women and children were lined up in a row before the rapidly mounting pile of wood upon which was poured oil," goes the *Bristol Herald Courier* account of the immolation of Tom Devert. "Men with pistols, shotguns and clubs stood before the lined up negroes to prevent their running away and as the last cross tie and the last dash of oil was thrown on the heap, one of the mob is reported to have turned to the cowering crowd and said, 'Watch what we are going to do here and if any of you are left in town by tomorrow night, you will meet the same fate.'" The mob lit the pyre and threw Devert's body onto it. Now, the cry went up to burn the Negro quarter.

But something extraordinary happened: That most conventional of men, L. H. Phetteplace, came forward. For Phetteplace, it must have been highly unnerving. The pursuit and death of Devert had occurred near dusk; by the time the pyre was built, it would have been evening. Phetteplace would have faced a nightmarish scene: In front of him was an angry mob, their faces lit by the burning railroad ties. Sprawled in the embers was the charred corpse of Devert.

Because he was general manager of the railroad, everyone knew L. H. Phetteplace, and he probably knew most of the people who made up the mob. To the extent that he was boss to many of them, he could exert some control. But mobs are fickle things, and Phetteplace could just as easily have done nothing, which was what the police did. As one reporter put it, the police did not interfere because they believed that Devert "deserved his fate." But at this critical moment, this dutiful man, who had spent years patiently climbing the rungs of a company ladder, spoke reason to the mob, and the Negro quarter was not burned down.

When John R. Shillady was appointed executive director of the NAACP in early 1918, one of the first things he did was to fire off a telegram to Woodrow Wilson demanding that the president come out against mob violence. The past summer, whites in East St. Louis had rioted, killing scores of blacks and burning black-owned homes and businesses. Shillady, a social worker who would be the last white to head the NAACP, apparently liked the idea of sending telegrams to governors and presidents. So it was not surprising that when he learned about the violence in Erwin, he would protest what had happened in a telegram.[18]

On May 23, 1918 Tennessee Governor Thomas Rye received a three-page telegram from Shillady:

Lynching and burning of body of Thomas Devert at Erwin Tenn Monday night again makes it patriotic duty of the National Association for the Advancement of Colored People to urge that you bring to trial in Tenn court lynchers who by repeated burnings of Negroes accused of crime are imperiling unity of nation at this most critical time. Five out of the six lynching occurring in your state since our country entered the war have been accompanied by burning either before of after death. This last case added to previous horrors that of forcing the whole Negro population of Erwin to line up and witness burning of Devert's body thus avenging crime of an individual by terrorizing innocent law abiding people whose only offence lies in their color. Every patriotic American must realize danger to nation [*sic*] welfare envolved [*sic*] in allowing lawless elements to believe themselves free to lynch and burn Negroes without fear of swift and certain punishment. Your state cannot sit back and say as you have in the past that your laws are inadequate to lynchers. We implore you in the name of our common country to exhaust every resource of law, money and patriotic endeavor to stem the peril which these burnings show to be one of terrible reality.

But Shillady said nothing about the expulsion although he very likely knew about it. In the NAACP file on the Erwin lynching there is a clipping from the *Montgomery Journal* of May 21, two days before Shillady sent his telegram, headlined, "All Negroes Leave Town After Lynching." The NAACP file also contains a clipping from the *Baltimore Daily Herald* of May 22, which describes the lynching and says, "The Negro population of Erwin, near this city, had fled to nearby towns as the result of threats made after the rioting Sunday." Yet when confronted with a clear example of an expulsion, the NAACP and Du Bois said nothing. In the months following the lynching and racial cleansing in Erwin, *The Crisis* did not even acknowledge that it had occurred.

This was clearly not a case of Du Bois or the NAACP trying to hide something. Du Bois spent a lifetime fighting bigotry and racial violence—sometimes at enormous personal risk. His courage and the strength of his convictions are beyond doubt. The record of Shillady and the NAACP are equally blameless. Shillady resigned from the NAACP in 1920 after he was severely beaten by racist thugs in Austin, Texas. He had gone there to protest the closing of the NAACP chapter by state officials. And the NAACP, from its very inception, was considered "radical" by its critics because it advocated full equality for blacks. Over nearly a century it has not wavered from that goal.

And yet when faced with a stark example of racial cleansing, they said nothing. Nor was this a momentary lapse. In the years that followed, the NAACP was largely silent when there were racial cleansings in places like Corbin, Kentucky. Occasionally there would be a perfunctory protest—a telegram was sent to the governor of North Carolina in 1923 when blacks were driven from Mitchell County. Instead, the outrage came from the white press.

The editors of the *Johnson City Staff* denounced the mob for driving off Erwin's black population. "Whatever may be the individual opinion as to the justice of the swift punishment meted out to the brute, or the method of it, the fact remains that an innocent population were done a fearful injustice and it will be long before the thrifty little city of Erwin recovers from the blot on its reputation as a law abiding and well conducted community."[19]

The editors of the *Knoxville Journal and Tribune,* after condemning the killing of Devert and the burning of his body, devoted half the editorial to a denunciation of the expulsion: "Why should the colored people be held to account for the act of this one fiendish criminal for no other reason than they were colored?"[20]

It is impossible to know if Shillady or anyone else within the NAACP ever saw the Johnson City editorial. But the Knoxville piece, which was printed one day after Shillady sent his telegram to the governor, was carefully filed away in the NAACP folder on the Erwin lynching along with the newspaper accounts printed before Shillady sent his telegram. It seems clear that the NAACP knew about the expulsion and, at the very least, could have drawn the same conclusions that at least two white, southern editorial writers had already arrived at independently. Which leaves a mystery: Why did Du Bois and the NAACP remain silent?

All of the people who could have shed some light on this subject are dead; now, there is only speculation. But there are some things we do know. When Walling reported on the violence in Springfield, he called it a race riot even though it was something more. To the extent that whites were rioting and they were attacking blacks, the term was accurate. But the intention of the rioters went beyond random violence. It was violence with a definite purpose: to drive all blacks from the city. Today we can look back and call it a racial cleansing because both the term and the intellectual construct exist. But these tools were not available to Walling, his readers, or to those who joined the NAACP. For them, the absence of the words to describe a class of actions—a type of conduct that was repeated in different places at different times—would certainly have inhibited their ability to understand what was happening.

Another factor may be that the expulsion of sixty or seventy blacks may have seemed like a minor skirmish in America's race wars. The history of the post-Reconstruction and Jim Crow South is littered with episodes of horrific violence committed against blacks. Lynchings were not simply executions. Often the victims were first tortured, sometimes for hours, before they were murdered. Men were castrated and women disemboweled. The form of execution was just as often burning at the stake as it was strangulation; the death throes were long and horrible. Afterwards, the corpses were sometimes ripped apart, and pieces of the victims sold as souvenirs. In this context, the fate of sixty or seventy unfortunate souls being sent off into the night may pale in comparison. If anything, they might be considered lucky for having escaped with their lives.

It is also possible that these expulsions were seen as part of a larger process—beginning with riots and lynchings—by which black communities were intimidated and also destroyed. Mary Ovington's history of the NAACP suggests this possibility. In her description of lynchings during the early years of the NAACP, Ovington describes a world in which "Maimed black bodies floated down the rivers and if recognized were never identified. After every rioting the black man fled the community, leaving behind him home, personal property, the bed, the table, that had been an integral part of family life." If racial cleansing was the consequence of lynchings and race riots, then perhaps the campaign to end lynchings and prevent race riots would put an end to racial cleansings.[21]

Whether or not one or all of these factors influenced the NAACP, there is one stubborn fact that intrudes. At a time when the NAACP was silent or at best murmured its disapproval, editorial writers repeatedly denounced the expulsion of blacks.

———

"Nothing."

Julian Bond, the current chairman of the NAACP, pauses before he says the word. The pause emphasizes just how little he knows about the history of racial cleansings in America. It is an odd moment for this man who has spent his life fighting racism. As a young man, he helped organize the Student Non-Violent Coordinating Committee (SNCC). He worked alongside Reverend Martin Luther King Jr., served in the Georgia legislature, and taught at Harvard, the University of Virginia, and American University. And he headed the Atlanta Chapter of the NAACP before becoming the organization's national chair. But when the subject turns to the racial cleansing in Forsyth County, Georgia—a place thirty miles from where he spent part of his youth—Bond confesses total ignorance.[22]

As he sits in a Washington, D.C. coffee shop a few doors from his office, he allows that he has "some vague memory of people saying that black people were run out of Forsyth County. But when, where, under what circumstances . . . nothing."

His willingness to admit what he does not know is part of Bond's charm. He is sixty-six, but he remains in some ways the studious, polite prep-school student he once was. When there was a brotherhood march into Forsyth County in 1987 to protest the continued exclusion of blacks, Bond did not participate.

"I've never been a big marcher," he says. The words sound hollow, and Bond tries to explain more fully why he failed to protest this glaring example of racism on his doorstep. "I really don't know why I didn't join the march. I think I remember assuming that it would be a production, effectively protected and guarded and a nice, wonderful occasion where these people on the march are saying, 'We are not going to tolerate this. We are going to show that it is possible for black people to go to Forsyth County and white people who are with them.' But I just didn't go."

For Julian Bond, a cultured and learned man and the chair of America's first and most eminent civil rights organization, the key facts are still missing. He ticks off the places in Georgia where it was not safe for a black to go, but he is at a loss to explain why.

"It was just something in the air."

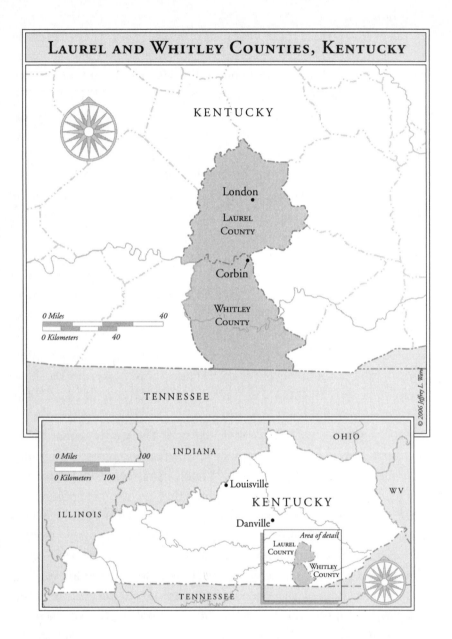

LAUREL AND WHITLEY COUNTIES, KENTUCKY

KENTUCKY

London

LAUREL
COUNTY

Corbin

WHITLEY
COUNTY

0 Miles   40
0 Kilometers   40

TENNESSEE

© 2006 Jeffrey L. Ward

INDIANA   OHIO

0 Miles   100
0 Kilometers   100

Louisville

ILLINOIS   KENTUCKY   W V

Danville

Area of detail

LAUREL
COUNTY   WHITLEY
              COUNTY

TENNESSEE

CHAPTER 9

A Dog Named Nigger

Laurel and Whitley Counties, Kentucky
1919

Some things are just meant to be. How else to explain the fact that, when a mob was rampaging through Corbin, Kentucky on the evening of October 30, 1919, it stumbled across the municipal band marching through town? The result was the first racial cleansing with musical accompaniment.[1]

The band's fifteen unsuspecting members, who had just finished playing at a political rally in the high school, had decided to end the night with a brisk march through town. But moments after they struck up the unwittingly prescient "There'll Be a Hot Time in the Old Town Tonight," they were overtaken somewhere between Main and Depot streets by a crowd of 125 gun-toting men. "This man, right out of a clear sky . . . here he come with this gang, with his six shooter," said Blake Killenger, one of the band members. "They were just, was just a-blazing on all sides and stopped us and told us they're running the blacks out of town." The bandsmen were ordered to serenade the gunmen as they rounded up the town's blacks and marched them to the railroad depot.[2]

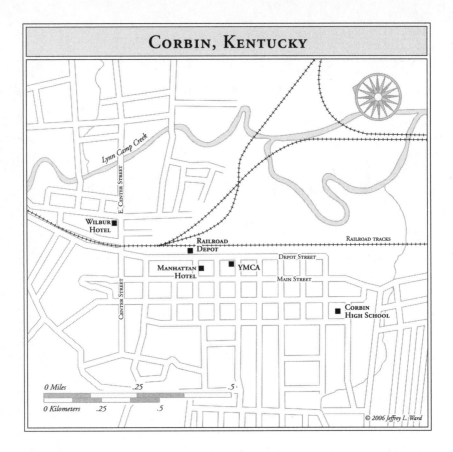

CORBIN, KENTUCKY

Lynn Camp Creek

E. CENTER STREET

WILBUR
HOTEL

RAILROAD
DEPOT

RAILROAD TRACKS

MANHATTAN
HOTEL

YMCA

DEPOT STREET

MAIN STREET

CENTER STREET

CORBIN
HIGH SCHOOL

0 Miles   .25   .5

0 Kilometers   .25   .5

© 2006 Jeffrey L. Ward

In addition to being the first musical racial cleansing, through a series of coincidences, it would also be one of the best documented. Killenger's account of the band marching through Corbin is one of several
oral histories collected in Corbin during the 1970s as part of the country's bicentennial celebration. These interviews are supplemented by an
unusually large number of documents at the Kentucky Department for
Libraries and Archives. For example, after Steve Rogers, one of the
ringleaders of the mob, went to prison, he twice petitioned the governor—once for a pardon and once to have his sentence commuted. In
his petition for a pardon, which is now in the state archives, he explains
what he did and tries to justify his role. Filed with it are the petitions of
others who supported or opposed Rogers; the petitioners also describe
what they saw the night of the cleansing.

The most unusual documents are a series of sworn affidavits collected by the railroad police. In 1920, J. B. Snyder, the commonwealth's attorney, asked the Louisville and Nashville Railroad (L&N) for help investigating what he called "The Corbin Mob." Snyder, who didn't have his own detective, wanted the railroad police to collect notarized statements from ten people he said had been in Corbin the night the blacks were driven out. The railroad lent Snyder its "Inspector of Police," who spent several weeks traveling the state locating witnesses and getting their affidavits. Those notarized statements of both blacks and whites, which were used before a grand jury in 1920, eventually made their way into the state archives.[3]

That the prosecuting attorney would have turned to the railroad for help is not surprising. The railroad was Corbin's lifeblood. When the L&N Railroad pushed its tracks through southeast Kentucky in 1883, a trio of land developers carved Corbin out of what had been called the Big Swamp. The developers also had little interest in political geography. When Corbin was incorporated in 1895, it straddled Laurel, Whitely, and Knox counties. What really mattered were the railroads and the lucrative freight business as long lines of hopper cars from the Kentucky coal mines rattled south to Knoxville or Atlanta and north to Cincinnati. Crews rested in Corbin, and trains were repaired in its sprawling yards. When the YMCA was built in 1902 across the street from the freight depot, it became an overnight stop for railroad men on their runs. There were saloons and whorehouses, and the local hotels hosted the parties of railroad fraternities.[4]

The railroad also brought blacks to Corbin. Although Corbin had some sixty long-time black residents according to the 1910 census, in 1919 the railroad had brought in a black work crew estimated at between 200 and 400 men. For a town of 2,800 people, this was a substantial increase. These laborers ate and slept on trains parked in the rail yard only a short distance from where they were building new facilities. In addition a paving contractor, hired to upgrade the town's dirt streets, had imported his own black work crew. The world had suddenly changed for a town accustomed to seeing only an occasional black face.[5]

Townspeople, unnerved by the sudden appearance of so many strange blacks in town, complained that the Negro workmen were responsible for a crime wave. After the cleansing, townspeople spoke of a "colored element . . . living in temporary abodes, rail road cars, and makeshift tenements." As one of the town's lawyers described it, the black population "was a menacing and floating one, very gregarious in habits, and lawless in acts."[6]

Fifty years later, in the 1970s oral histories, the same anxieties emerge. W. R. Stansberry, a lifelong resident, recalled that there was "a terrible lot of meanness going around." He said there was "robbing and so forth in town. I just heard about it. I was never concerned with it." Another resident, John Garrett, said, "The event that led up to it was hold-ups, breaking-ins, and what have you. They accused these colored people of being the principal offenders of these acts." There was also the sense that the blacks were intruders who were bent on changing the town. Oscar Little said the expulsion occurred because "colored folks was trying to force themselves on the white people here and they just wouldn't stand for it."[7]

Whether it was true or not, band member Blake Killenger had heard another and more immediate reason for the expulsion.

> I understand that what led up to this, these colored fellers over there, they liked to gamble. They'd shoot dice and play poker. And I understand that some of the switchmen and railroaders went over to their camp to gamble with 'em. I don't know why but a fight ensued. Whether they lost their money or what, a fight took place and this gang of switchmen led by Pistol Pete didn't like the situation so they just ganged up and a whole gang went down to the railroad station and told 'em to get out of town.[8]

Others claimed in their oral histories that a robbery the day before sparked the cleansing. In these versions a thirty-four-year-old railway switchman named A. F. Thompson was heading home from work around eleven P.M. on October 29 when he noticed that he was being followed by two men. After he crossed a bridge near his home and headed down an embankment, the pair attacked him. In the brief fight that followed they stabbed Thompson in the side and left a gash on his hand. Thompson said one of the men held the knife to his throat and told him to be quiet or they would cut his head off. After grabbing his money, the pair ran off.[9]

It would have been little more than a routine mugging except that Thompson claimed the robbers were black. As Stansberry put it in his oral history, "After they found Thompson cut up over there in the yard and he said the Negroes did it, tension began to build."[10]

Whatever the cause, it is clear from the affidavits that on the morning of October 30 there was a sense that something was going to happen. William Fugate, a railroad construction foreman, said that he had "heard rumors prior to this time that an attempt would be made to run the Negroes out of Corbin as soon as the construction work was completed." His first inkling that something might be imminent was when Steve Rogers, a flagman on the L&N, appeared at Fugate's railroad car with a crowd and began asking him about a black who had left the night before. Rogers said a trunk was missing from a carnival that had come to town and a black was suspected. What Fugate faced was not yet a mob, but in that moment Fugate could see its outlines. How else to explain Rogers, a railroad worker, and his crowd of men questioning people about an alleged robbery?

We know little about Rogers beyond the facts that he grew up in Corbin and was nicknamed "Pistol Pete" because of the gun he liked to wave around. But in the hours that followed, he would become the most powerful man in Corbin: He would decide who could stay and who had to go. For now, though, he and his men contented themselves with quizzing Fugate. As Fugate and Rogers talked, Police Chief Boggs shouldered his way through the crowd and began his own round of interviews. Only this time the chief grilled Fugate's black work crew both about the trunk and the Thompson robbery.[11]

The questioning apparently went nowhere, and, although Boggs told the black laborers to go back to work, Fugate was uneasy. He asked the chief and then members of the crowd of whites if they were planning "to molest the negroes that were working for me." If the blacks were going to be run out, Fugate said he wanted to arrange to evacuate them. Fugate does not say what he was told, but he was apparently satisfied because he said he dropped the idea of moving his men.[12]

Still the rumors persisted. Alex Tye, a black janitor in the master mechanic's office, said he became so alarmed by the rumors during the day that he hurried home and with his wife and stepson tried to figure out what they could do. Whatever plans they made are not described, but they were inadequate. In a matter of hours he and his family would be trapped in their home by a mob.[13]

As the day wore on, Fugate noticed that his work crew was growing increasingly uneasy. To calm them and allay his own fears, Fugate went looking for the chief again. This time he found a police officer named Barker who said that "nothing would be done to the Negroes." Reassured, Fugate returned to the railroad car that doubled as his office.[14]

But already the situation was beginning to worsen. John Turner, who had gone to the carnival with two friends, found they were running a gauntlet as they walked back to town that evening. Twice they were stopped by whites who cursed them and told them they would be run out of Corbin that night. Terrified, Turner raced home and locked himself in his house. Under his bed he had stashed his gun.[15]

Meanwhile Fugate, who was finishing up paperwork in his railroad car, was interrupted by a worker from one of the other crews. Fugate said the man "informed me that trouble had begun and white folks were shooting all the Negroes down there." He was only partly correct. No blacks had been shot, but the cleansing had begun.[16]

For John Turner, the cleansing began when a mob kicked in his front door. Turner grabbed for his gun but was not quick enough. "Bob Smith held a gun to the back of my head. Steve Rogers had me covered with a gun and Bryant had a gun in his hand, which he kept in his pocket while standing in front of me," Turner said. Even if he had fought back, it would have been suicidal. While five or six men ransacked his home, Turner could see a large mob outside. The mob was armed, and they were firing wildly as if celebrating.[17]

In a ritual that would be repeated throughout the night, Turner was marched at gunpoint to the train station while the mob went through his home stealing or destroying what they pleased. At the station Turner and others who had been rounded up were guarded in the Colored Waiting Room. As different trains pulled in, some of the unlucky captives would be hustled aboard. Where each one was sent was a matter of chance.[18]

At the YMCA, where train crews normally stayed, a white railroad worker named Alfred Walker was collecting a maintenance crew when the mob arrived. "There was a black man working there at the YMCA," Walker said in his 1977 oral history. "When they came up in front of the YMCA, there was a shot fired. They began piling in, looking for this black man that worked there." Walker said the mob was eventually faced down by one of the maids. "When the crowd came in the YMCA door, they started upstairs and there was a lady there by the name of Mrs. Putnam. She worked upstairs and she made up beds. So Mrs. Putnam, she wouldn't let them upstairs. Then they left the YMCA."[19]

The black man Walker was referring to was a janitor named Tom Good, and the mob's next stop was his house. At sometime between 10 and 10:30 P.M., "the mob began by throwing rocks at the house and broke out most of the window lights," said Good in his sworn statement. When the mob started trying to break down his front door, Good opened it and was confronted by Rogers. "We are driving all you damn Negroes out of this town tonight," was how Rogers greeted the janitor. He then ordered Good and his wife to the train station.

Thanks in part to Good's white neighbors, this particular expulsion didn't go as smoothly as the others. When they saw what was happening, three of Good's neighbors rushed to the house to help Good's wife, who had been bedridden for the past two weeks. Rogers suddenly found himself confronted with whites as well as Good who were all pleading that Good's wife could not be moved. Rogers made a small concession. They still had to go to the depot, but he would not force them to leave immediately as long as the white neighbors promised it would be "as soon as possible." With that Rogers and his mob left in search of their next victims.[20]

It was during this hunt that the mob fell upon the band. "I soon observed that a crowd was falling in behind the band and was making a great deal of noise and firing guns and pistol," said T. D. Thomas, one of Blake Killenger's fellow band members. Although they didn't realize it immediately, they had fallen into the mob's grip. When the band tried to turn toward Sutherland's drugstore, Thomas said that they were instead ordered by Rogers to head in the direction of the Wilbur Hotel. "Fearing personal violence," Thomas said, "we complied with the orders." The route to the hotel took the band past the depot, where Killenger saw a strange sight. It was "full of colored people," Killenger recalled. "I don't know where they had come from. They were from everywhere, some of them even in night clothes."[21]

Once past the depot, the mob and its captive band marched north alongside the railroad tracks for a short distance and then crossed the rail line to head east up Center Street to the Wilbur Hotel. J. A. Walker, the white foreman for the black work crew that was paving Corbin's street, was in bed at the hotel when the mob arrived. His first inkling that something was wrong was a call from the night clerk. When he went downstairs he found pandemonium. Outside there were ten or fifteen heavily armed men "shouting, shooting and using very profane language, the purport of which was to the effect that 'the black sons of bitches' all had to leave town." From time to time some in the mob would make forays from the hotel to hunt down blacks. Inside the hotel, mob members were holding two of his work crew. Walker said his men told him, "They were being run out of town and wanted sufficient money to pay their railroad fares." Walker advanced the two men money for tickets. Later that night, he would hunt down the rest of his crew at the depot to give them money as well.[22]

While Walker was inside the hotel trying to help his work crew, Killenger and the rest of the band were outside trying to figure out how they were going to get away. Killenger had hoped that he could slip off in the confusion of the search, but he said Rogers made it too dangerous. Rogers and his fellow mob members were, in Killenger's words, "just blazing away." A newspaper account the following day estimated the mob fired at least 500 shots as they roamed the town.[23]

Once they were finished at the hotel, the mob, with its fifteen-piece band in tow, struck out in search of more black victims. This time they headed to the home of Fanny and Alex Tye at the north end of town. Tye, who had left work early when he heard rumors that the blacks would be driven out, lived near the hotel with his wife and stepson, Cearney Parks. At around eleven P.M. Fanny called her husband to the window. Outside the mob was moving down the street hitting home after home. The first to fall was the Turner house. Then they moved to the Lyttle home next door to the Tyes. Rogers began banging on the Lyttles' front door ordering them to open up. He alternated between threatening to lynch those inside if they did not open the door and ordering the mob to break it down. As Alex Tye watched, it dawned on him that Rogers thought he was actually besieging the Tye house. But Tye realized that once Rogers discovered his mistake, it would be only a matter of time before the mob would come crashing through the Tyes' front door. Their only hope was to escape. But as they ran out the back, they were spotted by some mob members. "As we were leaving the house some one guarding the front door of our house fired two shots and called to the rest of the mob to follow us," Tye said. Although no one was wounded, somewhere during the frightening escape Fanny became separated from Alex and Cearney. In the dark of night Alex tried to find his wife. Mob members were everywhere. After giving up the search, Alex and his stepson worked their way across town to the Manhattan Hotel. It was dangerously close to the depot, but they knew the owner because Fanny Tye worked there as a cook.[24]

Years later Bill Early, son of the hotel owner, recalled in his oral history the night Alex Tye and his stepson suddenly appeared. "My father had a restaurant right there across from the depot. We had a colored woman cook and she and her husband lived up on Railroad Street. And they had a son. The son was about my age. The night they run the colored people out, her husband and her son came to the hotel and my father put them upstairs in one of the rooms. They stayed there all night and the next day."[25]

The Earlys were not the only whites to hide the mob's prey. The company that had the contract for paving Corbin's streets had set up seven tents to house its black workers, among them Will Jones. Jones, who was sleeping in his tent when the mob descended on their encampment, was able to slip away in the confusion. For reasons that are not clear, he ran to the home of O. A. Miles, who owned a garage in town. In his affidavit Miles said, "As I returned to my residence, a Negro came to my front door, pleading for protection. I took the Negro over to the jail and asked that he be allowed in the jail for protection." It proved to be only a brief respite. Later that night the jailer appeared with one of the mob members, and, despite his protests, Jones was escorted to the depot.[26]

At the depot raucous whites surrounded an ever growing crowd of blacks in the colored waiting room. While they waited, small dramas played out around the station. When the night baggage agent found some of his black employees being detained, he spirited them into the baggage room to hide. It took the mob only a few minutes to discover what was happening and storm the baggage room.

Sometime during the evening, after gathering together a few possessions, the janitor Tom Good brought his sick wife into the depot. They had kept the promise made by their white neighbors to the mob. At around ten P.M., a physician, B. J. Edwards, outraged by what was happening, stormed in and "protested as vigorously as circumstances permitted." When he warned the rioters that they could be arrested, he was hooted down by a mob member who said the doctor should go to Richmond, Kentucky where "there were plenty of Negroes to live with." When the doctor continued to argue with the mob, Police Chief Boggs told him to keep quiet because, "I would not be able to accomplish anything." The chief was certainly living proof of that. A number of people mentioned in their affidavits that Boggs spent most of the night wandering around town saying there was nothing he could do. His attitude, according to one witness, was that "he did not mind the Negroes being run off, but that the shooting would be dangerous and that some white person might be hurt."[27]

Outside the depot, the hunt continued. "We were just marching in different places in town," Killenger said. "They's trying to get all the colored people together to get out of town. He didn't let us loose until well after dark." When the mob finally allowed the band to stop playing, Killenger said, "The railroad station was full of colored people—children, women and everybody else. They were making efforts then, making plans to get 'em out of town. The railroad company sent two or three passenger coaches out to the station and they were to hook those on train number 24."[28]

The blacks were loaded on to at least two different trains. According to a newspaper account, one group went on a train headed for Knoxville that left at about two A.M. But a railroad worker who passed the depot that morning recalled "seeing them all lined up on the railroad to get out of here as I went to work." Blake Killenger said he thought this second trainload that left in the morning was sent to Louisville. "What they did in Louisville, I don't know."[29]

While the last of the blacks at the depot were waiting to be loaded on a train, Alex Tye and his stepson decided to leave the safety of the hotel and try to make their way back home. Once again they were able to evade any marauding whites, but when they arrived home they found it ransacked. Their white fellow citizens had stolen everything from opera glasses to a shotgun and what they had not taken lay smashed on the floor. As they poked through the rubble, Ben Egner, a white neighbor, came by with good news. Fanny, who had disappeared while they were being chased by the mob, had found shelter at the Egner house.[30]

The Tyes escaped the mob's dragnet, but as they stood in the rubble of their home, it was clear they could no longer live in Corbin. The fate of a few other blacks was not as certain. "Some members of the mob advocated allowing the family of John Barry, who has been a resident of Corbin for thirty-two years, to remain saying he was a 'good nigger,'" the *Lexington Herald* reported. "Others favored ridding the place of all Negroes." In the end some blacks were allowed to stay. "There were two old Negroes that stayed," recalled W. R. Stansberry. "One of them was, we called him 'Nigger' Dennis. He was old at the time. He had lived here all of his life and they told him to just to go to his room and stay there. He wouldn't be bothered. And another old lady by the name of Emma Woods."[31]

In fact, census records show that the black population in Corbin, which had been sixty in 1910, was exactly three in 1920: Emma Woods and her sixty-five-year-old boarder Steve Stansbury and the affectionately nicknamed "Nigger" Dennis. Beyond the city limits, there was a lesser but still substantial drop. Laurel County saw its black population cut in half from 657 to 333 between 1910 and 1920. Whitley County's black population went from 1,111 to 600. By 1930 it would be cut in half again, and after 1960 it would never again rise above 150.[32]

In the first few weeks after the cleansing, a few blacks tried to return. For example, A. C. Martin, a white baggage agent in Corbin, talked some of his former black employees into returning to work. One of them, Pete Frakes, described what happened. "We worked one shift and saw from the demeanor of the crowd on the street that it would not be safe for us to remain. We left on the following evening."

There were, however, two small but significant changes in the way whites reacted to the cleansing. A year earlier the editor at the Knoxville paper had denounced the Unicoi County expulsion. Now, in the wake of Corbin's cleansing, the editor of the local paper also attacked the mob's handiwork. "Our name has gone out over the nation with a black spot that can never be removed," the editor said. "We are glad that the minister and other good people are openly expressing their condemnation of the mob spirit." It was not much, but it was better than the editorial silence or racist screeds after earlier cleansings in Lawrence County, Missouri and Forsyth County, Georgia.

More importantly, the state decided to prosecute the leader of the mob, Steve Rogers, aka Pistol Pete. A decade earlier Kentucky had arrested and convicted Dr. Emelius Champion, the leader of the Birmingham raid. But that was as much about stamping out an insurrection as it was about protecting black citizens. It is clear from the letters of commonwealth's attorney, Joseph B. Snyder, who handled the prosecution, that he wanted the people in Corbin to know that attacking innocent blacks was no longer acceptable. In a letter to the governor in December 1920, Snyder described the "antediluvian" racial attitudes in Corbin:

> The opposition to the Negro in Corbin is something fierce. Negroes are not permitted to live in the town and are not permitted to pass through the town without being run, shot and whipped." Snyder said the government had to make it clear to whites that "the Negro is in this country to stay and that they will have to deal with him with the laws

instead of by force. This theory is not race equality but it is a later day theory of inter racial relations that will bring about a better feeling among the races and to keep each race in its place.

For his part, Snyder won a conviction against "Pistol Pete" in 1920 for his role in the riot. Rogers was sentenced to the state penitentiary for two years, but the punishment had little impact on the people in Corbin. A year after Rogers went to prison, Snyder told the governor that "the anti negro sentiment is as strong there as ever before." Rogers's conviction, in fact, became a cause célèbre. Three hundred townspeople signed a petition supporting his pardon saying Rogers was "an unfortunate victim of circumstance." The townspeople also explained to the governor that "hundreds of good citizens quietly and in a very orderly way assisted in driving out this lawless element, in putting them on trains, and sending them out of Whitley County, in a quiet and determined way, and it is evident that such action was at the time demanded and sanctioned and approved by the whole community of law abiding citizens."[33]

The governor denied the pardon.

———

Glenda Livingston locked herself in her hotel room. It was admittedly an odd thing to do. The day she had spent in London, Kentucky was at worst uneventful. No one had threatened her or had even said anything that could be termed unkind. In fact, everyone at the local elementary school had been very solicitous. She had expected that. As leader of a school accreditation team, she had come to London in 1990 to inspect the Bush Elementary School. The last thing local school officials wanted to do was upset her. But that didn't matter. She was afraid.[34]

Livingston was not easily frightened. As a young woman in the late 1950s she had gone from the small, all-black college of Kentucky State to the sprawling campus of the University of Kentucky at Lexington. This was before the March on Washington, voter registration drives, or the freedom rides, and she was the only black in all of her classes. No one was rude to her, but, then again, few were kind. She was simply ignored and spent a very lonely year at the university.

Glenda Livingston is a warm, engaging woman with a ready laugh; she says that she wanted her master's degree and, if that meant being lonely, so be it.[35]

But London, Kentucky was different. "There were absolutely no blacks. I saw one teenager when we had the opening dinner but then the school that I was sent to with my team—Bush Elementary—there were no blacks on the faculty. No black students. Not nothing." She had grown up in Lexington, about an hour's drive from London. But it could have been the moon, because this was a county where blacks didn't go. The stories, stories that Glenda Livingston had heard, were a matter of legend among blacks. And all of those stories centered around one town, Corbin, just a few miles from London.

Livingston said she first heard about Corbin when she went to college at Kentucky State in Frankfort. "I went to college with kids who lived there and who talked about it. You didn't go inside the city limits of Corbin," Livingston said. "There were signs even posted that said you couldn't come in to the city limits. . . . I don't know if anything happened to cause that or not, but it was pretty well understood by all those guys from Eastern Kentucky that you just did not go into Corbin."[36]

For Livingston, who rose from elementary schoolteacher to school administrator, and her husband, Joe, an electrician, Corbin had been a world away. They and their only son, Shawn, lived a comfortable, middle-class life in Lexington. One of their rituals was to have breakfast together every morning. "My husband has to be at work at seven. He always got it started," Mrs. Livingston recalled. "Saturday was the big breakfast because we weren't running to get places. We were a threesome. I mean we did everything together." It wasn't until Shawn turned sixteen that places like Corbin would loom large over their breakfast table.[37]

Mrs. Livingston and her son remember the moment differently. She thinks they were watching television when a story sparked a conversation about dangerous places in Kentucky. Shawn says the conversation took place over breakfast.[38]

"I was sixteen, and I had my license, and I was driving everywhere just so I could drive," said Shawn, who is now a reference librarian at the University of Kentucky. "We did a lot of talking around the break-fast table before we went off to go to work. And this was I guess January. I got my license, we were still in the midst of school so I was spending my weekend driving and they set me down. I wouldn't say it was deathly serious but it was a very serious conversation."[39]

Whether it was in front of the television or over breakfast, both Shawn and his mother agree on what was said. "You are never to drive to Corbin or Morehead. If we find out, you are in more trouble than you can get from the police."

Neither Shawn nor his mother are sure of why Morehead was included. Shawn said his father, who has since died, always warned his family about Morehead without saying exactly why. "We had talked earlier about stories that my dad and also his family told him about one night the blacks being run out of town in Morehead," Shawn said.

"Those places in eastern Kentucky didn't welcome blacks," Mrs. Livingston said. "And we told him that, you know, when you are driving around with friends and in particular because he had lots of friends that were white. They did things together and went places together and so that was the reason we kept emphasizing that you cannot go into those areas. You are not accepted like the others."

For whites, the idea that their town is considered dangerous can be galling. Mrs. Livingston said that when she was an administrator with the Lexington school system, two of the people she worked with were from Corbin. "They denied that there was ever a time when blacks were not welcome."[40]

Allen Dizney, eighty, who grew up in Corbin, goes even further. He says the blacks were never run out of town. Dizney is a history buff and the man the public library recommends when a history question comes up. Dizney says the story about blacks being run out is an invention of the "damned media."[41]

The damned media in this case was Robby Henson, a documentary filmmaker, who came to Corbin in 1987. Henson, who grew up about fifty miles away in Danville, had heard about Corbin's reputation as a child and thought it would be interesting to do a film about the town. Unaware of the information in the state archives, Henson had to rely on a few old newspaper clips that gave sketchy descriptions of a "race riot" in Corbin. Instead Henson spent much of the film chronicling the racial attitudes in all-white Corbin in 1987. The town was not pleased.[42]

"Some reporter wrote that story without ever coming down and finding what was happening," Dizney says.

The truth to that is Corbin did not run the black people out of town. Now the truth is that there was a work crew that came in here that was about forty men and they were black with white bosses. Now we got a bad crew in here and they were drinking and they were carousing and some feller got his throat cut one night, a white man, and he claimed he was robbed and what not. But anyway they decided, since they were having so much trouble with this crew, that they would remove 'em from Corbin. There was no guns fired. It was all false. They just run this crew out. Black wasn't the situation. It just happened to be a black crew. It could've been a white crew but it wasn't.

According to Dizney, reporters invented the stories that were published about the riot in Corbin. "It was the damned media," he complains, "and I'm cussing you because it was the damned media that done all the bad stories that they didn't know the hell what they was talking about." And it is because of those stories, Dizney says, that Corbin is forced unfairly to live with the reputation of being racist.

When he worked in Cincinnati after World War II, Dizney says his black co-workers picked on him. "I wanted to know what the heck was going on so I cornered one of them one night and he told me. He said, 'Well, you're from Corbin. You all run all our people out of town back in the twenties and what not.' He said you can't go through there on the passenger train unless you duck down because people'll shoot at you and what not. I told him that was the biggest bunk I've ever heard and I told him what the deal was."

In Dizney's telling, his black co-workers eventually went to Corbin and found out there was racial harmony. "They come down here on their own and found out that all of that was a damn lie, that Corbin did not look down on black people."

"Makes me madder than hell," Dizney says. "You people in the media come up some time and you want to make a big fancy story so you make it sound like hell and that ain't the truth."

He also explains how, until the man's death, he was good friends with one of the blacks in town named Howard Nolan. It was Nolan, Dizney says, who told him what really happened in 1919. As he talks, Dizney's outrage grows. He rattles off the names of black people who lived in Corbin. He claims the trains were not segregated. His wife breaks in to say that Harry Nolan was well treated at the old age home. Dizney recalls how he was misunderstood by a filmmaker who was making a documentary about racism in Corbin. The memory still rankles. "He talked about me being a racist and that sort of thing." For some reason, Dizney says, the film even bothered with the name of his dog.

The dog was named Nigger.

The damned media.

VERMILLION COUNTY, INDIANA

INDIANA

ILLINOIS

OHIO

VERMILLION
COUNTY

WAYNE
COUNTY

Jackson
Richmond

EARLHAM
COLLEGE

Blanford
Clinton

★ Indianapolis

Helt Township

Wabash R.

0 Miles   50

0 Kilometers   50

© 2006 Jeffrey L. Ward

MICHIGAN

INDIANA

ILLINOIS

OHIO

VERMILLION
COUNTY

★ Indianapolis

KENTUCKY

0 Miles   100   150

0 Kilometers   150

CHAPTER 10

The Horse Thief Detective Association

Vermillion County, Indiana
1923

Even before the killings, the people of Blanford, Indiana must have been on edge. For Blanford, a gritty coal-mining town, 1923 had started badly. Throughout the first two weeks of January there had been a series of liquor raids in nearby Clinton. It was only a matter of time before police would also descend on Blanford, a place one federal judge in Indianapolis declared "the worst city in the world."

Since 1920, when Prohibition was passed, the judge had seen a steady stream of Blanford's residents shuffle through his court after being caught making moonshine. The judge was obviously exasperated, a feeling no doubt shared by Blanford's immigrant miners. Having grown up in Europe, where wine and beer were as common as table salt, they saw making moonshine as both an economic necessity and a labor of love. Between miner and judge, there could be no compromise, only an unyielding war of attrition.[1]

But during the third week of January and before the police could launch another raid, Blanford was hit by racial troubles. Whites were pitted against blacks in a tense standoff that lasted nearly five days. The outcome was never in doubt, however. Only a few hundred blacks lived in Vermillion County at the time, and most of those in Blanford.

When Sheriff Harry Newland got a call about gunfire in Blanford at a black-owned store on the night of January 28, he decided that, before he ventured out, he needed help. In addition to his deputy, he decided to take one of his prisoners, a trusty. But they were not enough. The sheriff made a phone call for more men.[2]

That single phone call provides a chilling insight into the hold that racist politics had on Indiana and the nation in the 1920s. The sheriff had called on the Helt Township Horse Thief Detective Association. The group sounds like something out of a comic opera, but it fact there was nothing funny about it. Sheriff Newland had called in the Ku Klux Klan. When the night was over two men would be dead.

————

The story of how the Klan became the police on that cold winter's night in Indiana reaches back to Reconstruction.

The original Klan was born out of boredom.

In May 1866 six former Confederate soldiers in Pulaski, Tennessee had too much time on their hands, and dreamed up a club characterized by outlandish rituals and little else. A new member, for example, would be blindfolded and dressed up in what he was told was a crown, but which was, in fact, a pair of outsized donkey ears. The members then put him in front of what they said was the "royal altar"—a large mirror. Next he was told to repeat a couplet by Robert Burns: "O wad some power the giftie gie us/ To see oursel's as ithers see us." Then the blindfold was whisked off. In 1866 that was considered pretty funny.[3]

Another ritual involved running around town in a tall cardboard hat, a mask, and a long flowing robe. Each costume was supposed to look as grotesque as possible; early taste in these outfits ran to calicoes. It all seemed harmless until someone noticed that the outlandish outfits frightened superstitious blacks. In a world where the old forms of social control—master and slave—had been swept away, this innocent fun could be adapted for an uglier end: intimidation.[4]

This first Klan had a brief life. As its aim shifted from entertainment to enforcement, Klan "dens" quickly spread across the South. But its secrecy and brutality were its undoing. In 1867 Nathan Bedford Forrest, the Confederacy's brilliant but ruthless cavalry commander, was enlisted to run the burgeoning organization. By 1869, unable to control its excesses, Forrest ordered all Klan chapters to disband and burn their files. Some did. Some didn't. It was not until 1871 that federal government troops were able to bring the last remnants of the Klan to heel.[5]

The first iteration of the Klan was rooted in the frustrations and social upheaval that followed the Civil War. The next version, which was to drive events in places like Vermillion County, fed off the same kinds of fears following World War I. The second Klan was far larger and more powerful than the first, thanks to that unique icon of American hucksterism, the publicity agent.

In 1915, D. W. Griffith directed a film entitled *Birth of A Nation,* based on two racist novels by Thomas Dixon, which glorified the post–Civil War Klan. Although harshly criticized by the NAACP and other black organizations, it was praised as the most artistically ambitious film in the young history of cinema, and remained the most profitable film in American history until another epic about the South, *Gone with the Wind,* came along in 1939.

When the film opened in 1915 in Atlanta, William J. Simmons, a minister turned salesman, saw his chance. As a child, Simmons had been deeply impressed by the Klan when his father had joined after the Civil War. Forced to convalesce after an accident, Simmons began to spend his days developing an organization chart, inventing titles and working out the ritual for the Klan's resurrection.

With fourteen others, Simmons scaled Stone Mountain, about fifteen miles east of Atlanta, in November 1915 and, with elaborate ceremony, announced the Klan's rebirth. By 1920, the Klan had several thousand members, a modest success but not nearly the organization Simmons longed for.

In hopes of vastly expanding the Klan, Simmons turned to Edward Clarke and Elizabeth Tyler, two publicity agents who had formed the Southern Publicity Association in Atlanta. This meeting was to be a turning point in the history of the Klan, as Clarke and Tyler worked their magic on their new "product." They retooled the Klan's message to match the tenor of the time. Sales territories were carved out. Agents were hired to make the pitch. They in turn earned a commission on each "sale"—a dues-paying member. Klan leaders were taught to stay on message. The messages themselves were carefully tailored to specific audiences. The press was enlisted to spruce up the Klan image, and snazzy brochures made the product more appealing. From a marketing standpoint this new campaign was a thing of beauty and was studied by marketing experts long after the Klan itself fell apart. Edward Clarke and Elizabeth Tyler had pulled off a miracle. It just wasn't a very pretty miracle.[6]

After the Southern Publicity Association began its work, the Klan signed up 48,000 new members within three months. At its height in 1924 it had millions of members nationwide and was able to recruit new members in the most unlikely places. Quakers, famed for their nonviolence, signed up in substantial numbers and, in fact, one of the Klan leaders was also a Quaker minister. By 1925 thousands of Klansmen in full regalia paraded down Pennsylvania Avenue in front of the Capitol building.[7]

The Klan's popularity was rooted in the discontents of America after World War I. The world that old-line America knew was passing, as Catholic and Jewish immigrants threatened Protestant hegemony; Bolshevism endangered the political order and the crime and cynicism created by Prohibition threatened the social order. The Klan's response was an upbeat message of support for law and order, religion, and the "American home." One Klan recruiting brochure said public education "must and shall be preserved supported and developed" and that the KKK stood for "full and impartial law enforcement" and the "upbuilding of Protestant Christianity." This was a kinder, gentler KKK.[8]

One of the opening shots in this publicity campaign was a story in the *Atlanta Journal*. Simmons told the reporter that the Klan was not anti-Negro. In fact, Simmons recalled Old Aunt Viney, his black "mammy" from childhood, and the beloved Uncle Simon, who "was a great hand at picking a banjo." Simmons did not hate blacks. He just believed along with most other whites that the white race should be dominant. That meant that the Klan was opposed to allowing blacks to vote "because such suffrage means political equality and is another way of saying that a Negro has as much right to occupy the office of governor or any other high position as a white man." By the same token, he denied religious intolerance. "We merely provide that no man shall become a member of the Klan who does not believe in the tenets of the Christian religion."[9]

But Simmons, who had been coached by Clarke and Tyler, kept returning to the idea that the Klan was a lawful organization with a corporate charter from the state of Georgia. "We are always silently at work for the maintenance of law," Simmons said. "In almost every community where the Klan is organized the sheriff is one of the first to join." The Klan's purpose in fact was "maintenance of our American institutions."[10]

For those who were worried about communists and foreign agitators, the Klan would be a bulwark. "We admit no member who is foreign born." Simmons said. "We know that some of our most loyal citizens are foreign born, but in the effort to make the Klan thoroughly American, thoroughly loyal to the flag, we have decided to draw a sharp line by saying that no one, no matter who he be, shall become a member of the Klan unless he was born on American soil."[11]

———

The wave of immigration to America in the late nineteenth and early twentieth centuries traumatized Vermillion County. In 1890, nearly all of the county's 13,000 residents had been native born. In 1920, nearly fifteen percent of the 27,625 people living in the county were foreign born. The majority of the immigrants were Italian, but there were also Austrians, Hungarians, forty-two people from the Balkans and two Finns. Italians were not enthusiastic about Prohibition, were usually not Protestants, and were considered potentially radical in their politics.[12]

Anyone who read the newspaper knew Vermillion County was under siege. In Blanford and the surrounding towns of the county, Indiana people subscribed to the *Daily Clintonian*. It was named after the town of Clinton, which though only a few miles down a winding road from Blanford, was a world away. Blanford was a tough coal mining town where Italians, Serbs, and blacks drank, fought, and struggled to stay alive. The people in Clinton, who lived in neat houses along the Vigo River, were descended from early settlers, were farmers and tradesmen, prayed in Protestant churches, and voted Republican.

The *Daily Clintonian* was a Republican paper. Patriotic, it had backed President Woodrow Wilson, a Democrat, throughout the war. But in its heart it yearned for a good Republican like Colonel Leonard Wood, considered the heir to Theodore Roosevelt, to run the country. The country needed a strong, steady hand because, thanks to the war, the world had become an infinitely more dangerous place. Bolsheviks, those spawns of war's chaos, had swept through Russia and were now, the *Daily Clintonian* warned in 1919, poised to strike Indiana. "Clinton Police report there was speech delivered at Seventh and Oak streets, Sunday night, which they understood to be of the Bolshevist type," the *Daily Clintonian* reported on February 17. "No arrests were made, but they warn the anarchists that, if evidence warrants it, they will investigate all such efforts to stir sentiment here which, in its last analysis, clearly has for its purpose the overthrow of the American Government."[13]

Three days later matters grew worse. On the front page of the *Daily Clintonian* a banner headline screamed, "BOLSHEVIKI PROPAGANDA SCATTERED IN CITY." To the *Daily Clintonian,* what this new propaganda campaign meant was clear. "The Russian Federated Soviet Government is now trying to get a foothold in this vicinity." While the speech and the handbills were ominous, the newspaper reassured its readers that "federal authorities are working on the cases and just waiting for a slip by the agitators before they take action."[14]

Two months later, and with still no arrests, the communists struck again. A front-page story warned "Anarchist Literature Scattered in Night" and described how copies of a pamphlet distributed around town extolled the new Soviet government. The "Anarchist" story was packaged with another feature that told readers "Some Soviets Plan to Seize Women Also: Official Testimony Quoting Proclamation, Indicate That Homes Are to Be Superseded by Plan to Raise Children by 'State Plan'; How Would Average American Like This Program?" And that was only the headline.[15]

Clinton was not alone. The rest of the country, which over the past few years had been whipped into a frenzy by government propaganda about the Hun, had become obsessed with the threat of foreign radicals and anarchists. In June 1919 the *Daily Clintonian* explained how U.S. Attorney General Mitchell Palmer was readying the country for possible anti-American outbreaks on Independence Day. At the same time the head of Army Intelligence briefed Congress on its efforts to monitor radical activity. "The General showed the committee maps of New York City, one of Manhattan and the other of Brooklyn on which were marked, he said, every rendezvous infested by dangerous radicals."[16]

If there were any doubts about the danger facing Vermillion County, they were dispelled in the first days of January 1920. Federal agents across the country began rounding up thousands of "radicals"—estimates range as high as 10,000 arrested—in what would become known as the Palmer Red Raids. Six were arrested in Clinton January 3 and another three on January 5. Clinton was in the crosshairs.[17]

The Red Raids cemented the impression in Clinton that all dangerous radicals were, in fact, immigrants. A headline in the *Daily Clintonian* in May 1919 said exactly that: "All Reds Are Foreigners." Quoting a Chicago judge, the story said that all the people arrested in a May Day disturbance were immigrants. "All such people should be forced to choose and choose quickly," the judge warned, "whether they want to stay here as American citizens or get out."

Vermillion County's growing uneasiness with its immigrant population was reflected in the shifting tone of the *Daily Clintonian* editorials. In an editorial on November 14, 1918 the newspaper chided Italian immigrants for talking "as though they were more Italian than American." It stressed, however, that native-born citizens and immigrants should learn to adapt to one another. "If native born Americans expect the World War to teach the foreign born Americans that they are expected to be for America first, last and all the time, it also should teach all native born citizens something of humility." The editorial then reminded everyone of the sacrifice made by other countries in the war.[18]

Four months later, the tone of the editorials had changed dramatically. "It safely can be said that public sentiment in Clinton, where live a considerable number of foreign born, is strongly in favor of the deportation of any man who comes to this country with the idea of helping overthrow the government."[19]

In Vermillion County and across the nation, the issues of temperance, religion, and immigration were inextricably linked. America's early immigrants were from Northern Europe, a cold, wet climate never known for its wine making. But many of the later immigrants arrived from the sunny, dry countries around the Mediterranean, where people had tended their vineyards for as long as anyone could remember. While Protestant ministers railed against drinking, Jews and Catholics from Italy and the Middle East used wine in their religious ceremonies. The Klan, which limited its membership to Protestants, naturally promoted temperance. Simmons noted how the Klan "could fill a book with what we have done in the way of furnishing information against bootlegging and offenses of that sort."[20]

Prohibition began on January 16, 1920. When the *Daily Clintonian* was not fretting over the "Bolsheviki," it was tallying the arrests from liquor raids. And an alert reader did not have to get much beyond the headlines to figure out that immigrants were involved in illegal stills. One headline read, "Booze Traffickers Are Caught in Net; Joe Trunko, Patketta and Carlvetta Nabbed." Just in case the reader missed the point, the newspaper would add a suspect's nationality. A story on an arrest of "booze haulers" ends with, "Pete Bibich of Clinton also was summoned for today, though he and his friends say he has not been mixed up in any way with any of this business. He is Serbian."[21]

But the crime engendered by Prohibition was only the leading edge of a much larger problem. The previous year, the population of Clinton had been shocked when George Cartwright, a local fifty-one-year-old businessman, shot his estranged wife and then put the gun in his mouth and killed himself. The murder-suicide came after what for Vermillion County was a crime wave. In 1919, six men were awaiting trial for murder. Reflecting on the Cartwright shooting, the *Daily Clintonian* noted that "there is a noticeable wave of crime in large cities and it is said it is usual after all wars for such crime waves to sweep over the country."

More to the point, the community worried that the crime rate was somehow linked to immigrants. The *Clintonian*, responding to these fears, told its readers in an editorial to "look at the facts calmly." While acknowledging that the community had "an unenviable record for murders," citizens should not despair of their "cosmopolitan population." The newspaper said that it was inevitable that some men will "go wild" where a large percentage of them "have left their wives or families," nevertheless "Serbians, as a nation and as a class of citizens, generally are desirable."[22]

Communism, crime, and alcohol were the interrelated problems facing Vermillion County at the beginning of the 1920s, and it was no wonder that the Klan took strong root there. The Klan, after all, stood for Protestantism, Prohibition, and Public Order. Its members were, as the Southern Publicity Association wanted everyone to know, "100 percent American."

Vermillion County became a Klan stronghold. Just how popular the organization was became clear when an enterprising Indianapolis reporter obtained a copy of a Klan memo in 1925 detailing the Invisible Empire's membership in the state. The county's 1,800 Klan members found on the list represented thirty percent of Vermillion's native-born, white males, one of the highest percentages in Indiana. This was not even the high point of Klan membership—because by 1925 membership had begun to fall throughout Indiana as the group was buffeted by one scandal after another.[23]

The Klan was more than just popular, however, in Vermillion County. By 1923, it had become the law.

The Klan's strategy for taking control in Indiana rested in part on an anachronism, which went by the name of the Horse Thief Detective Association (HTDA), a vigilante organization unique to Indiana that operated with the blessing of the state government. As its name implies, the HDTA's job was to track down horse thieves, and it had been formed before the Civil War. If local citizens wanted to form a chapter and could get the approval of the county government, the state was willing to grant them the same powers as the police. In other words, its members could investigate crimes and make arrests.

The HDTA may have made sense in the 1850s, but as cars rolled off Detroit's assembly lines, the association's fortunes began to sink. By 1916 its membership had dwindled to 9,027 and the association appeared ready for oblivion. But then something magical happened. The membership numbers began turning around and by 1924, had climbed to 15,500. Along with the new members, new chapters formed every month. Vermillion County had only one chapter before 1920, but there were four by 1923. There may have been fewer horses, but that didn't seem to matter. Business was booming.[24]

In fact, the leaders of the Klan looked at the HTDA and realized it was everything a Klansman could hope for. If the Klan could create chapters of the HTDA, it would have armed vigilante bands with police powers that, while sanctioned by the government, were answerable to the Invisible Empire of the Ku Klux Klan. Klan members masquerading as the Horse Thief Detective Association would organize chapters in each county and ask the government for a charter.

Although no order has ever turned up in Klan records, the Klan takeover of the HTDA was one of the era's open secrets. *Tolerance,* a newspaper formed specifically to battle the Klan in Indiana, headlined one article in August 1923, "Ku Klux Morons Police Indiana! State Reaping Whirlwind from Klan's Revival of Old 'Horse Thief' Law." In another article in April of the same year the newspaper noted, "The St. Joseph County Commissioners fail to see the urgency for granting constabulary powers to the Ku Kluxers who recently organized the South Bend Horse Thieves Detective Association." By 1923 organized labor, which opposed the Klan, started passing resolutions condemning the HTDAs. The machinists' union, for example, "requested all union men now members of such associations to withdraw."[25]

In Vermillion County, the four chapters of the HTDA were riddled with Klan members. In 2001, a piece of Klan stationery turned up with a list of what were likely some Vermillion County Klan members. When the roster was compared with HTDA membership lists, four of the fifteen members of the Cayuga chapter of the HTDA were Klansmen. There were at least fourteen Klansmen in the Helt Township chapter, and three of the seven members in the Rileysburg chapter were KKK.

If there was trouble—and there would be—the Klansmen/police of Vermillion County were ready.

When the trip hammer fell, it was probably as much coincidence as anything else that it came down first on Vermillion County's blacks. The Klan was prepared to do battle with Catholics, Jews, immigrants, and blacks. But in Blanford blacks were a minority even within the town's immigrant community. Of the sixteen hundred people in Blanford in 1920, less than forty were blacks and four hundred were immigrants. There were blacks living outside of town, but their numbers were negligible. Yet to the whites living in and around Blanford, blacks and immigrants were two distinct groups and both were a threat.

There is still bitterness in his voice when Eli Skorich talks about the "Americans." They were the whites of the Klan and the Horse Thief Detective Association who, Skorich says, ran the town. Of Serbian descent, the eighty-five-year-old Skorich has lived in Blanford most of his life and is one of the last people alive who remembers what happened to the town's blacks.[26]

"We didn't have anything against the coloreds," Skorich said. "Them horse thieves just didn't like the colored. If you weren't American there was no place for you to live here."[27]

The newspaper version of what happened in January 1923 is very simple. On Thursday, January 18, 1923, Thelma Bales, twelve, told her parents that, while returning from the grocery store, "she was seized by a Negro, carried about a quarter of a mile, mistreated, and then permitted to go home." When the parents took the child to a hospital in nearby Terre Haute Friday night, news of the attack leaked out. On Saturday, newspapers reported several hundred men attended a mass meeting in Blanford and issued an ultimatum to the town's blacks that "unmarried adults must be out of Blanford by 7 o'clock [Saturday] and that married persons and their child would have until 7 P.M. Wednesday to leave in case the fugitive is not produced."[28]

Almost immediately blacks began to flee. The *Indianapolis Star* reported on Sunday, the day after the ultimatum, that "all available automobiles operating between Blanford and Clinton were filled with Negro passengers and a number of trucks were filled with household goods." On Friday, two days after the deadline, the *New York Times* noted that "when the 'zero hour' approached the last of the Negroes were on their way to Terre Haute and Clinton." There had been 235 blacks living in Vermillion County before the cleansing. By the next census there would be sixty-nine.[29]

But there are odd gaps in the story that the newspapers reported. On Monday John Bales, the father of the girl who had been attacked, went to the *Daily Clintonian* to talk about what had happened. Bales, who had been born and raised in Indiana, described all blacks as troublemakers and Blanford as a community living in fear. He cited the Fantone family as one of the victims of this black crime wave. But when the editor called people in Blanford, a community supposedly united against the blacks, he got a very different picture.[30]

"I don't think the majority of people think [the entire black population] should suffer for a crime committed by one colored man—especially as he is not a resident," Barney Fantone, an Italian immigrant, told the newspaper. His lack of concern was especially odd because, according to Bales, Fantone's daughter had supposedly been pursued by a Negro only days before the assault on the Bales girl. But, when questioned by the newspaper, Fantone shrugged off the incident. His daughter had been frightened by a black man, but "We don't think there was anything to this. He never hurt [her] nor tried to do so far as we could learn."[31]

If Blanford was supposedly seething with rage against all blacks, there is also not a single account in any newspaper of whites attacking blacks during the five-day grace period. Instead during this period the newspapers describe Blanford with one word: "quiet." Men like Bales, born in America and steeped in its culture of racism, might be upset, but Fantone and his fellow immigrants, who made up much of Blanford's population, were less impressed with the black menace.[32] In fact, on the day the ultimatum was issued, the *Indianapolis News* reported that "Willis Satterlee, prosecutor, and Harry Newland, sheriff of Vermillion county, accompanied by a number of deputy sheriffs and several members of the Horse Thief Detective Association of Dana visited Blanford Saturday night, but lingered only long enough to ask, 'Is everything quiet.'"[33]

Throughout the five-day period, newspapers reported local stores coming to repossess furniture that blacks had purchased on credit, black laborers gathering their tools from the mines, and blacks packing their belongings. At the same time there is no mention of the sheriff doing anything. On Wednesday, with only hours until the deadline expired, Governor Warren McCray sent a telegram to Newland asking if he needed help from the National Guard. "No group of citizens in a town have the right to issue an ultimatum to another group to get out, the governor was reported as saying to the Vermillion County sheriff," the *Indianapolis News* noted. As with Corbin, Kentucky, when the leader of the mob that drove out the blacks there was prosecuted, this was another sign that racial cleansings were falling into disfavor. But this was not to say that everyone agreed with the governor. Sheriff Newland, for example, declined the offer.

In all the gaps in the newspaper accounts, this was perhaps the strangest. With the minutes ticking away until the deadline, the sheriff turned down offers of help and yet did nothing himself. If a reporter had questioned him about his inaction, there is no record of it. Instead there was silence. The press never learned Harry Newland's secret.[34]

The Bales girl was allegedly attacked on January 18. The ultimatum was issued on the 20th. By January 24, a Wednesday, the blacks were gone.

It had all happened so quickly that there were bound to be loose ends. One of these was a clothing store in Blanford owned by two black men, named in news accounts only as Brown and Hale. Having sold the store, they came back to Blanford on the Sunday after the cleansing to do an inventory. It was a risky thing to do, but they may have figured the town would be quiet on a Sunday night. If that was their plan, they were wrong. Mike Trkula and Kristina Ciraj had gotten married earlier in the day, and on Sunday evening, while the two store owners counted their stock, a Serbian wedding celebration was underway at a nearby dance hall.[35]

It is not clear who fired the first shots. According to one account, one of the store owners called the prosecuting attorney around ten P.M. because three or four shots had been fired into their store. Another account says only that a few shots were fired, and it is unclear who called the police. But this first round of gunfire was enough to rouse the sheriff with a warning that a riot might be underway in Blanford. It was at that moment that Harry Newland called Ed Sturm, captain of the Helt Township Horse Thieves Detective Association.[36]

Aside from what were presumably two thoroughly frightened haberdashers, the sheriff and his band found no evidence of a riot. But as they made their way through town, the Serbian wedding was in full swing. There are two versions of what happened next. The police version is that, when the police entered the dance hall, Newland and Sturm stood by the door and told partygoers why they were there. At the same time Deputy George Price and another officer walked to the stove at the back of the hall to warm themselves. In the police version, as they waited, someone, without any provocation, fired at Price through a window from outside the hall. Within seconds two Serbian mineworkers were dead, and both the sheriff and Price were wounded.

The second version is described in the *Daily Clintonian* only as one "going the rounds." In this account while Sturm and Newland were waiting by the door, Deputy Price walked to the stove, ordered everyone to hold up their hands, and then fired into the ceiling. The wedding goers, assuming they were about to be robbed, started shooting at the police.[37]

Both versions leave out one salient fact. Although they came to town as police, the sheriff and his men were, in fact, the KKK. At least fifteen members of the Helt Township Horse Thief Detective Association had ties to the Klan. More importantly Ed Sturm, the captain of the group, was a leader of the Klan. In a 1925 Klan membership list for Indiana, Sturm is "Klexter," a kind of sergeant-at-arms for the Vermillion County chapter of the KKK. His name appears along with that of the "Klaliff,"—"Harry Newlin" of Newport—apparently a phonetic spelling of the sheriff's name. (While Harry Newland lived in Newport, there is no Harry Newlin listed in either the city directory for Vermillion County or in census records for the period.) The 1925 Klan list also notes that in Vermillion County, "All county officers favorable except the prosecuting attorney." The sheriff was a secret member of the Invisible Empire.[38]

When the KKK/police entered the dance hall within days of a racial cleansing, it is not hard to imagine that the Serbian wedding party saw this as a provocation. Even after all these years we can hear an echo of that outrage in the voice of Eli Skorich, one of the last survivors from that era. "They had no business to come into this wedding. They just wanted to disrupt it. When they run the coloreds out, they were the same guys that come into the wedding. They were after the foreigners."[39]

———

Time has not been kind to Blanford. When the coal mines played out in the 1940s, the rot set in. Streets emptied, shops closed, and cheaply built homes, staggering under the weight of neglect, collapsed into vacant lots. What remains today is the residue of a town: a few homes, a post office, a ball field.

And that is where Jon VanSant comes in. As towns like Blanford loosen their grip on life, VanSant prises out the keepsakes, mementoes, and heirlooms. He is an incongruous figure. In a world that is exhausted, VanSant is indefatigable. An engineer by trade, the thirty-four-year-old VanSant's passion is the history of Vermillion County. He grew up near Perrysville, a small town in Vermillion County twenty-seven miles north of Blanford, and, although he moved to Davenport, Iowa, he returns to the county every few weeks searching for artifacts of a lost world. He talks to elderly residents about memorabilia they might want to part with. When they die, he approaches their heirs. If, by chance something slips past him, antique dealers know to call VanSant with their interesting finds. And bit by bit, Vermillion County gives up its past: an old revolver, a badge of the Helt Township Horse Thief Detective Association, and in 2001 a list of members in the Vermillion County KKK.[40]

Vermillion County Klan memorabilia is not uncommon, but as he scanned the list he stumbled on the name of Frank Crist. It was his great-grandfather.

"What do you think of that," he asked his grandmother.

"Oh, he was a member."

"Was grandpa a member, too?"

"Well as a child," she replied. Doubtless they had thought it would be a cute idea. Father and small son went off together to cross burnings. She remembered they had even made his grandfather a little Klan robe for the occasion.

Some things change; others don't.

According to VanSant, people in Blanford don't like to be reminded of their town's history as a Klan stronghold. But, like many in Vermillion County, they are still leery of blacks. The 2000 census found only forty-four living in a county with a total population of over 16,500.

"Let's say you are a black man and you were to drive through Perrysville, Indiana. Nobody's going to say anything to you," VanSant said. "They will be very congenial, very nice. If you are to move into town, that's probably not a good idea only because the people will not be very friendly to you. A whole group of [black] families move in, you'd probably have a cleansing."

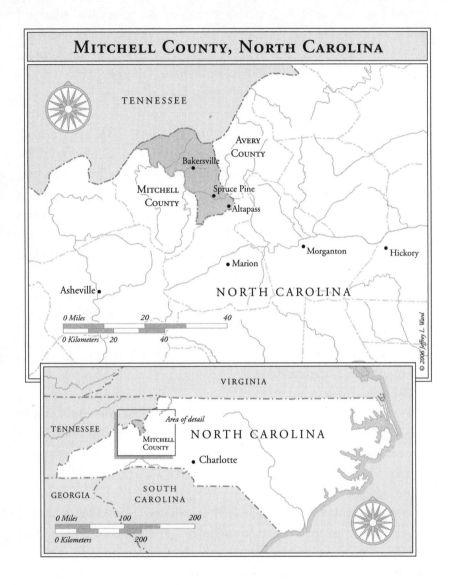

MITCHELL COUNTY, NORTH CAROLINA

TENNESSEE

AVERY COUNTY

Bakersville

MITCHELL COUNTY

Spruce Pine

Altapass

Morganton

Hickory

Marion

NORTH CAROLINA

Asheville

0 Miles 20 40

0 Kilometers 20 40

© 2006 Jeffrey L. Ward

VIRGINIA

TENNESSEE

Area of detail

MITCHELL COUNTY

NORTH CAROLINA

Charlotte

GEORGIA

SOUTH CAROLINA

0 Miles 100 200

0 Kilometers 200

CHAPTER 11

Bedtime Stories

―――――――――

Mitchell County, North Carolina
1923

In the Thomas family, bedtime stories were a bit different. Lloyd Hise recalls one in particular. It did not have a formal title as such, but to this day he refers to it as "The Day Granny Thomas Was Raped by a Black Man." The children would listen spellbound as they were told the story of how in 1923, when she was in her sixties, Alice Thomas, Hise's great-grandmother, was raped. It was an exciting, heroic story because it ended with two of Granny Thomas's sons helping the sheriff to track her attacker for several days before capturing him just outside of Hickory, North Carolina. And the story had a moral, too, since the attacker was not lynched but rather tried in a proper court of law. After the jury deliberated for five minutes, they settled on electrocution.[1]

By necessity, stories were a tradition in the Thomas family. Aunts, uncles, cousins, and grandparents all lived along a small stream a few miles from the town of Spruce Pine in the western mountains of North Carolina. Hise said that, when he was growing up there in the 1950s, they still didn't have electricity along the creek. At sundown

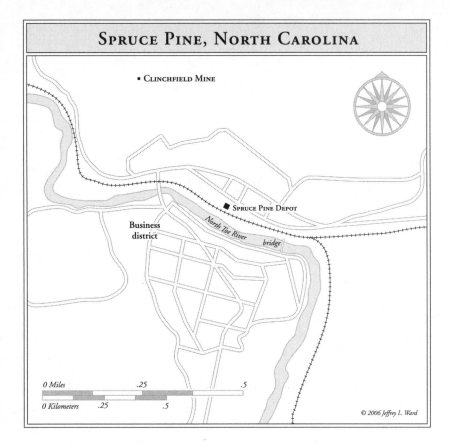

Hise's grandfather, the tall, taciturn Wilburn Thomas, one of the sons who tracked his mother's rapist, would simply go to bed. If grandchildren had come to stay the night in one of the straw tick beds, it was up to Wilburn's wife, Charlotte, to amuse them. That was when the stories began.[2]

"They would tell all of us children about the old days," Hise says. "Most of these stories were told—you know you go visit and you spend the night—and they were told at eight or nine or ten o'clock at night. Granddad was always in bed by then. I can remember him from the bedroom, 'Hold it down in there. I'm trying to sleep.' She would tell me stories you know as a little kid to frighten you. She could really spin a yarn and get you so scared you couldn't sleep at night."[3]

The story about the rape of Granny Thomas—Charlotte's mother-in-law—was especially frightening because she had been attacked along the creek where the Thomas clan lives. That was only a few hundred yards from where the children listened to Charlotte Thomas tell the story.[4]

After the rape, a posse had been formed to search the hills for her attacker. And when they came up empty-handed, the same posse went into Spruce Pine later that day to drive out all the blacks. Hise remembers that was the odd thing about the story. The rape, pursuit, capture, and eventual execution of the man who raped Granny Thomas were often discussed. But, if the subject of the expulsion ever came up in conversation, Wilburn Thomas, unsmiling and remote, could not bear to hear about the fall day when the blacks were herded into boxcars at the Spruce Pine Depot and sent packing.

"That was just a subject he didn't talk about," Hise explains. "He would talk about the rape but now he would not talk about the riots and the problems that happened subsequent to that. If that subject came up he would leave the room."[5]

Like some ancient redoubt, Mitchell County, pitched along the top of the Blue Ridge Mountains, looks out over the plateau that is North Carolina's Piedmont. Although worn down by time, the Blue Ridge Mountains still stand sentinel along the western edge of North Carolina. The road into Mitchell County—Highway 226—runs north across the Piedmont and then zigzags up the escarpment of the Blue Ridge. This escarpment faces roughly south, and when it is lashed by storms, the water retreats back into the streams and creeks of the Piedmont. Where the road surmounts this ridge line, Mitchell County begins.

There were slaves in Mitchell County before the war. Elvira Jennings, who traces her family back to one of the first families in the county, says her great-grandfather was a slave owner. But the practice was not very widespread. In 1870, the census found only 213 blacks living in a county of more than 4,000 people. When the county more than doubled in population in 1880, the number of blacks increased as well to 503. But well before 1920 that number had dwindled to fifty-six when the county's total population stood at about 11,200. Aside from an abandoned gravesite above Bakersville, the county seat, there is little to indicate blacks ever lived in the area. There are scattered stories in the local paper of two blacks dying in the flood of 1901 or an anecdote about Sam Silvers, the last black man living on Cane Creek.

The only story that gives a sense of what life was like for blacks in Mitchell County was published in the *Lenoir Topic* in 1886. The ostensible subject of the article is a white man who shoots a black miner working near Bakersville. But soon the story veers off into an anecdote about another shooting that occurred on Big Rock Creek just above Bakersville. The writer recalls how "a man from Rock Creek met two Negroes just over the state line" in Tennessee. Without ever explaining why, the writer says the Rock Creek man, "made them put their heads together so he could kill them both at one shot." It apparently did not go well. One man was killed instantly, but the other was unharmed. The killer then bludgeoned the surviving black with his gun and dragged both bodies to the side of the road where he hid them. In one of those "believe it or not" codas, the writer says the bludgeoned man "crawled out and recovered." The moral of the story: "You will hardly ever see Negroes on Big Rock Creek."[6]

But not all interactions between blacks and whites in Bakersville were so violent. Wilburn Thomas's daughter, Georgia, recalls a small settlement of blacks that lived near them close to Gouge's Creek Road. "There was a bunch of them that lived up here," she says. Her mother and aunt would go up on the hillside to pull galax, a leafy plant that was used to decorate at Christmas. "The blacks, they didn't have no way to make any money," she explains. The Thomas women would bundle the galax the blacks pulled together with their own, sell them together, and split the profits. It was a neighborly gesture, but, she quickly adds, "They didn't let my daddy or my uncle know it."[7]

The first hint that this world might be changing came in 1915 when J. E. Burleson, a wealthy businessman, bought the first car in the county, a Carter Car with its patented "friction drive." The friction drive never worked very well, but it might not have made much of a difference to Burleson. The only road in the county ran a little over a mile from the Spruce Pine Depot to the Burleson Mica House. Even if Mitchell County was not on the cutting edge of transportation, it was clear that cars were the future. Or at least that was the opinion of Cameron

Morrison, who, when he was elected governor in 1921, convinced the legislature to float a $50 million bond issue to build roads throughout the state. Mitchell County's principal link with the outside world, the railroad, was about to be overtaken by the car.[8]

In Mitchell County what this meant was that the state hired contractors to begin building roads from Spruce Pine and Bakersville to surrounding counties. Porter and Boyd Construction was in charge of the section from Spruce Pine to Bakersville, while O'Brien Construction had the contract to extend the road in the opposite direction to Avery County. At the same time, the state Department of Corrections opened a work camp in Mitchell County, presumably to use convict labor in the road-building program. While the supervisors and foremen were white, the work crews for the construction companies and the convicts at the labor camp were black. In addition to the road building, the town of Spruce Pine had hired the D. W. Adams Company for a water and sewer project. The workers on this project, who also were black, had set up a temporary camp on the banks of the Toe River that meandered through the downtown. And at the Clinchfield Mine near Spruce Pine—the county was rich in deposits of mica and feldspar—management had begun importing black workers. In 1920 the census found fifty-six blacks living in the county. Three years later, that number had quadrupled.[9]

No local newspaper survives that might indicate how the county's whites felt about the sudden influx of black laborers. But in 1928, five years after the expulsion, Muriel Sheppard, the wife of a mining engineer, moved to Mitchell County and, fascinated by this strange and insular world, began writing a book. "Anyone who comes from outside the mountains is a 'furriner' in mountain parlance whether he comes from Knoxville or New York or London," Sheppard wrote in *Cabins in the Laurel*, published in 1935. "They are willing to admit white furriners into their country-within-a-country, but they have no intentions of being colonized by colored people. The mountain people would almost rather not have the highway than let in the Negroes."[10]

At about noon on September 26, 1923, the two worlds collided when John Goss, a black trusty at the nearby convict work camp, wandered into the Thomas hollow off of Gouge's Creek Road. The story handed down in the Thomas family was that Goss stopped at one house and asked for a drink of water. Georgia McClellan, who still lives in the hollow and is a granddaughter of Alice "Granny" Thomas, said it was her mother who "gave him the dipper and told him to go to the spring and get him a drink of water . . . my grandmother was coming up the road or was supposed to have been and he met her and he was supposed to have raped her."[11]

Alice Thomas herself gave a more graphic account to a reporter from the *Asheville Citizen*, who interviewed her a few days after the attack. She described how "a negro came by and spoke to her, following her for some distance." At some point Alice Thomas said Goss grabbed her and, when she screamed, pulled a knife and threatened to kill her. According to the story, "she was dragged about 75 yards into the woods." After the rape, Alice Thomas quoted Goss as saying, "If you tell, I will kill you." Although Thomas was overpowered, held at knife point, and dragged into the woods, the reporter does not mention seeing any cuts or bruises.[12]

What happened after the assault is unclear. Presumably Goss ran off and Alice Thomas returned home. But there is no indication of when Alice Thomas revealed the attack or whom she told. Sheppard only says, "As soon as her kinfolk found out about it, they started after him." And a story in the *Asheville Times*, which sent a reporter to Spruce Pine, is equally vague. "When the news of the assault upon the woman reached Spruce Pine early Wednesday afternoon, a crowd formed for the purpose of searching for the guilty Negro."[13]

But they were too late: Goss had already escaped. Scores of men began combing the hills around Spruce Pine. The men who began this futile search included Mack Thomas, the husband of Alice Thomas, and several of their sons, including forty-year-old Wilburn, an experienced hunter. But in these first few hours they and their neighbors were searching for vengeance. "This crowd started as a posse but after a few hours' futile search for the negro, it became a potential mob," the *Asheville Times* reported. "Thwarted in its attempt to apprehend the assailant, it set itself the task of driving all negroes from the community."[14]

The mob's first target was the black miners. Between fifty and a hundred men descended on the Hawkins mine and then the Wisemen mine, which was owned by the Clinchfield Products Corporation. The *Asheville Times* made the mob's order to leave sound like an almost fatherly admonition. "The leaders of the mob made no loud threats. They merely assured the negroes that their presence was not desired and that the next train should find them in transit. Moreover, they appointed delegations to see that their orders were strictly complied with." In fact, as events later that evening would prove, the mob was heavily armed and spoiling for a fight. What the newspaper called a "delegation" was most likely a group of angry, gun-toting backwoodsmen who guarded the black miners and their families until they could be loaded on a train. And, if other cleansings are any guide, the "assurance" the mob offered was presumably a pledge that any blacks who did not leave would be murdered.[15]

With the mines cleared, the mob turned its attention to the black laborers building water and sewer lines in Spruce Pine. The black work crew had set up a camp on the banks of the North Toe River, which loops past Spruce Pine on its way to Tennessee. The town's business district sits on the northern bank and a bridge, since demolished, crossed to the work camp on the opposite bank. As the mob moved through the town and toward the bridge, it was met by the mayor, A. N. Fuller, and Herbert Hickey, a private citizen. While the mayor stood at the front of the mob begging it to disband, Hickey circled to the rear and in the words of one newspaper was "appealing to the members individually and as friends." With Fuller and Hickey distracting the mob, L. H. Wright, the chief of police, and D. W. Adams, the head of the construction company working on the town's sewer and water lines, raced to the bridge in what would be a last-ditch attempt to block the mob from crossing. Whatever the mayor said, it had little effect. After a brief pause, the mob shouldered past Mayor Fuller and ninety men armed with an assortment of weapons faced off on the bridge with Wright and Adams.[16]

For Wright this had been a very long day. During the afternoon he had gone to Altapass, a small village near the southern end of the county, on the theory that Goss would try to hop a freight train there. Goss did not materialize, but the chief, caught in the Blue Ridge tunnel as a train passed, had nearly been overcome by the exhaust. Now, as night fell, he was back in Spruce Pine trying to hold a bridge almost single-handed against an angry mob. Wright first tried to reason with them. But when one of the ringleaders aimed his shotgun at the chief, Wright drew his pistols. As the ringleader fired, someone in the mob yanked at the gun and the shot went wild. Although Wright did not return fire, the mob retreated. Bloodshed had been averted but only by the narrowest of margins.[17]

The next day began badly. Armed men enforcing curbside justice were wandering the downtown or guarding the blacks being held at the train station. An automobile dealer from Asheville who rode into town with a black chauffeur quickly discovered what mob rule was like. Someone stopped the car and ordered the chauffeur to the train station, where he joined the others waiting to be shipped out.

That Thursday morning, with no one guarding the bridge, mob members were finally able to cross to deliver their ultimatum to the black work crew camped on the south bank. As the day wore on the mob grew in strength and ambition. At three in the afternoon P. H. O'Brien, the president of the O'Brien Construction Company, which was building the state road from Spruce Pine to neighboring Avery County, found himself facing 150 armed men. As the mob, which had apparently marched the five miles from Spruce Pine, came into view, part of O'Brien's work crew ran off. But the thirty who remained were now being ordered at gunpoint to Spruce Pine. "I begged and pleaded with them," O'Brien said in a letter to state officials, "and told them that our Negroes were law abiding citizens and did not go out of our camp at night and absolutely they knew nothing of a rape committed on an old lady by a Negro in Mitchell County." The mob granted O'Brien a small concession: Instead of driving the blacks out immediately, they gave the blacks in the camp until noon Friday to get out of the county. But when O'Brien tried to use this brief delay to call for help, he discovered the extent of the mob's control. The sheriffs of Mitchell and Avery counties both told him there was nothing they could do to protect his men.[18]

Back in Spruce Pine, town leaders were also beginning to realize they had lost control. While some mob members were going through the countryside rounding up blacks, others were busy at the Spruce

Pine train station loading them on anything that could roll down a track. One observer estimated that on Thursday two box cars and three passenger cars left the Spruce Pine Depot with their unwilling passengers. As blacks were being shipped out, the police did nothing. Finally late Thursday afternoon, town officials telegraphed the governor's office and admitted the obvious: The town was in the hands of a mob that was "driving colored labor away from the place."[19]

The governor, Cameron Morrison, was an avid proponent of business interests. He had been a corporate attorney, and in labor disputes as governor he sided with the company, in one case going so far as to call out the National Guard to break a strike. A champion of economic development, Morrison borrowed millions to improve public services such as roads and education.

Morrison's record on race was mixed: He by turns prevented blacks from voting and protected them from white violence. In North Carolina's disgraceful 1898 election, the Democratic Party declared itself the White Man's Party, railed against "Negro domination," and, to make sure it won, formed the Red Shirts, a paramilitary group that prevented blacks from voting. Morrison was a leader of the Red Shirts, and he and his thugs spent Election Day heavily armed and lounging around polling places to intimidate black voters.

As governor, however, Morrison clamped down on mob violence, and for the last three and a half years of his term, there were no lynchings. The attack on the black laborers in Spruce Pine challenged the governor's policies on race, interfered with business activity, and foiled his pet project to improve the state's roads. His response was swift and unequivocal.[20]

Shortly after noon on Friday, the fire bell in Asheville, thirty-six miles south of Spruce Pine, tolled with the code that ordered the immediate assembly of the city's National Guard unit. In Morganton, twenty-four miles to the east of Spruce Pine, a similar alarm sounded and Company "B" of the 105th Engineers was also called out. The orders for both companies were to march on Spruce Pine. As the troops assembled, a National Guard official in Asheville assured a reporter that his men were "in splendid shape" and the officer in charge was "every inch a soldier."

The activation of the guard followed a burst of activity late Thursday afternoon in the governor's office. When Morrison first learned that the mob controlled the town, he immediately ordered Adjutant General J. Van B. Metts of the National Guard to go personally to Spruce Pine as the governor's eyes and ears. At the same time he sent a telegram to the Spruce Pine officials making it clear the mob would not have its way. He also released a brief statement to the press that he would "afford the community ample protection, in order to safeguard the rights of all its citizens, both white and colored." Friday morning the governor called in one of Metts's subordinates to discuss the situation, and by noon, after Metts arrived in Spruce Pine, he was ready to act.[21]

In Spruce Pine the first inkling that anything in the wider world was happening came at eleven P.M. Thursday when an Asheville reporter phoned Mayor Fuller. For some reason the governor's telegram, sent late Thursday afternoon, had not arrived, and it was left to the reporter to deliver the message. By the time it was relayed, most if not all blacks had already been shipped out, and the mob members had gone home to bed.

With the town now quiet, the mayor told the press he didn't see any need for General Metts to visit. But Fuller agreed something would have to be done to protect the black construction crews if they returned. It is doubtful that the mayor or anyone else in town imagined that in twenty-four hours armed troops would be patrolling the town with fixed bayonets, and machine guns would be trained on the main street.[22]

The Asheville company, which had boarded a special train around three P.M. Friday, was the first to arrive at eight P.M. Within a half hour they were joined by the Morganton contingent, which had endured a bone-jarring ride through the mountains in trucks. The force of a hundred men quickly pitched tents, set up a guard at the depot, and commandeered a warehouse where they could sleep. The soldiers were ordered not to fraternize with the local population and, for their part, the residents of Spruce Pine maintained a respectful distance. Spruce Pine was now under martial law, a first for the town and a first in America's history of racial cleansings. The only problem was that they had arrived too late. There were no blacks left in Mitchell County.[23]

While the troops were settling in for an uneasy night in Spruce Pine, more than twenty miles to the south another group of men were spending that Friday night also trying, as best they could, to get some sleep. For the past two days a posse of five men led by Deputy Sheriff Mack Buchanan had been pushing south on foot through dense woods and down the rock-strewn trails of the North Carolina mountains searching for Goss. Among the posse members was Wilburn, the son of Alice Thomas. This small band was now just outside of Morganton, one of the beads on the necklace of towns strung out along the railroad tracks that ran east and west. The posse assumed that Goss had either hopped a southbound freight from Mitchell County or had simply walked out of the mountains to get to this all important rail line. Once on the east/west line, Goss could catch a freight train and, in a matter of hours, lose himself in the more densely populated cities and towns at the eastern end of the state such as Greensboro, Durham and Chapel Hill. The rail line out of the mountains actually intersected this track about eighteen miles west of Morganton at the small town of Marion. By approaching the line further east at Morganton, the posse might be able to get ahead of Goss. But that rested on two assumptions: that Goss had either walked or hopped a freight that landed him near Marion, and that he too would eventually head east.[24]

Saturday morning the small posse walked into Morganton, enlisted the help of the Burke County sheriff there, and began pressing eastward. They had one encouraging bit of news: A man fitting Goss's description had been seen around the Morganton depot early that morning. If it was indeed Goss, they were only a few hours behind him. While the posse moved along the tracks, a deputy sheriff tried to get ahead of Goss by taking a passenger train to Hickory, a town more than twenty miles east of Morganton. At the same time, police up and down the line were warned that Goss might be heading their way.

The deputy sheriff's instincts were correct, but it was the local police in Hickory who eventually stumbled over Goss on Saturday afternoon. In an anticlimactic ending, they found him peacefully munching cheese and crackers.[25]

To forestall a lynching, Goss was hustled off to the state penitentiary in Raleigh. In the meantime, Governor Morrison began to stage-manage the trial. He fired off telegrams to Spruce Pine asking that Alice Thomas and her husband be brought to Raleigh at the state's expense so that she could identify her assailant. Other telegrams to county officials insisted that a special session of court be called to quickly try the case. When local officials objected to a special session, the governor made it clear who was in charge. Unable to persuade, he ordered the county to hold a trial on October 22.

Morrison also took some time to deal with a relatively new organization from out of state that had sent the governor a telegram. On September 28, just two days after the cleansing began, Walter White, the assistant secretary of the NAACP, had fired off a message asking if it was true that blacks were being rounded up and shipped out of Spruce Pine. If it was true, the NAACP demanded assurances that the state would protect its colored citizens. The governor sent a curt telegram back saying the NAACP would have to get its information from the Associated Press along with the rest of the public. There the matter was apparently dropped. There is nothing about Spruce Pine or Mitchell County in the files that the NAACP donated to the Library of Congress and there is nothing further in papers of Governor Morrison in the North Carolina State Archives.[26]

On Sunday September 30, there was a banner headline in the *Asheville Times:* "John Goff Captured." The newspaper's confusion over the convict's last name was understandable. Until he was actually arrested, everyone from the governor on down thought his last name was Goff. The newspapers were also under the impression that he was twenty-two. Although he was thirty-seven, it was later reported that he was middle aged.

Other basic facts also eluded the press. On Monday the *Asheville Citizen* ran two different accounts of the rape on its front page. One story by the Associated Press reported that Goss had come to the Thomas house "and under the pretense of asking for food, attacked her." Another story by a reporter for the *Citizen* ran only inches from the AP story but described a different scenario in which Goss came upon Thomas outside, followed "her for some distance," and then dragged her into the woods to assault her.

Covering the story was also complicated by the fact that events moved in fits and starts. One luckless reporter, who had rushed to Spruce Pine to cover the excitement, discovered that by the time he arrived on Saturday nothing much was happening. The lead on his story reflected his predicament. "All is quiet tonight in this little mountain-girt town. Everything is placid, perhaps ominously placid on the surface. It may be the lull before the storm."[27]

There was, in fact, a brief flurry of excitement on Sunday night. After they heard some gunfire, troops combed the hills around Spruce Pine. Nothing was discovered, but Governor Morrison, not taking any chances, ordered another National Guard company into Spruce Pine on Monday.

Morrison also began to move the black workers back to Mitchell County. Disdaining the offer of a military escort, Mrs. Clarence Laughridge, the daughter of a former state senator, brought in the first contingent of blacks in her own automobile. One was her cook, and two others had worked at the hotel in town. Next to arrive were eight blacks from one of the construction companies. They came in by train and were met by two companies of guardsmen and a crowd estimated at 200 men. The crowd watched quietly as thirty soldiers on horseback escorted eight "badly frightened" men to their camp.[28]

The governor cracked down hard on the mob of Mitchell County. On October 10, fourteen men were arrested in Spruce Pine for their role in driving the blacks out of Mitchell County. These arrests were followed in late October by a grand jury indictment against eighty-six people, including Mack Thomas, Alice's husband, and their son Wilburn, for their part in the September 26 rampage through Spruce Pine. None of the cases ever went to trial, and if they had the state probably would have lost when faced with an all-white jury. All of those charged pled guilty and with only a few exceptions were freed after paying court costs.[29]

John Goss was not so lucky. Guarded by troops, he returned to Mitchell County for his trial on October 22. In less than an hour, he was tried, convicted, and sentenced to death. Only three people testified. The superintendent of the work camp identified Goss and said he had escaped; Alice Thomas briefly described the rape; and a neighbor testified that she had seen Goss minutes before the assault. If Goss's lawyer put on a defense, it is not mentioned.

When he was arrested, Goss had denied assaulting Alice Thomas. At the trial he told a reporter that he wanted to plead guilty to "attempted assault," but his lawyer advised against it. He continued to insist that he had not actually raped Alice Thomas. The jury saw it otherwise. They deliberated about five minutes before finding him guilty.[30]

The slang term for death in the electric chair is "fry." In Goss's case the word is entirely apt. Before the execution, the newspapers said Goss made a "complete confession" to a minister. However, he said nothing at his execution. After he was strapped in the chair, the executioners made three attempts to kill Goss. After each cycle of electricity, a doctor would check for a heartbeat. By the third round, a reporter said "the air of the room grew heavy with the odor of burned flesh." It took five minutes for the state to kill Goss—the same amount of time it had taken the jury to convict him. The next day the *Raleigh News and Observer* pronounced Goss "a mean nigger" and said that when dead, "he stared with solid indifference at the ceiling."[31]

With Goss dead and the troops long gone, life returned to normal in Mitchell County with but one exception. To no one's great surprise, when the troops left, the blacks, with memories of rioting whites threatening them, left as well. On the southern edge of the county near Altapass, a small black settlement remained. But they lived just inside the county line and were all but invisible to the rest of Mitchell County. When Muriel Sheppard, the mining engineer's wife, arrived in the late 1920s, she described the county as "white man's country." She romanticized the people living in the county as a hardy, independent, and hardworking yeomanry and their attack on the blacks as a principled stand. "Through all the confusion of the mob passion the people of the Toe River had kept sight of their original purpose, to run the blacks out of the country. The state had carried its point and demonstrated that Negroes have a right in the mountains but the hill people showed so unmistakably what their reception would be that since then the Negroes have not wanted to come up Toe River."[32]

Sheppard's story rests on what might be called the Dred Scott premise: The humble whites, because they were the masters of Mitchell County, were entitled to drive off the black intruders. This was the same argument that Supreme Court Chief Justice Taney had made in 1857: America is white man's country, and blacks are, at best, guests. With blacks as guests in the white man's house, he who rapes trespasses against not only the victim but also white hospitality. The offense is further magnified by the fact that it is a sexual assault. It is no coincidence that half of the cleansings in this book were precipitated by a black man allegedly attacking a white woman.

Casting blacks as guests also makes collective guilt seem reasonable. By his actions the offender has brought shame upon his fellow guests in the same way that one family member both represents and is the responsibility of his family. In this way guilt, which is individual, is made to appear collective. Ejecting all of the guest's kinfolk from the house is not only reasonable but expected by society. Naturally when hospitality is violated, the host's attack on the offending guest is almost mandatory.

This formulation of black as "guest" is appealing to whites because it lends legitimacy to racial cleansings. Whites did nothing wrong because the expulsion was dictated by the norms of society. But leaving aside for the moment the idea that blacks are not guests in America, one has to wonder why every "outrage" against a woman did not end in a racial cleansing. Thousands of blacks were murdered by mobs for allegedly raping white women, yet not every lynching ended in a cleansing. Why?

One answer comes from the Mitchell County businessman J. E. Burleson, who was upset with his fellow citizens for attacking black workers. Burleson warned the governor in an October 8 letter that, having lived in Spruce Pine all his life, "I know the disposition of people." At the time Burleson wrote the letter, the crisis appeared to have passed. With little to occupy them, on October 9 the troops would be withdrawn. But Burleson was still wary. Fearing the letter "would make enemies to me," Burleson asked that it be kept "strictly confidential." His dark secret was that "people that were into this are people that don't want to work." The blacks were run out because "they want to drive this labor away because they think they were working at a lower price then they would work for." Burleson's writing skills might have been a little shaky (he wanted to say that whites feared competition from cheap black labor), but his solution was straightforward. "If these people are prosecuted, this will stop it and anyone can take labor and work in peace." Burleson ended the letter by hoping the governor "will take the right view of the situation."[33]

An attack on a white woman might be a convenient rallying cry, but more often than not what separated a single lynching from a mass expulsion was economic rivalry.

Even happy families have secrets. In the Thomas family, the Civil War and its legacy were best not mentioned. Shortly after the surrender at Appomattox, Alice Thomas's father—Lloyd Hise's great-great-grandfather—died of the wounds he had received in the trenches at Petersburg defending the South. But another of Hise's great-great-grandfathers had joined a cavalry unit made up of North Carolina men loyal to the Union. Hise's grandparents didn't talk much about that, he recalls.[34]

But there were other things, secret things, that would be hinted at from time to time. For a curious child like Lloyd Hise, these secrets were like marbles you worked in your hand, comforting and precious. In one of her bedtime stories, his grandmother had let slip just such a secret. It was a story about a cross burning, and somewhere deep in the midst of it, Hise recalls, his grandmother hinted that Wilburn had been there and seen that fiery warning. Could it be that his stern, unsmiling grandfather was a member of the Invisible Empire?

With morning came the question. "I asked her if grandpa was a member of the Ku Klux Klan and she never said a word," Hise said. "She just got my hand and led me back in the back bedroom and opened the closet and opened the trunk and showed it to me." In the old, black trunk were his grandfather's Klan robes. "She said don't tell anybody."

Wilburn's secret died with him. No one knows why he would get so upset about the story of the blacks being driven out of Spruce Pine. But one possible explanation can still be found in the courthouse archives. In one of the folders are the indictments of eighty-six men who rampaged through Spruce Pine that day. The name of Wilburn Thomas can be found partway down the list. There are four counts to the indict-

ment. The men conspired to "drive away" blacks from town, used guns
to terrorize some blacks, pursued others, and assaulted both black
workers and their white bosses. What exactly Wilburn did is not mentioned, but this proud, silent man eventually pled guilty to the charges.
Admitting guilt must have been as incomprehensible as it was bitter.
He had avenged the rape of his mother not only by helping to capture
Goss but by driving off all blacks. To Wilburn it must have been self-
evident that, after such a fundamental violation, blacks did not belong.
But now he was being punished. He would never be able to speak of it
again. Wilburn's daughter, Georgia McClellan, has another secret. As
she sits in the sunny porch of her home, talk turns to the days her father would tell her to stop by Granny Thomas's house.[35]

"I didn't like to go there because everything had to be so quiet and
you know a child can't be quiet," she says. "And it had all these clocks
that just ticked away and I can remember thinking I hate those clocks.
And I don't want a clock that dongs. I can't stand that."

Granny Thomas, who lived into her nineties, would sit in a straight-
back chair and simply stare at the stove. And as her granddaughter recalls those brief, uncomfortable visits, she starts to talk about what had
happened to Granny Thomas. The story she had heard was that Goss
had come by one house asking for a drink of water. As he did, Granny
Thomas, who was walking up the road, encountered Goss. "He was
supposed to have raped her," McClellan says.

But there was something more to the story, something passed down
in the Thomas family. After the riot, manhunt, trial, execution, and
campaign to drive out the blacks, McClellan says that doubt lingers that
Alice Thomas was actually raped.

"My mother thought she must have just got scared."

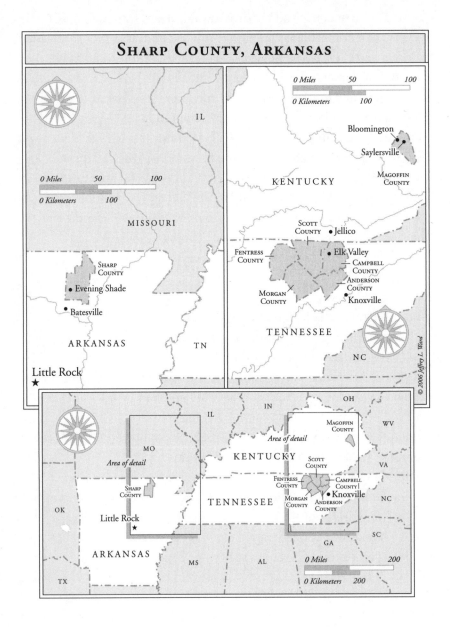

SHARP COUNTY, ARKANSAS

IL

MISSOURI

0 Miles 50 100
0 Kilometers 100

SHARP
COUNTY

• Evening Shade

• Batesville

ARKANSAS

TN

Little Rock
★

KENTUCKY

0 Miles 50 100
0 Kilometers 100

Bloomington
Saylersville

MAGOFFIN
COUNTY

SCOTT
COUNTY   • Jellico

FENTRESS
COUNTY   • Elk Valley

CAMPBELL
COUNTY
ANDERSON
COUNTY

MORGAN
COUNTY

• Knoxville

TENNESSEE

NC

© 2006 Jeffrey L. Ward

OH

IL   IN

MO

Area of detail

SHARP
COUNTY

Little Rock
★

ARKANSAS

OK

TX

MS   AL

KENTUCKY

MAGOFFIN
COUNTY

WV

Area of detail

SCOTT
COUNTY

VA

FENTRESS
COUNTY   CAMPBELL
COUNTY
MORGAN   • Knoxville
COUNTY   ANDERSON
COUNTY

TENNESSEE

NC

GA

SC

0 Miles 200
0 Kilometers 200

CHAPTER 12

Lost, Stolen, or Strayed

Sharp County, Arkansas
1906

You don't see the graves immediately.

At first it looks like a field that long ago went to seed. Where the plow might have cut, trees grow, and beneath them, where crops took root, a thick mat of leaves and briar. But as you stand in a neighboring pasture and look over the rusted, barbed-wire fence into this neglected field you are able to see them among the trees. You do not notice them all at once. They appear singly, each a mound covered with gray fieldstones. But look closely and nearby you see another mound. Then another and another. Some mounds have a flat, angular rock at one end that someone had carefully upended and partially buried in the ground. It is a crude marker. Other mounds have no marker but are simply covered in stones. One has a tree growing out of it.

It isn't until you vault the low fence and walk among the mounds that the truth dawns on you. These are graves, scores of graves, scattered like bird seed in one corner of a field just outside of Evening Shade, Arkansas. You are standing in an abandoned burial ground. Elmer Runsick, a raw-boned farmer who owns the land adjacent to the burial ground, explains that a black man owned the field long ago and donated a corner as a cemetery for his fellow blacks.

If it weren't for these graves, one could almost believe blacks never existed in the county. In the local histories, blacks are barely mentioned. There are a few passing references to slaves and, following the war, a story about Negro troops being quartered in the county. Beyond that there is silence. All the chatty anecdotes center on white farmers, businessmen, doctors, and outlaws. The old photographs in these books show only white faces, and the town landmarks are places where whites lived, did business, or went to school.

But in this cemetery, a few hundred feet from the fence line, there is a small clue to the fate of the black community. Lying close to two other graves with headstones is the last resting place of Sara Shaver. Her date of death—1902—is the most recent. After her burial it appears the graveyard was never used again. There could have been a few more of these crude, anonymous burials, but census records suggest otherwise. There were 212 blacks living in the county in 1900, only eighty-three a decade later, and by 1920 only fifteen. Whatever end came, it followed the demise of Sara Shaver.[1]

In its way, Sharp County is the exemplar. There are scores of counties in the United States like Sharp that have a similar story. Census records show a sudden drop in the black population. In some counties, there are bits and pieces of evidence that blacks, who once lived there, left suddenly. The local histories, almost always written by whites, do not even hint at how or when the blacks left. But, despite signs that hint at a racial cleansing, the proof lies just out of reach. That is except for Sharp County. There is no doubt that on Christmas Eve 1906 there was a racial cleansing.

Almost everything we know about the Sharp County racial cleansing rests on a single news story. It appeared on December 28, 1906 in the *Sharp County Record,* and it is at once cryptic and detailed, revealing and maddeningly vague. In the style of the time the headline—"Negroes Leaving"—is followed by a much longer subhead that says

"Mysterious Threats Have Driven Almost Every Negro from Evening Shade." The story begins briskly with a nice, compact sentence. "There is scarcely a Negro left in Evening Shade or the immediate vicinity." Then things go awry. The story describes two threats to what it calls "a small colony of negroes [that] lived just on the outskirts of town." The first threat came four days earlier when "Joe Brooks, a negro man, who lived with his family two and a half miles north of town, was called to his door by unknown parties and fired upon." Brooks was wounded but survived the assault. The second threat was a "notice" that "was posted to the effect that these negroes must leave the country at once, and all but a very few have gone." It is unclear whether the attack on Brooks came after he ignored the notice or whether Brooks was for some reason attacked first and then the notice was posted. In either case, the newspaper thought it unwise to probe too deeply. *"The Record,"* it admits with refreshing candor, "does not know who is responsible for this exodus among the negroes." More to the point, the newspaper says, "We have no desire to know."[2]

Having missed the "why" of the story, the writer nevertheless paints a brief but revealing picture of the expulsion. "Some of these negroes own a few acres of ground on which they had built residences. Those who have left have abandoned their property or disposed of it at whatever figure they could secure and left on foot. Some of these negroes, now old, have lived here since the war and are peaceable and harmless." The detail that these people left on foot and that they only owned a few acres is telling. A few acres of land points to subsistence farming and, in fact, because they left on foot they were undoubtedly too poor to own a carriage or a wagon. The nameless mounds in their burial ground only add to this picture of grinding poverty. For all but a very few, the cost of a headstone was a luxury.

Having painted a picture of this sad exodus, the author of the article seems not to know what to think of it. After noting that the people being driven out were "peaceable," the writer declares, "No man had a right to cause them to abandon their property and flee the country." On the other hand, the writer looks across the generation gap and grumps that "Some of the younger ones were Smart Alecks and characters not desired in the community. The community is better off without them."

Even so the newspaper says it cannot endorse the expulsion because "it is lawlessness of a dangerous character." Having zigged toward opposing the cleansing, the story zags away from embracing the victims. "We have little use for the negro as a citizen and on general principles." Just to make sure no one get the wrong idea the story stoutly declares, "We are not a Negro defender." But unless the Negro interferes "with white people's business" the writer says, he "ought to be allowed to go his way and have the right of life and liberty." As if exhausted by these vacillations, the story collapses in a heap in this final line: "We trust sincerely that no serious trouble will result from this thing."

The following week the newspaper ran a brief story saying that the few blacks that had not left—estimated at about a dozen elderly people—were going about their business unmolested. However, the story said another notice was posted warning blacks to leave. Who was harrying the blacks was still a mystery.[3]

There the story of Sharp County's racial cleansing might have ended except for an odd postscript. A few months after the blacks were driven out, the *Sharp Country Record* reported that two men by the names of Caleb Evans and J. D. May got into an argument during which May accused Evans of being involved in the expulsion. Evans then sued May for slander. The newspaper reported that a crowd filled the courtroom but "there was no startling developments during the trial and who ran the negroes is still a question." May was acquitted.[4]

Whites had driven blacks out, and yet the memory of this expulsion worked at whites like a stone in a shoe. To accuse a fellow white of being involved was a slander. And yet, as the newspaper writer observed, "we have little use for the Negro." For the whites of Sharpe County, the general proposition that blacks were inferior was a settled question. When in 1901 President Theodore Roosevelt invited Booker T. Washington to dinner at the White House, Sharp County and the rest of the South were scandalized. "President Roosevelt can never lead the people of this section of the country to believe that the black man is the equal of the white man," the *Record* thundered, "and the oftener he dines the coon the greater he will be held in contempt in the South where negroes come near growing on trees."[5]

At the same time whites felt a kinship with blacks they knew person-ally. A year after the expulsion, one of the elderly blacks, who had re-fused to leave, died. "An unusual sight at Black Rock one day last week was observed," the *Record* noted, "when a number of white citizens of the town carried flowers and placed them on the grave of an old negro man who was being buried."[6]

And there was the problem. How do you honor a man in death while at the same time hounding his children? The expulsion was wrong—the newspaper story had admitted as much—yet the community acqui-esced in the face of something evil. To discuss this event was to face the evidence of one's own moral failure. In that context the closing line in the newspaper story—"We trust sincerely that no serious trouble will result from this thing"—sounds more like a plaintive plea. Unable to find any peace in the memory of the cleansing, Sharp County chose to forget.[7]

Scores of communities where there had been racial cleansings, when faced with the same dilemma, made the same choice. They decided to forget. In those places where the artifacts of a cleansing endure, the community's past is like a restless sleep. No matter how much they would like to forget, terrible things tug and prod at them. But what about those communities where the newspaper story or the diary or an oral history did not survive?

In places like Magoffin County, Kentucky or Scott County, Ten-nessee, to name only a few, what little remains of the past taunts the present. Although they are not counted in this book as examples of a racial cleansing, what we know about them is unsettling. As you exam-ine the stories of these places, what becomes clear is that the history of racial cleansings exists on a continuum.

While in this book I have drawn a line between what is and is not a racial cleansing, in reality the line is not so easily made. Expulsions like those in Forsyth County, Georgia and Lawrence County, Missouri are well documented and beyond doubt. But there is very little that sepa-rates a Sharp County from a Magoffin County save a single newspaper story. The evidence in Magoffin County may be circumstantial, but as

Henry David Thoreau once noted, "Some circumstantial evidence is very strong, as when you find a trout in the milk."

The first clue that something happened in Magoffin County, a rural backwater in Eastern Kentucky, comes from census records. In 1900 there were 136 blacks living in the county, and ten years later there were only fifty-four, a drop of sixty percent. It is an interesting fact but by itself means little. Given the relatively small black population, anything from a disastrous fire to a crop failure could account for the fluctuation. But a closer look at the census figures reveals some surprising things.[8]

Most people know the census as a blizzard of numbers that appear every ten years as painfully detailed newspaper stories. The number of Americans rose by so much, and there was a population shift from north to south and back again. But after seventy years, the census bureau releases the actual records the census takers use to compile all those numbers. Each page of the census shows the name of every individual in town, along with age, race, sex, and position in the household; son, daughter, husband, etc. These rolls show generally where people live in a community and what they do for a living, whether they rent or own, whether they are literate, and their place of birth. It is a comprehensive snapshot of the nation one person at a time. And in Magoffin County that snapshot shows in 1900 their black population looked pretty much like the black population in any other county in the country. With segregation in full swing, blacks no longer lived in town alongside whites as they had in Comanche County in 1886. Within the city boundaries of Salyersville, the county seat, there was not a single black. Instead, like Sharp County, where the blacks lived a short distance from Evening Shade, there were ninety-one blacks living outside of town in the Salyersville District. The balance of the black population was scattered on farms across the county.[9]

Ten years later the picture changes dramatically. In the Salyersville District where the majority of the blacks once lived, the census only found eight people, all members of two families. In the outlying areas, whole families have disappeared. In the Bloomington District where there had once been the Keeton, Wilson, and Higgans families, only the Keetons remain. In the Meadows District all fifteen members of the Caudle family are gone. In their place are the Gipson and Nickels families, who once lived close to Salyersville. The pattern looks suspiciously like what would have happened if there had been a racial cleansing.

In most racial cleansings there is some sudden and violent event in the county's major town or city that is followed by an ultimatum: Leave or die. The black population closest to this epicenter, like the one near Salyersville, all but disappears. Most, but not all, move to another county and are never seen again. However, some blacks, hoping to hang on to whatever life they had, settle at the county's periphery like the Meadows District. These refugees from the city or town join black farm laborers who are being protected by their white employers. When the next census arrives, the white population has remained steady or risen slightly while the black population has been at least cut in half. In Magoffin County the white population rose by about 1,600 people between 1900 and 1910 while the black population dropped to fifty-four. For those hiding on remote farms and settlements, life becomes increasingly problematic. Barred from the major trading center, mundane tasks like buying farming supplies or clothes or getting medical care become major logistical headaches. If the black church was in town and is still standing, it is now off limits. Shared experiences that give meaning to life like funerals, weddings, religious education, and social events are curtailed. Two decades after the cleansing, census figures show the black community is either reduced by half again or disappears altogether.[10]

Magoffin County fits this pattern but only up to a point. When the census canvased the county in 1910, it found something very strange: Between 1900 and 1910, several black people became white. People who said they were black in the earlier census now claimed to be white. The entire Nickels family, for example, who had lived outside of Salyersville, went through this amazing transformation. In the 1900 census they were black, and in 1910 the six family members became white. In total fifteen people experienced a racial conversion. All, save one, became white. Sidney Gipson, nineteen, became an Indian.[11]

The most remarkable pilgrimage was taken by Sambo Gipson. Although he does not show up in the 1900 census, you can find his other family members. They are black. In 1910 Sambo and the rest of the Gipson family become white. In the 1920 census Sambo reverts to being black. But when he died in 1945, his death certificate said Sambo was a white man.[12]

As strange as the racial transubstantiation of Magoffin County may seem, the truth is that race in America has always been fungible. Races come and go like fall fashions and people are moved from category to category depending on who is doing the counting. One year Hungarians are of the "Mongol" race and another year they are white. Some whites—Italians or Jews—are less white than other whites while some white people become black because they have "protruding heels." (That was how one witness in a trial said you could tell if a person was a Negro.)

Ironically, it was in the course of trying to codify race that its malleability came most clearly into focus. The strange story of Dr. Walter Ashby Plecker illustrates the point. In 1912 Dr. Plecker, a native son of the Old Dominion, became the head of Virginia's Registrar of Vital Statistics, a seemingly innocuous post, unless, of course, you were Dr. Plecker. A humorless and aloof man, Plecker was convinced that the white race faced disaster from "mongrelization." When the different races lived near one another, Plecker warned, there would be interracial sex. And the only result of interracial sex would be "the final deterioration or complete destruction of the white or higher civilization." Faced with this apocalyptic vision of the future, Plecker and his supporters convinced the Virginia legislature in 1924 to pass the Racial Integrity Act. The law prohibited a white person from marrying anyone but another white person. Since by state law every person's birth certificate had to list their race, the man who would decide which people could legally marry was Dr. Plecker.[13]

That was when the fun began.

A Lynchburg woman who listed her baby's race as white got a curt letter from Dr. Plecker. "This is to inform you that this is a mulatto child and you cannot pass it off as white." On another occasion, he spied twins in an orphanage. Although they appeared to be white, Dr. Plecker tried to get them evicted. He reasoned that, because they were born out of wedlock, "chances are 10–1 they are of negro blood." He decreed that anyone in Amherst County with the last name of Adcox, Johns, Branham, Hicks, Hamilton, or Redcross should be classified as Negro. Because there was no appeal, in the end your race was whatever Dr. Plecker thought it should be.[14]

What drove Dr. Plecker was the fear that his race would be "destroyed." By the same token it is possible that what drove Sambo Gipson was the more immediate concern that he would be destroyed. Gipson may have changed his race because he thought he could "pass" in a hostile white world. From his death certificate there is evidence that he could have been light-skinned. On the census rolls his mother and father are listed respectively as white and mulatto.

But in a county of only about 13,000 people, how easy would it really have been to "pass"? Perhaps there is another explanation for these cases of racial transformation. If Magoffin was anything like Sharp County, people may have been conflicted about what happened. In that context either Gipson or sympathetic whites might have decided that it was better for everyone concerned to pretend that he and his family were white. When time and the danger had passed, the charade could be dropped.

The truth is that we do not know. Unlike in Sharp County, there are no newspapers or contemporary accounts that describe what happened in Magoffin County at the turn of the century. Until something surfaces, we are left with the fact that the black population collapsed, and of those that remained, a number chose to become white.

———

As with Magoffin County, there was a dramatic drop in the black population of Scott County, Tennessee. In 1900 there were 335 blacks living in the county. Ten years later the black population had fallen by seventy percent. By 1920 there were only sixteen blacks in the county, and even today the 2000 census shows only nineteen blacks living there.[15]

And again, as with Magoffin County, the census numbers contain some interesting clues, although nothing as dramatic as racial conversions. In some counties when there is a dramatic drop in the black population there is a corresponding drop among whites. Typically, this means that there was some kind of economic catastrophe like a drought or a factory closing. But in Scott County while the blacks were leaving, the whites were moving in. Between 1900 and 1910 the county's population grew from 9,700 to 12,900. If the county had fallen on hard times, for some odd reason the depression only affected blacks.

In fact, economic figures indicate the county was thriving. Scott County, which sits on the Kentucky border about forty miles northwest of Arkansas, was busy mining coal at the turn of the century. In 1900 coal production was 87,000 tons. Ten years later it had reached 132,000 tons. And working in the coal mines was one of the top three occupations of blacks in the 1900 census. While the majority of blacks (fifty) listed "laborer" as their occupation, twenty-seven said they worked in the coal mines. Thirty blacks were employed by the railroad—the other most common occupation. Only seven people said they were farmers. Given the steady increase in coal production, there was no immediate reason that blacks, who mined coal or who worked on the railroad transporting coal, would have had to leave for new jobs.[16]

The next clue is the odd demographic signature that is left by counties that went through a racial cleansing. Typically, the county that has driven out its black population becomes the "donut hole." While it has few if any blacks, the African-American population in surrounding counties either remains roughly the same or increases. That is exactly what we see in the four counties surrounding Scott County. The numbers are as follows:

	1900	1910	1920
Scott	335	97	16
Fentress	25	98	42
Morgan	700	691	497
Campbell	616	1,887	1,272
Anderson	1,118	921	595

By 1920 the "donut hole" which was evident in 1910, becomes even more pronounced. Probably because of the "great migration" that occurred during and after World War I when about one million blacks moved to the North, there were black population declines in all four counties between 1900 and 1920. But Scott County experiences the greatest percentage drop and the greatest imbalance between whites and blacks. In 1920 there are only sixteen blacks remaining in Scott, a county that had a total population of 13,400 people.[17]

The census numbers are suggestive, but, like Magoffin County, they do not prove that a racial cleansing occurred. While copies of a newspaper survived in Sharp County, unfortunately there are no newspapers in Scott County from the period from 1900 to 1910.

There is only one tiny piece of evidence to suggest what *might* have happened in Scott County. It can be found in a story that ran in the *Knoxville Journal and Tribune* on June 25, 1903. A reporter in Knoxville, who had heard about a lynching in northern Tennessee, went to the train station and began interviewing arriving passengers hoping to find an eyewitness. When J. T. Dixon, a stone mason from Jellico, stepped off the Southern Railway train, he mentioned that, when the train passed Elk Valley, he saw a black man hanging from a tree near the railroad track. "The Negro's toes lacked by a few inches of touching the ground," was how Dixon described the scene.

According to the article, Charles Jones, a railroad worker, had been grabbed the night before by a mob in Elk Valley, marched a half mile east of town, and murdered near the tracks. The killers had left his body hanging there most of the day in full view of passing trains and, when the coroner cut him down, they dug a hole and buried him near the murder scene. The coroner concluded he had been killed by "unknown parties."[18]

Jones was lynched for the usual reasons. He allegedly tried to rape thirteen-year-old Margaret Bruce, who had gone berry picking with her younger sister. A farmer, attracted by the screams of the two girls, drove off a black man. When Jones was arrested and identified by the Bruce girl, his fate was sealed. Or as the *Clinton Gazette* noted, "The citizens of the little village of Elk Valley did what any other community, who honors the home, would have done." But, according to the Knoxville newspaper, killing Jones was not enough for the citizens of Elk Valley. "Following the lynching, the people who had engaged in it notified the members of three crews of railroad negroes that they would all be treated in the same way, that all would be strung up of a limb if they were not gone by nine o'clock yesterday morning. This notice had the effect of causing all of the negroes to leave on the local train, and the railroad work in that immediate section has been suspended."[19]

Like Evening Shade's untended graves, there is nothing to tie the lynching in Elk Valley to the black population collapse in Scott County. Elk Valley, which is no longer shown on state maps, was in Campbell County—about a mile from the Scott County line. But census records also show that the railroad maintained a work camp in Scott County. In 1900 and again in 1910, about twenty-five black men are listed as railroad workers living together at the camp. It seems almost inevitable that the news of the lynching of a black railroad worker in nearby Elk Valley would have gotten back to the whites in Scott County. At that point, whites in Scott County may have decided that, for the safety of their families, they had to drive off the blacks. Alternatively vigilantes from Elk Valley could have joined with their Scott County neighbors to expel the blacks. Either possibility would not have been unusual.[20]

It is, in the end, the discovery that racial cleansings were not unusual that is so hard to believe. Scott, Sharp, and Magoffin counties lie undisturbed like the graves outside Evening Shade. Half-remembered stories of blacks being assaulted and chased away litter the abandoned fields of our past. And like the burial ground, it is hard to distinguish one story from another through the tangled undergrowth. If there was something, for example, that once marked Scott County as the site of a racial cleansing, it was long ago dragged off into the night. But does it matter?

The illusion is that there is some fence that separates the past from today. In truth, we live out our past every day. When Hurricane Katrina drowned New Orleans in 2005, newspapers termed the mostly poor blacks trying to flee the city "refugees." To the disbelief of most whites, blacks were furious. "These are not refugees," Rev. Jesse Jackson insisted. "They are citizens of Louisiana and Mississippi, tax-paying citizens." Some newspapers dropped the word while others did not. William Safire, then a columnist at the *New York Times*, agreed that "refugee," which connoted a person from another country, was not accurate. But then he added, "In my judgement, refugee is neither racist nor ethnic nor in any way demeaning."[21]

Blacks looked over their shoulders and could see a past where they were driven from town to town. They were fair game because they could not vote and were not considered citizens. To now call them refugees and once again imply they were less than citizens was outrageous. Whites who looked back saw only an abandoned field.

It matters very much.

To get to the abandoned black burial ground outside of Evening Shade, you have to cross Elmer Runsick's farm. He takes people bouncing across his pastureland in a beat-up Jeep while he gives a running commentary on the life and history of Sharp County.[22]

Evening Shade itself experienced its fifteen minutes of fame in the 1990s. The story goes that Hollywood producer Linda Bloodworth Thomason was developing a situation comedy about a high school football coach and needed the name of a place in the United States where it could be located. Among her friends were Bill Clinton, then the governor of Arkansas, and his wife, Hillary. It was supposedly Hillary who suggested they use the name Evening Shade, a town in northeast Arkansas. The idea stuck, and for four years the town basked in the reflected glory from the glowing TV set. Burt Reynolds, one of the show's stars, attended a high school graduation in Evening Shade in 1991 and when two cast members married, Evening Shade hosted the event. The show died in May 1994, and with it, the town's bubble of fame burst.

Before the TV show, the town boasted about its natural spring that burbled away near the center of town. At first they built a wooden scaffold to shelter the spring and later a stone cupola. Inexplicably the spring dried up in the 1960s, and now the stone cupola looks more like an elaborate grave marker for a defunct tourist attraction.

As the conversation turns to the people who drove out the blacks, Elmer Runsick grows thoughtful. Runsick is rooted to his land, and it is obvious that he has a deep affection for Evening Shade. In Runsick's moral universe, the expulsion is an anathema. He grapples with words to make sense of what happened and, as the jeep hits another rock and bounces forward, he touches at the heart of things.

"White people back then," Runsick says, "they just weren't civilized."

Conclusion:
Esta's Gift

"I didn't see it as an institutional attempt to whitewash or to cover up. I saw it more as half-assed."

It was January 24, 2006, and Andy Alexander, the Washington bureau chief for Cox Newspapers, was struggling. For the last twenty minutes he and a handful of other Cox Newspaper editors had been on a conference call grappling with how to edit a story that involved the *Atlanta Journal-Constitution*, the flagship of the company's newspaper chain. Tall, thin, and unfailingly polite, Alexander was trying hard to fashion some consensus about how to deal with one of the stories I had written. Scheduled to appear in the *Austin American Statesman*, the story was critical of the way the *Journal-Constitution* had covered the legacy of the racial cleansing in Forsyth County, Georgia, coverage that Alexander himself acknowledged was "half-assed." The story presented a delicate problem because, if printed in its current form, it meant that one Cox-owned newspaper would be criticizing another. And race was an especially sensitive topic for a newspaper chain based mainly in the South.

"So it would be all right with you then if we simply described the [*Journal-Constitution*] coverage as half-assed?" asked David Pasztor, the projects editor for the *Austin American-Statesman*.

"I wouldn't use that word," Alexander allowed. But what could they say?

When I had begun researching the history of racial cleansings in America, I had no idea that the trail would lead back to the company where I have worked for fourteen years. But as I reconstructed what had happened in Forsyth County, just twenty miles from downtown Atlanta, I found the series of stories published by the *Journal-Constitution* in the wake of the brotherhood march in 1987. Rather than deal with the legacy of racial cleansings, the newspaper urged its readers not to dwell on "what happened in the past." At critical moments when solid reporting would have helped advance the public debate, the newspaper's coverage was incomplete and misleading.

But most of those involved in the conference call seriously doubted that one Cox newspaper could criticize another. Alexander tried to argue that Atlanta's coverage was not all that important. Newspapers like the *Journal-Constitution,* Alexander argued, don't have "a major responsibility for the community not coming to grips with this."

John Erickson, an editor at the *Dayton Daily News,* suggested that simply reporting the material that the *Journal-Constitution* had missed would be sufficient. A sharp-eyed reader who bothered to compare the coverage could see the shortcomings of the *Journal-Constitution.* Another editor wondered if we could judge since we didn't know what had been in the editors' minds.

The longer they talked the clearer it became that the *Atlanta Journal-Constitution*'s checkered coverage of race was taboo.

"This is not to get beyond this room," warned Fred Zipp, the managing editor of the *Austin American-Statesman,* before he hinted that political pressure from inside Cox would doom any critical look at the *Atlanta Journal-Constitution*'s role. "I don't think we are going to get [the series] into any newspaper that is owned by Cox." The problem, Zipp said, was that, if Atlanta's role was discussed, the publisher of the Austin paper, would get "a call from somebody saying, 'You know we really think it is a bad idea to put that series in the paper the way it is written now.'" When that happened, Zipp said, "What I will be required to do is take it out or not publish it."

Over the course of the eight years I spent researching this book, I had been struck again and again by the fact that America's racial cleansings had remained hidden for so long——hidden from historians, hidden from public memory, and sometimes even hidden from the communities in which they had occurred.

It seemed impossible that events that, by their nature were so public, could disappear so completely. How could that happen?

I was about to get a demonstration.

———

What is striking about this story is that Cox Newspapers is such a good corporate citizen. It is seen as solid and responsible. Its newspapers in Dayton and Atlanta have won Pulitzers, and the company hosts yearly awards within Cox meant to encourage good journalism. It is not shy about spending money to take the government to court when it feels public information is being withheld, and Cox executives have testified before Congress to make government more open. It treats its employees fairly, provides a generous health care plan, funds a solid pension plan, and racial diversity is a company-wide goal. The number of minority employees in the newsrooms at its four largest newspapers ranges from thirteen to twenty-three percent, and a 2005 study found Cox ranked fifth among the top twenty-six newspaper companies for the number of non-white employees it has hired. The company holds diversity seminars, works to find minority employees, and would, I have no doubt, fire any employee guilty of discrimination. Yet, when confronted with missteps in its own past, the company lost its head.

When, by way of my article on Forsyth County, the issue of racial justice came into direct conflict with the company's historic reputation, Cox Newspapers jumped back as if it had brushed against a hot stove. The stories I had written were edited to obscure the Atlanta newspaper's lackadaisical coverage of race. Editors ignored clear conflicts of interest while editing the racial cleansing series. Procedures designed to protect the integrity of the reporting process were dispensed with. And finally the head of the company's newspaper division overrode the judgment of editors in Austin and Washington and ordered that a different term be substituted for "racial cleansings." It is a cautionary tale about the lingering shame that trumps honest discussion of the full history of America's racial cleansings.

———

The story of Forsyth County's racial cleansing is fairly clear: Over several months in 1912 more than a thousand blacks were driven out of the county. Some were able to sell their land. The majority lost everything. With their expulsion, Forsyth County became a sanctuary for racism in northern Georgia. While counties surrounding it had black populations that numbered in the thousands, in Forsyth County the number of blacks never went above fifty. In 1960 the census only counted four, and that drifted down to one in 1980. The county's racism was hard to ignore. It was hard but not impossible.

Throughout the 1960s and 1970s, the *Atlanta Journal* and the *Atlanta Constitution,* which were both owned by Cox Newspapers and merged in the 1980s, usually discussed the county's racism only when there was an incident, such as an attack on black campers at a local park. Invariably in the description of the incident the newspaper would quote a resident saying racism was a thing of the past in Forsyth County. Even when there was an incident, the newspapers might not cover it. In 1980, for example, neither newspaper reported that a black Atlanta firefighter had been shot by whites while attending a picnic in the county. The only way the public learned about it was a brief article buried in the back pages describing the conviction of one of the assailants.

In 1987 when whites in Forsyth County created a national uproar by attacking a biracial brotherhood march, the *Atlanta Constitution* ran a series of stories about racism in America that included Forsyth County. It seemed like a good first step except for the editor's note at the top of the story.

> The racist feeling expressed during recent events in Forsyth County had a Southern voice and inflection, shaped in part by the history and culture of that county. But racism is not a Southern or even a regional phenomenon. Today's is the first of three articles, reported from Forsyth County, New Hampshire and Ohio, exploring the currents of white bias in America.

The newspaper was reassuring its readers that they were no worse than anyone else.

But it was in its coverage of the issues raised by the 1987 march that the newspaper reached its nadir. The stakes were high: The issue was whether or not blacks would be compensated for land now worth millions of dollars that had been stolen from them when they had been run out in 1912. Whites in Forsyth County claimed to be mystified about rumors of stolen land and produced a local historian who said all or nearly all black-owned land had been purchased by whites. It was an opportunity for the newspaper to dig through state and county records, examine competing claims, and write a story that would shed light on a contentious history. Instead the newspaper produced one very lightly researched story, which, while claiming to have exploded the "legends" of the expulsion, was misleading and incorrect. When members of the black community objected to this shoddy reporting, the newspaper did not respond.

If the *Atlanta Journal-Constitution* learned anything from the events of 1987, it was not reflected in its news coverage in following years. It returned to the pre-1987 pattern of describing racism in Forsyth County as a thing of the past and predicting a rosy future. In 1990, it announced that "Rapid industrial development may bring a significant number of black residents to the county." Three years later, when a store opened in Cumming with two black store clerks, there was a near riot in lily-white Forsyth. Although the two blacks were evacuated, the *Journal-Constitution* quoted a local official as saying "that [racism] isn't Forsyth County." The newspaper sounded the same note in 1997 when it announced, "Today, [Forsyth] county leaders say blacks are welcome." Apparently not everyone got the message. "Jose Ramirez awoke Friday to the worst attack of vandalism yet against his family," began a story in 2000. "Graffiti, including racial slurs, was scrawled in yellow, black and red paint across the 6-foot-tall, 200-yard-long cedar fence enclosing the family's yard in south Forsyth County. The incident Friday marked the third time vandals have targeted the family."

In 2002 when the latest census found 684 blacks living in Forsyth County, the *Atlanta Journal-Constitution* wrote a front-page story about how "Past Racial Tension Ebbs." Although the new census numbers showed that there were still fewer blacks living in the county than had been driven out in 1912, the newspaper thought the number was highly significant. True to form, the story quoted residents who said the county's racist past was the work of outsiders. "Locals tell newcomers that those events [of 1987] were created by outsiders and did not represent the true Forsyth County."

As I sifted through the *Atlanta Journal-Constitution*'s coverage I was struck by how important the "fable" is in the aftermath of a racial cleansing. When a racial cleansing occurred, most white residents applauded the fact that they had created a racially "pure" community. But as time passed and attitudes changed, this history became, at best, inconvenient. One way to deal with a painful past is to simply fashion a different and far more pleasing story of what happened. In Corbin, Kentucky, for example, the fable was that blacks were not driven out. It was a rowdy railroad crew that just happened to be black. No one hated blacks, the story went. People just wanted a little peace and quiet. In this fable the idea of the "railroad crew" is the story's center of gravity. By limiting the universe of victims to this one small, distinct group of outsiders, what happened was not so bad. A railroad crew was acting up, and their expulsion had nothing to do with race. What we did should be forgiven. It could even be seen as reasonable.

In Forsyth County, the fable's center of gravity was the idea of compensation. After much provocation, the story goes, whites forced most, but not all blacks, to leave. However, those who did leave were compensated for their property. Because they were compensated, the fable shows that the whites were fair-minded, even benign. And, if whites were fair-minded, then what happened was not so bad. In the end the fable must deposit us at that most important of destinations: redemption. And because they promise redemption, these fables are enduring. The Forsyth County fable has never been seriously challenged by anyone or any institution, including the *Atlanta Journal-Constitution*. In fact, I would soon discover to my surprise that the *Journal-Constitution*, which had assiduously defended the fable over the past several decades, would spring to its defense yet again.

What made the *Atlanta Journal-Constitution*'s coverage problematic was that at the same time as I was reporting on what it had done, it was also a paper that might publish the stories I was preparing. As a member of the Cox Newspapers Washington Bureau, I worked for the chain rather than any specific newspaper. What this meant was that, on any particular story, whatever I wrote would be sent "over the wire," and each paper would decide whether or not to print it. But when working on a large project such as racial cleansing, it was important to have a sponsoring newspaper. While other newspapers would be able to run some or all of the stories in the project, the sponsoring newspaper would shape the direction of the reporting, edit the stories, and publish the entire package. As the largest newspaper in the Cox chain with a county in its circulation area that had undergone a racial cleansing, the *Atlanta Journal-Constitution* was the logical candidate to be the sponsoring newspaper. It was not to be.

I had already been working on the project intermittently for a couple of years when the Washington Bureau approached Eric Sundquist, one of the editors at the *Atlanta Journal-Constitution,* about the racial cleansing story. As Alexander, the Washington bureau chief, later wrote, "his reaction ranged from coolness to outright skepticism." I was disappointed, but I continued to work on the project. Another opportunity seemed to present itself when Shawn McIntosh was hired as the new deputy managing editor for special projects at the *Atlanta Journal-Constitution.* When she visited the bureau, I developed a PowerPoint presentation along with handouts and walked her through several examples of racial cleansings including Forsyth County. She listened attentively and at the end announced, "It's a story with no impact." Although she continued as a projects editor, I never saw her again.

It wasn't until about four years after I began working on the story that it finally found a home. At Alexander's urging, I approached Maria Henson, an editor at the *Austin American-Statesman,* who jumped at the idea. When Henson left the paper, the project was passed to David Pasztor, who was, if anything, even more enthusiastic. By September 2005, with nearly all the stories written and edited, our goal of beginning publication on Sunday, October 2 seemed within reach. On September 13, Alexander sent an email to the other Cox Newspapers announcing that within a few weeks we would begin to move a major series. Along with the announcement, he sent copies of the series to Hank Klibanoff, managing editor for news at the *Atlanta Journal-Constitution*. In what was fast becoming a tradition at that paper, Klibanoff said he had little interest in the series. "I do not for a minute wish we were doing it," Klibanoff explained in an email. However, the editors in Atlanta, Austin, and Washington agreed that Klibanoff should go through the stories and in his words make "some observations I would make to our projects editors if they had brought this story to me."

It is not unheard of to have one newspaper in the Cox chain ask editors from sister newspapers to review a story it is about to be run. Alexander, for example, had asked an editor in Dayton to review the racial cleansing series that was slated to appear in Austin. But I found it troubling that Klibanoff or anyone else at the *Atlanta Journal-Constitution* would vet the racial cleansing series. I became even more uneasy when I was ordered to meet with Klibanoff so he could quiz me on my reporting. One of the unwritten rules of journalism is that a newspaper, before it publishes, never allows the people it is writing about to see an advance copy. And giving the subjects of a story the opportunity to edit what is being written about them is un-thinkable. Yet that was precisely the opportunity being given to the *Atlanta Journal-Constitution*. Not only was this bargaining away edi-torial independence, but it tampered with the basic fairness of the editing process. The "courtesy" offered to Atlanta was not being given to anyone else I had written about. It was as if we were allowing the Republicans to review any political stories while denying the same op-portunity to the Democrats.

What blurred the line was that, while we were writing about the *Atlanta Journal-Constitution,* we were also asking the newspaper to publish the racial cleansing series. One could easily argue that the *Atlanta Journal-Constitution* had the right to edit anything that appeared on its pages. But, if the cost of getting into the *Atlanta Journal-Constitution* was bargaining away editorial independence, it should have been too high a price for any newspaper to pay. In retrospect it was a bad bargain, and I should have ob-jected. What I did not realize was that the bargain would grow worse.

Klibanoff began by marking up the copy, spent a day questioning me at a meeting in Austin, and then finished with a seven-page, single-spaced memo to the top editors in Washington, Austin, and Atlanta "in-corporating the concerns I raised in earlier emails and the questions I asked inside the manuscript." But most interestingly Klibanoff spent the greater part of the memo on one issue: Was the black-owned land stolen? Whether intended or not, his memo attempted to shore up the key claim of the fable—the land was not stolen.

There is an inherent problem in such an argument. If one accepts the premise that angry whites terrorized blacks into leaving, the idea that any land sale was somehow valid, even if it did occur, is far-fetched. But the only other alternative—the sales were valid because the blacks were not driven out—is equally implausible. Klibanoff was careful not to claim he was denying anything. "I raise the questions fully aware that they could be unfairly interpreted to put me in league with the deniers," Klibanoff wrote. "I am not a denier." He was, however, a doubter. And those doubts centered on what he saw as the impossibility of proving that black-owned land was stolen. "Were blacks cheated? I am not talking about whether any of us THINK they were cheated. Do we show or prove they were cheated."

In the newspaper story, I wrote that, while some blacks were able to sell their land, the majority did not. Those who did not sell simply abandoned their land leaving a gap in the title history. In other words, there are no deeds showing that black owners transferred title to someone else. Instead a white appears a few years later claiming ownership. But the fact that there are no deeds, Klibanoff argued, did not show the land was stolen. In fact, the lack of a deed, Klibanoff wrote, "allows a false positive to dictate our conclusion."

I found that some white landowners without a clear chain of title went into court years later to "cure" the title through an "adverse possession" hearing, whereby the judge can declare someone the legal owner if that person openly used the land for a set period of time. That meant nothing, Klibanoff wrote, because much of the land "lay fallow for years and years and years—maybe so long that anyone who later moved onto it could rightfully claim it through adverse possession."

At the time Klibanoff wrote his memo, I had just found the Forsyth County tax rolls covering 1912 through 1915 in the state archives. They showed that one year after the cleansing, whites began paying taxes on nearly two-thirds of the black-owned farmland for which they had no deeds. Although this contradicted his theory of the land lying fallow for "years and years," Klibanoff said it was not good enough. "It doesn't prove land was stolen," Klibanoff argued. "It gives us a good lead, a lead that is better than anything else we gathered in three years (as far as proving). . . . I don't know how many parcels are involved, or even if he [Jaspin] had confirmed the links he was making."

But the fact that I had found the records raised questions in Klibanoff's mind about whether I was a competent reporter. "I was, and am, more than a little concerned," Klibanoff wrote, "that after more than three years of reporting, and after the stories were written, edited, slotted, rimmed, designed and headed to publication, we finally get the first bit of evidence that puts us on a path to prove, perhaps, that the land was stolen." It was, at best, a strange criticism. Before I had tracked down the tax rolls, I had spent weeks doing a title search on every piece of black-owned land in Forsyth County. I had reviewed oral histories, interviewed local attorneys and historians, and sifted through papers in the state archives. My reporting on the stolen land had been reviewed and accepted by the editors in Austin and, far from being the "first bit of evidence," the tax rolls were only the most recent in a long string of documents I had collected. More to the point, the tax rolls confirmed all the work I had already done.

Up to this point Klibanoff only thought about land where there was no deed. What about land that had been sold? Could it be considered stolen? If the blacks were forced to sell their land for a song, then it could be termed stolen. But the stories didn't address whether blacks who sold had gotten a fair price. "I don't think we attempted to establish a prevailing rate for the land that was sold," Klibanoff wrote. "Nor do we compare other factors that may have weighed heavily on price." Klibanoff wondered if the farm economy was "running hot" or perhaps "the value was slipping." There were obviously an awful lot of complicated factors that had to be considered. He decided that the "the biggest gap in our reporting is an overall measurement of the value of the land that was sold."

In all of this ruminating, the one thing barely mentioned was that the blacks had lost their land at gunpoint. Klibanoff alludes in one place to blacks who were "flushed off their land" and at another point to being "run off," but he never goes beyond that. If he did acknowledge the wave of terror, the entire intricate structure of doubts, questions, and imponderables he had so carefully constructed would have come crashing down. It is a stubborn fact that in the end cannot be ignored: When the racial cleansing began in Forsyth County, the blacks had no choice. These people were forced either to sell what they had or, barring that, to abandon their land. In either case, they were harmed. As Eduardo Penalver, visiting professor of law at Yale University, put it, "If I threaten you and say sign over the deed to your house, even though I have a written deed that records a purportedly voluntary transaction, I've stolen your house." It made no difference whether the market was "hot" or "cool," deeds were filed or not, or land was taken after a day or a decade. Our idea of legal commerce is built on a willing buyer and a willing seller striking a bargain. When the only alternative to selling is death, a willing seller does not exist.

It was an argument I made to Klibanoff, and it was one that he did not refute. The only way he could have done that would have been to deny that a racial cleansing had occurred. That was a place he could not go. Nevertheless, in his memo he said, "I do not accept [that sales were made under duress] as sufficiently prima facie to assert in print that the land was stolen." He does not say why.

Klibanoff made two other arguments as well. One was that, my reporting to the contrary, the *Atlanta Journal-Constitution* covered racism in Forsyth "in a pretty big way." It was not a claim that got much traction inside the company. As David Pasztor, the editor in Austin put it, "Why are [we] pounding on the *Atlanta Journal-Constitution* for being apologists who look at race relations in Forsyth County through rose colored glasses? The reason we are doing that is because the *Atlanta Journal-Constitution* have been apologists who look at the race relations in Forsyth County through rose colored glasses. It's just true."

The other argument was that the term "racial cleansing" was in some way wrong. Klibanoff never explained why it was wrong besides saying "it has a zealot's ring to it." But it was clear he was unhappy with the term. "I think it needs to be analyzed and discussed more." As it turned out, Klibanoff would see his wish come true.

In the weeks after the Klibanoff memo, editors in Austin and Washington fashioned a strategy for countering the objections of the *Atlanta Journal-Constitution*. Alexander laid out a plan that involved several steps. I would work with Pasztor, the editor in Austin, to address the objections that Klibanoff had raised. In the meantime Alexander would talk with a variety of experts about the propriety of using the term "racial cleansing" and use their comments to counter any objections Klibanoff might raise on that issue. Then the revised stories would be sent to John Erickson, an editor at the *Dayton Daily News,* who was considered one of the best project editors in the chain, for his comments. After Erickson's blessing, the entire package and a lengthy cover letter from Alexander would be given to Jay Smith, the president of Cox Newspapers. Alexander reasoned that by gathering support within the company as well as getting the imprimatur of Smith, he could overcome any opposition from Atlanta.

Alexander had a substantial investment in the racial cleansing series. In part, it was a newsman's love of a good story—although it went far beyond that for him. Alexander projects an air of sweet reasonableness, but in his bones is the fierce desire to break major news. In the racial cleansing series he found a story he called "marvelous." At the same time he had invested a huge amount of my time and the company's money in reporting the story, and it was important to justify that investment.

Balanced against his desire to run the story, however, was the fact that the goodwill of the *Atlanta Journal-Constitution* was key to the bureau's continued well-being. Every few months Alexander issues a "Factory Report" that totes up how many stories each reporter had gotten into one of the Cox newspapers. The story count is one indication of how well or poorly reporters are doing. The usage numbers are also reworked into statistics on how many stories run in the *Atlanta Journal-Constitution,* the chain's flagship paper and the bureau's most important consumer. Dips, trends, and spikes are followed with a stockbroker's zeal. Bureau editors are on the phone everyday with their counterparts in Atlanta testing the cross currents of office politics and gauging how receptive the *Atlanta Journal-Constitution* is to different story ideas. If the personal relationships between Washington and Atlanta sour, it threatens story usage. And if Atlanta doesn't run Washington's stories, it undercuts the bureau's reason for being.

Initially, Richard Oppel and Fred Zipp, the editor and managing editor respectively of the *Austin American-Statesman,* backed what I had written about the *Atlanta Journal-Constitution*. When Klibanoff raised his objections during September, Oppel defended the stories. At the same time, he delayed publication, which was to have begun in October, ostensibly to give Atlanta more time to hash out any problems as well as to allow it to plan what it was going to publish from the package. But as time wore on, Austin grew skittish. I would get calls from Pasztor that his superiors had decided that this sentence or that paragraph that mentioned the *Atlanta Journal-Constitution* had to be cut. The edits were troubling.

By the same token there were signs that the company might resist Atlanta's "edits." One of these signs came in the form of a media training seminar. Management reasoned that, when the series ran, television as well as other newspapers would want to interview me. I was told to fly to corporate headquarters in Atlanta on January 20 for a day of training on how to deal with the press. When I arrived, I was amazed to find the company had assembled a team of six people who spent an entire day coaching me. As well as the ubiquitous PowerPoint presentation, the public relations team put me through a series of mock interviews that they videotaped and critiqued. The company obviously saw the racial cleansing series as a public relations bonanza. I hoped that also meant Cox executives would persuade Atlanta not to tamper with the copy.

But four days after I returned from my media training, I would get a rude surprise. As the final step before the series was sent to the president of Cox Newspapers, I and editors from Austin, Dayton, and Washington would teleconference to review the stories one last time. Alexander, who was visiting the Dayton newspaper at the time, joined the call from there with Erickson, who at the time was the *Dayton Daily News* projects editor.

Erickson, a phlegmatic, fifty-year-old midwesterner, had spent much of his career at the Dayton paper, where one of the stories he edited won a Pulitzer Prize. He is a man of infinite patience renowned within the company for his ability to work with temperamental investigative reporters. His counterpart in Austin, David Pasztor, although about the same age, is Erickson's opposite. Where Erickson sprawls in a chair, Pasztor fidgets endlessly. In one meeting he absent-mindedly grabbed some scissors and whatever other office detritus was at hand to create a kind of doodle lashed together with a rubber band. Quick-witted and acerbic, he likes to project the image of a cynical, tough-talking wise guy. But away from work he lavishes endless care and attention on a collection of dogs that could only generously be called mutts.

With Pasztor in Austin was Fred Zipp, the paper's managing editor. Zipp had come to Austin from the *Palm Beach Post,* where he and his wife both worked. Once in Austin, his career blossomed. Short and wiry, he rarely temporizes. He will listen to a debate among his subordinates and then issue a judgment with the finality of a death sentence.

Although the *Atlanta Journal-Constitution* was not included on the conference call, I soon learned it was there in spirit. The meeting opened with Alexander objecting to the emphasis I had placed on the *Journal-Constitution*'s role. After the 1987 march, the newspaper had entered the public debate on stolen land with a story that ran on page one. It came at a critical moment because, in the wake of the civil rights marches into Forsyth County, both races were finally talking about the racial cleansing and its aftermath. Instead of a fable, there was a chance for the community to deal honestly with its past. Unfortunately, the story the *Atlanta Journal-Constitution* published was a disaster. It referred to some of the events surrounding the 1912 racial cleansing as legends and gave a wildly inaccurate and misleading account of what had happened to black-owned land. It was in part because of this shoddy coverage that Forsyth County did not have to come to grips with its past.

Apparently trying to steer what he thought was a middle course with his fellow editors on the call, Alexander said that, while we should mention the *Atlanta Journal-Constitution*'s role, it should be downplayed. The newspaper, he argued, was "not on the same par" with everyone else who was looking at the issue of reparations for stolen land. Alexander thought it was significant that, in the wake of the march, a biracial commission had been formed to look into various issues including the stolen land. Since they were "quasi-governmental," he thought they bore greater responsibility for what later proved the failure to sort out the matter of black-owned land.

Alexander's math was questionable. With the exception of the Georgia attorney general, who promised, but failed, to investigate what had happened to the stolen land, the biracial commission and the civil rights groups were volunteers with small or nonexistent budgets. By contrast, the *Atlanta Constitution* and its counterpart, the *Atlanta Journal*— their staffs merged in 1982—had hundreds of reporters, researchers, banks of computers, an annual budget of millions of dollars, and a masthead that boasted that it "covers Dixie like the dew." It had the resources in its pocket and on its shoulders the mantle of the fourth estate. All it lacked was courage.

Zipp said he was uncomfortable "trying to characterize what [the *Journal-Constitution* editors] were thinking" when they tried to cover Forsyth County's racial problems. He worried that the story was impugning the motives of the *Journal-Constitution* editors. In fact, the stories never discussed what motives the *Atlanta Journal-Constitution* might have had. It only described what the newspaper did.

Alexander tried to defend the *Journal-Constitution* coverage by saying, "They would have done more on it, if [the story] was huge." When Pasztor reminded Alexander that the 1987 march and subsequent turmoil was "a big-assed story," Alexander argued that, given a long history of racial strife, it would have not been immediately apparent to an Atlanta editor that the newspaper needed to provide in-depth coverage of yet another racial fracas.

Zipp, having switched from the idea that we were impugning the newspaper's motive, introduced two contradictory arguments. He at first said that the *Atlanta Journal-Constitution* "in broad outline" actually did cover the same things I had in my stories. On issues like whether or not land was stolen, Zipp said, "I would argue that some disagreement remains possible." After I pointed out the numerous factual errors in the *Atlanta Journal-Constitution* reporting, Zipp later in the call tried a different tack. In this version, Zipp said the newspaper's failure to cover things like racial attacks in Forsyth County was because it "just didn't know what the fuck was going on."

For over an hour, editors raised objections, but like a stray piece of furniture that guests kept stumbling over, the newspaper's shoddy coverage kept getting in the way of arguments that we should soft-pedal the *Journal-Constitution*'s role. Alexander himself described the coverage as "half-assed." Nevertheless, he declared, "I can't justify in my own mind that the newspaper is that important to the situation." Whether or not it did a miserable job, the newspaper's role was secondary, and writing about it at any length was pointless.

It may not have dawned on those on the conference call—all of whom had worked in newspapers most of their adult lives—but it was a demeaning moment. We would not discuss the newspaper's coverage because what we did for a living was inconsequential. After the conference call was over, Pasztor called me back and summed up the meeting in two words. "We lost."

The decisions made during the conference call had a momentous impact on the way in which the story was subsequently edited. In a version of the story before the teleconference, one of the passages about the *Atlanta Journal-Constitution* read as follows:

In a lengthy June, 1987 front-page story headlined "Tale of white Forsyth not fully factual," the paper set out to debunk the "legends" that had come to surround the county after the 1912 expulsion.

"For generations, Forsyth has been known as the place where blacks were not allowed to live. None," the story said.

But at least two blacks—a married couple—lived in the county in 1933, the article noted. In 1986, "county officials sold automobile license plates to 15 black people," it reported.

The presence of at least some blacks, the article said, showed that "Forsyth County's racial history, as it gradually unfolds from courthouse documents and state records, is not quite living up to its 75-year-old reputation."

The newspaper said, "It was the legends that drew civil rights marchers and segregationists alike to the courthouse square in Cumming last winter and fixed the world's attention on what seemed a defiant bastion of racial exclusion."

The newspaper also reported that, contrary to legend, most blacks forced from the county were able to sell their land, some at a profit.

The newspaper's characterization of what happened to black-owned land largely rested on research conducted by Donna Parrish, identified as a genealogist from Forsyth County.

Parrish, an amateur historian who runs a small water company in Forsyth County, emerged as a pivotal figure in 1987. In addition to the newspaper story, she testified before the Biracial Commission, was cited in the Attorney General's report and her conclusions are quoted at length in one of the commission's final papers.

But Parrish's research was incomplete, a fact she herself would later acknowledge on a web site she created.

Parrish said, and the newspaper reported, that there were 42 black landowners in 1912. In fact, there were 58 according to a 1912 tax roll obtained by Cox newspapers. Only 28 were able to sell their land.

After the conference call it was reduced to:

In a lengthy June 1987 Sunday front page story headlined "Tale of white Forsyth not fully factual," the paper reported that some characterizations of the 1912 cleansing were overblown because a few blacks remained in the county. It incorrectly concluded that most blacks forced from the county were able to sell their land, some at a profit.

Reporting on the newspaper's current coverage of race matters in Forsyth County met an even worse fate. The pre-teleconference version read:

In a 2002 story headlined "Past Racial Tension Ebbs," the *Atlanta Journal-Constitution* reported that the county's black population had "skyrocketed" since 1990.

The 2000 census found 684 African Americans—or about 0.7 percent—among the more than 98,000 people living there, compared to 14 blacks, or .03 percent, in 1990.

The article described Forsyth as the "whitest county in metro Atlanta," and reported that locals felt the troubles of 1987 were caused by "outsiders and did not represent the true Forsyth County."

That part of the story was simply eliminated. A few months later those last three paragraphs re-emerged in another draft of the story but without any mention of the *Atlanta Journal-Constitution*.

I could not abide the publication of the article in this expurgated form. A few weeks earlier I had written the closing piece for the series in which I argued we must face our past and come to terms with what happened. Instead of a white history and a black history, there should be an American history. Yet if I agreed to these revisions I would be perpetuating the problem I was writing about. It was the very soul of hypocrisy. I could not control how Cox Newspapers edited the series, but at least I could have my name removed.

But before I took that step, I made a final try at heading off what would be an ugly confrontation. The day after the teleconference I said to Alexander that we should bring in an outside editor before we began cutting references to the *Atlanta Journal Constitution*. I argued that we faced a conflict of interest because those editing the story were either directly or indirectly beholden to Atlanta. As a result editorial decisions were not being made in an objective way. Although I didn't say it, I also wondered if that section of the story should be re-reported by someone who was not a Cox employee. In that way Atlanta, which had twice rejected my story idea, could not claim that I, as the reporter, was biased.

Alexander dismissed my idea out of hand saying two other Cox editors agreed with him that the story should be toned down. He then warned me that if I took my name off the series, it would mean that the company would not be able to use a story it had spent a great deal of time and money on. Alexander told me that I was "an absolutist" and said that if I refused to attach my name to the articles there would be a "rupture in our relationship." I understood that he was threatening to fire me.

From the outset, Cox knew that I was writing a book on the broader subject of racial cleansings in America. They had even granted me a leave of absence in which to write it. Now, when I threatened to remove my name from the bowdlerized articles, Alexander warned me that Cox would also do what it could to prevent the book from being published. Although I would later check with lawyers as well as my book publisher, I had no doubt that a company owned by a couple of billionaires could field a squadron of lawyers who could tie the book up in litigation for years. I was boxed in.

There was, however, one last thing I could do. When Alexander handed me his revisions, I wrote a memo to the *Austin American-*

Statesman. In the memo I went through my objections to the story and ended by saying that I felt that the story as edited was "incomplete and misleading." In the normal course of things such a memo would raise alarm bells at any newspaper. It did not.

I was left with two unappealing choices. I could refuse to put my name on the series, be fired, and hope that I could somehow get the book published, or I could allow the series to go forward and use the book in part to correct what had been printed under my name. In weighing my choices I had one overriding interest: The story had to be told. If that was my goal, the latter choice was the safer route. But what I did not reckon with was the series of ethical compromises I suddenly faced.

In the normal course of editing a story, a reporter is asked to make changes to the copy. These changes are usually to provide greater clarity or improve the writing. But now I was being asked to make changes that obscured the story and misled the reader. Having agreed to let the series go forward, did I now become a willing participant? It seemed as if each day presented a new ethical puzzle. One of the first was what to do with the phrase "racial cleansing."

When the "edited" series was sent to Jay Smith, the president of Cox Newspapers, Alexander sent it along with a lengthy cover letter that tried to anticipate any objections. As unhappy as I was with the expurgated version, I did not expect any problems from Smith. There was a tradition in Cox that each newspaper was given editorial independence. I had been at the meeting in Austin when the editors there decided "racial cleansing" was an appropriate term. And Alexander, in his cover letter to Smith, had argued that the term should not be tampered with. Once again I had miscalculated.

On March 1, Alexander called me into his office and said that Smith, after carefully reading the material, had come to a decision that would be final. Smith felt that in the popular mind "racial cleansing" meant genocide and what I was describing was not genocide. Although he did not have any alternatives, Smith decreed that we could not use the term "racial cleansing."

Alexander told me that we had to come up with a substitute. I was appalled. Time and again I had noted the euphemisms that whites had used to hide the reality of what they had done. Driving off your neighbor at gunpoint, for example, was a "disturbing situation." Now I was being asked to continue this sorry tradition. My solution was to parody Smith's order. I created what I called a "euphemism generator" that consisted of three columns of words. By picking a word from each column, it was possible to come up with a phrase such as "involuntary African-American relocation." I emailed the generator to Alexander and suggested he should pick his euphemism from among the generator's more than four hundred possible combinations. Probably because the people at Cox knew how disgusted I was, I was left alone after I gave them the generator. Instead someone in Austin hit upon the substitute of "racial expulsion." It came close to describing what happened without being meaningful.

But just how broken things had gotten only became clear when Rich Oppel, the editor at the Austin paper, called to console me about Smith's decision to expunge the term racial cleansing. "Having been on the Pulitzer Board five years now and reading fifteen different public service projects and fifteen different investigative projects," Oppel explained, "you never object to the words you never saw. Nobody but us will be talking about the racial cleanings."

Journalistic success now depended on what people didn't know because we never told them.

"The Pulitzer board will settle on Jaspin and Cox and whatever that chooses to be called and most importantly the substance of the story line," Oppel, who was reelected to the Pulitzer board in April 2006, continued. "I know you don't do things for a Pulitzer but it's nice to get them. And I can tell you what is being discussed here in no way impairs the strength of this in Pulitzer competition from my perspective."

About a month later the Austin paper sent me a new version of the series, this time edited by Oppel himself. The section on the *Atlanta Journal-Constitution* had now shrunk to four paragraphs along with a few scattered references elsewhere. In one of the paragraphs there had been the statement that the *Atlanta Journal-Constitution* "incorrectly concluded that most blacks forced from the county were able to sell their land, some at a profit."

Oppel ordered the word "incorrectly" deleted.

If all the deletions, revisions, and omissions were intended to mollify the Atlanta editors, they failed. In late May, Julia Wallace, the newspaper's executive editor, told Alexander that the *Atlanta Journal-Constitution* would not publish a single word of the series. As Alexander explained it to me, Wallace felt that there was nothing new in what I had written. Alexander also said she had doubts about my credibility, raising the specter that I was a zealot. Nor, apparently, was Wallace going to do anything to correct the erroneous reporting like the "legends" story that ran in her newspaper. No one at the *Journal-Constitution* asked me for documents like the tax rolls and deeds. Nor has the newspaper to this day run its own story that re-examined what happened to black-owned land. Wallace's refusal to run the series rankled Alexander. "I think we both know what's going on here," he told me in frustration at one point. "They are afraid of angering white people."

Wallace's decision had some unintentionally hilarious results. In a meeting on June 16 to discuss how best to promote the newspaper series, Cox executives debated an "anti-marketing" campaign. The problem, as Alexander explained it, was that any marketing that involved Atlanta would raise some ugly questions. If the people in Atlanta learn about the series, Alexander said, they will ask, "why didn't they run anything here and the *Atlanta Journal-Constitution* will have to offer an explanation." That would be "kind of a sticky situation," agreed Robert Jimenez, a Cox executive who was spearheading the marketing campaign. But no one seemed quite sure of how to keep the citizens of Atlanta in the dark. Worse yet no one knew what to tell the public if, after Cox published the series in Austin and promoted it around the country, news somehow leaked into Georgia. Even by the low bar of most corporate meetings, the discussion was absurd. It was, however, instructive.

In the coming days that meeting on promoting the series would take on a far more ominous tone. For all the silly discussions about how best to tiptoe past Atlanta, both Alexander and Cox officials in Atlanta, who over the last year had discussed marketing the series, were now at the June 16 meeting talking in detail about how it should be done, including my appearance on TV shows like *Oprah*. Once again I had been handed an ethical puzzle. It would be bad enough trying to glide past the fuzzing of the *Atlanta Journal-Constitution* role or the excision of "racial cleansing." But what if I were asked about Atlanta's decision not to run the series? When Alexander had originally told me Atlanta refused to publish my stories, I asked him what I should say if I was interviewed by reporters from other papers. He assured me he would field those questions. Now everyone assumed I would be happy to defend editorial judgments I considered unethical or, at best, wrong-headed.

Unsure of what I should do, I said nothing in the Friday, June 16 meeting. But Monday morning I sent Alexander an email. "I gave this a lot of thought over the weekend and I do not feel that in good conscience I can be part of the promotion effort. Aside from deep reservations about the series, I think my decision is in the best interests of the company. No one in Cox would be pleased by my answers to questions regarding everything from the name of the series to the fact that the AJC is refusing to run it."

Alexander was furious.

He began with an email that said, "I hope you're not telling me that after keeping you free to work on this for years, after a considerable investment of time on the part of the top public relations people at Cox, after countless internal battles over content and timing, after thousands of dollars of travel and legal fees, and after deep involvement of the top editors and many staffers at the *Austin American-Statesman,* that you don't think you can be diplomatic enough to handle a few difficult questions." From there the discussion went downhill. Over the next few weeks and during innumerable meetings, I was, among other things, called an "idiot," asked if I wanted to continue working at Cox, and told that, if I felt so strongly about the issue, I should resign.

When I did not budge despite threats, harangues, and even a call to be "reasonable," people simply stopped talking to me. I would come into work, putter around the office, and at the end of the day go home. As far as Alexander was concerned, I was a pane of glass.

Which still left the question of how Cox would handle Atlanta's refusal to run the series.

On July 7, the Friday before the series was to begin, I got my answer. Alexander came into my office with "talking points." Cox had abandoned the idea of a promotional campaign, but the talking points were a list of things I should say if anyone interviewed me. The last of the talking points was, "Do not proactively mention Cox Newspapers or the *Atlanta Journal-Constitution*'s past coverage of racial expulsions. If any inquiries arise about why particular papers did not run the series, go back to messages about how each paper makes its own editorial decisions and that the series wasn't made available outside of the [*Austin American-Statesman*]."

————

I had started my research on racial cleansing puzzled by how something so public and traumatic could remain so hidden. Now what unfolded in front of me was a demonstration of exactly how racial cleansings had come to be concealed in a thicket of lies, half-truths, and euphemisms. The *Atlanta Journal-Constitution,* although its own involvement was once removed, acted like the white people of any town who had driven out their black population. It constructed its own fable that its role was minor, not worthy of mention. At the same time it tried to shore up the larger fable that blacks in Forsyth County had been compensated for their land. Contradictory facts were ignored or minimized. I, as the bearer of that information, was pronounced a zealot or an absolutist. And others within Cox for varying reasons fell in behind this parade of folly.

The truth is that the memory of these racial cleansings remains acutely painful. Black shame and a sense of helplessness at being driven out is matched by white embarrassment over an unpardonable act. The conventional wisdom says there is nothing to be gained by talking about these long-ago events. It will only cause trouble. Besides race relations are just fine today. Silence sweeps the board. But maintaining silence comes at a terrible price.

Cox Newspapers, like almost any reputable media company, has a variety of safety checks to prevent errors or omissions from tainting editorial copy. Alexander, who is fastidious about maintaining the highest possible standards in the Washington bureau, has promulgated a bureau code of ethics that prohibits conflicts of interest. The *Atlanta Journal-Constitution* has an elaborate procedure for dealing with any mistakes that make their way into the newspaper. Cox Newspapers itself has a long tradition of promoting editorial independence. Yet it was as if these rules, procedures, and policies did not exist. It was not that rules were bent. They were swept away. When it was over, not even the words "racial cleansing" would be spoken.

But the failure here runs deeper than a breakdown in institutional checks and balances. The failure is one that mirrors a larger problem of American society. Despite the company's good-faith efforts over a period of years to promote diversity, it is striking that everyone involved in the key decisions regarding the series was white. A century earlier, segregation, disenfranchisement, and racial cleansings had established a white man's country. And one of the legacies of this white hegemony was an all-white group of managers who, in un-self-conscious irony, now grappled with how to talk about America's history of racial cleansing. It is not that the people in Cox Newspapers are racists. They are not. But it is hard not to wonder if these same people would have reached the same conclusions if one among them had been black. What diversity brings to the table is more than the self-congratulatory affirmation that we are all equal. It brings people who can speak with an authority informed by a different past to challenge the conventional wisdom. Would it have made any difference in this case? We have no way of knowing. Yet it leads to another question: Having recounted the entire history of burnings, killings, and terror, could any white person in good faith tell any black person that these were not racial cleansings?

For Cox, having printed the expurgated series, there was now one loose end to tie up. Before the series ran, Alexander asked if I would be mentioning Cox Newspapers in my book. I told him I would not discuss what I was writing. Now that the series had been published, he raised the issue again, and again I refused to discuss it. The company's response was to have Dale Cohen, a Cox attorney who normally works on first amendment issues, call my publisher on August 28. Lara Heimert, who is my editor at Basic Books, fielded the call. According to Heimert,

Cohen first asked if there was any signed agreement with Cox that allowed me to use material I had gathered while working on the newspaper series. There was not, Heimert explained, but it had always been her understanding that Cox News had been aware that the articles were being developed simultaneously with the book project. Although he made no explicit threats, Cohen suggested that Basic Books and Cox Newspapers would need a formal written agreement before book publication could proceed. But then he got down to business. He told Heimert that any memos, emails, or conversations within Cox were the property of Cox, and neither I nor Basic Books had permission to use that material.

It was gratifying to know I finally was right about something. My guess that Cox would use its legal staff to attack the book now seemed prescient.

As if to underscore the company's point, the next day Alexander told me after fourteen years as an editor I was being demoted to reporter.

———

History does not permit alternate endings. But there are times when the ending we think we see is, in fact, an illusion. The jubilant citizen dragging a wooden horse into the city thinks he is celebrating a victory for Troy. Concealed in that moment, however, is another story that ends instead with the city's destruction. In the same way, the story of Forsyth County and its fable would seem to be settled history. It begins with Mae Crow being raped and beaten and dying of her injuries, and it ends with the expulsion and a long, sullen night of hate, division, and deceit. Its legacy is so powerful that nearly a century later it is still able to trip up the *Atlanta Journal-Constitution* and a clutch of newspaper executives. Yet concealed in what we think we know about Forsyth County is another story that begins almost at the same time and place as Mae Crow's murder. It promises a far different ending.

I encountered this different past on an early spring day in 2005. Following what I thought was an unlikely lead about the 1912 rape and murder of Mae Crow, I turned off Brown's Bridge Road about a mile from where it crosses Lake Lanier in Forsyth County and found a simple, white-frame house at the end of a long gravel drive. From the driveway I followed the path that gently slopes down to the home's well-worn door. When the door swung open, it was like finding a passageway to another world. There stood ninety-four-year-old Esta Wetherford, Mae Crow's sister. Stooped with age and growing deaf, she supports herself as she moves from place to place using the kitchen counter, chairs, or tables. Although her daughter lives next door, this fiercely independent woman prefers to live alone. On one wall, captured for all time as a young girl, is a picture of her murdered sister, Mae.

When Mae Crow died, Esta had just come into the world. Tethered as they are to the same family, their lives have the symmetry of a photograph and the stark contrast of its negative. While Mae, through the manner of her death, was yoked to the fame of victims, Esta is anonymous after having lived a life of great courage. Those who killed Mae, like thieves of the soul, stole the purpose of her life, while Esta, because she lived, was able to fashion her own purpose.

The legacy of Mae's life—Forsyth County subtracted of its black citizens—is what we see before us today. The legacy of Esta's life is largely hidden. Yet, because it is so important, it demands its own telling. Esta's life stands not so much as a rebuke as an alternative to Cox Newspapers. The dilemma that Cox Newspapers faced is the dilemma that we struggle with every day.

The tenth of eleven children, Esta had always been different. She says her brothers called her a "smarty pants" when she was growing up. It was more than being a showoff. She had a sly sense of fun mingled with a complete indifference to convention. It has stayed with her. When she turned ninety, for example, Esta started taking naps in the afternoon. On her front door, she would post a sign. "Do Not Disturb. I'm in the Back with Mel Gibson."

The term "smarty pants" implied something else as well: Esta was willful. A better term might be indomitable. In the 1930s, shortly after she was married, her husband, who owned a sawmill, was diagnosed with a heart condition. He would be unable to work for the next year. In the depths of the depression, Esta devised a simple plan. "I just gathered up some flowers and cooked some cakes and went to town and stood on the sidewalk and sold it," she said. "I think that was four dollars I brought back home and I thought I was rich. So from that I went selling things and, you know, cooking cakes, killing chickens. And from then on ever since I have sold things. You make a living with that no matter what."

It was when she was "selling things" that Esta, without even knowing it, passed on her legacy to her granddaughter. At least that is how Debbie Vermaat remembers it. Today Debbie is a suburban matron living near Philadelphia in a large, graceful home overlooking a forest. But when she was a child, both of Debbie's parents worked, and she spent most of her time with her grandmother, Esta. Wedged between her grandparents in the cab of their pickup truck—the Wetherfords always drove a battered pickup truck—Debbie was the skinny, little girl off to help them sell their crops at the produce market outside of Gainesville. In this rigidly segregated southern world the produce market was one of those unique spaces where commerce trumped race. Farmers, white or black, each had their own space, and their customers, white or black, were still customers. Beyond making change or running errands, Debbie recalls how her grandmother treated everyone. She treated them the same. As Debbie apprehended the lesson in the way that only children can, Esta gossiped, joked, bargained, and made friends with both whites and blacks. In Georgia of the 1950s and especially in the Crow family, what might seem ordinary was, in fact, extraordinary.

It was extraordinary, in part, because of the wound that Mae's death created in her family. Like some wounds that never heal, the grieving for Mae never stopped. Whenever Mae's name was mentioned, Esta said her mother would start to cry. More ominously, some in the family blamed all blacks for what had happened. "Some of my older brothers and sisters, they didn't hardly ever get over that," Esta said. "My brother was about two years older than Mae. He never did get over it. He hated black people." Although after the cleansing it was dangerous for a black to be in Forsyth County, what, if anything, her brother, Major, might have done was not clear. Because Major is long dead, Esta does not want to talk about that part of the family's past. However, it is not hard to imagine. In 1980 when a black firefighter from Atlanta was shot in the neck after he attended a picnic in Forsyth

County, one of the men arrested was Melvin Crowe, part of the extended Crow family. Asked about his involvement in the shooting, Melvin Crowe shrugged and said, "Somebody has got to keep the niggers out of Forsyth County."

Yet Esta's life served as a kind of firebreak. The hatred burned up to her but not beyond. It was not so much that Esta defied convention as she worked around it. Some things had to be kept secret.

Esta's close friend, Lillian Koch, was one such secret. Esta helped out in the small store that Lillian owned in Gainesville. "I had been told Lillian was Jewish but I had also been told not to tell anybody that she was Jewish," Debbie said. "If people had known she was a Jew, people wouldn't have done business with her."

When Debbie grew older, her grandmother began telling her the family history. When she was twelve, her grandparents took Debbie to where Esta's sister, Mae, had been raped and killed. Near the site, someone had long ago placed a rock in the crook of a tree. When Esta brought her granddaughter to the site, she pointed out the rock. "I can still see the rock in the tree," Debbie said. "She told me it was used to beat Mae over the head, that Mae was hit repeatedly with the rock and that she was left there very badly beaten. I guess they didn't find her for twenty-four hours." The tree, as if not wanting the murder forgotten, had grown around the rock, grasping it as tightly as any killer had.

For a child looking up at the rock, the lesson was clear. It revolved around one of her grandmother's family boasts. Esta liked to say that her sister Mae had been the prettiest girl in the county. Later she had said the same thing about her daughter, Debbie's mother. As Debbie stood by her grandmother, the lesson for the child was that pretty girls would be murdered. "I was thinking this could happen to my Mom. This could happen to me." In time, though, Debbie would find in this moment of her family's history a more complex and even darker meaning.

When they visited the site where Mae had been attacked, Esta had warned her granddaughter not to "let hate make a place in your life." It would be a warning Esta would come back to repeatedly. In 2000, Esta sent her granddaughter a picture of Mae. On the back, after briefly describing the murder, she wrote, "My oldest brother hated all

Black people as long as he lived because of what happened to his sister. But I didn't—they are just like us, GOOD AND BAD." What Esta said was one thing. What was hinted at within the family was quite another matter.

Debbie never pressed for answers, but what little she learned was disturbing. While two men were executed after a trial, a third man was taken from the jail in Cumming and lynched. Did her family have a hand in the lynching? If it was talked about, it was only discussed obliquely, but Debbie said she is "99 percent sure that some arm of the family did participate." There was also the matter of guilt. Three men had died for Mae's murder, but were all three guilty? Debbie learned that even Mae's mother was unsure of the guilt of one of those executed. Although Debbie doesn't know which man her great-grandmother was referring to, Oscar Daniel went to the gallows protesting his innocence.

"As horrible as what happened to Mae, what happened afterwards was equally horrible," Debbie said. "If you understand anything about the history of lynching, that even though these two young men were given a trial there was no guarantee of their guilt. So I think what always sat with me is the fact that my family might have actually participated in the death of somebody who was innocent."

The uneasy family history was matched for Debbie by the uneasiness of the South in the waning days of segregation. Like so many children before her, Debbie was baptized in the waters of segregation on her first day of school. It was disconcerting. Up until that first school day there had been no distinctions. When Debbie needed to make change at her grandmother's produce counter, she turned for help to another counter and an older girl, who was black. In the weeks before school was to start, she and her friends, both black and white, talked about the lunch boxes (Lassie or Snow White) they would bring. Debbie just assumed she would see her black friends on the first days of class. "When I came home from school I asked, 'Where are my black friends? Why aren't they at school?' Well, my mother said, you know they have their own school. I remember somebody else saying to me at one time, 'Well the reason they have their own school is black people aren't as smart as we are.'"

Sometimes it takes a child's logic to make sense of the world. Debbie knew the black girl who helped her make change at the farmer's market was smarter than she was. If she was smarter, Debbie reasoned, then what she was being told about blacks could not be true. But she did not see her black friends in school again until desegregation began during her high school years. And then, instead of friends, the races eyed one another in chilly silence.

Desegregation was only the latest flashpoint in the uneasy truce between the races. Like ill-fitting clothes, Debbie found that as she matured the strictures on race grew increasingly uncomfortable. Her family had deep roots in Georgia, but, as her grandmother had broken with her family's bias, Debbie severed her ties to the world she had grown up in. Married during her senior year at the University of Georgia, she and her husband dropped out of school and in 1975 moved north, in part to escape the old hatreds. Their children would not be tutored in the old shibboleths.

It was a forlorn hope. They soon found that they had traded the overt racism of the South for the more subtle but equally pernicious bigotry of the North. It was, however, a lesser concern as Debbie's husband built a business as a realtor and she cared for a family that would eventually grow to four children. But for Debbie there was something that was yet to be settled. As much as she might live by Esta's warning about hate, it was Mae's unintended legacy that chafed. These contradictory worlds she had inhabited as a child were, as an adult, still unresolved. Debbie might push it all to the periphery of her life, yet it remained there, a presence that only needed to be jostled back to life. In 1987 it awoke.

When Debbie and her children visited her family in Georgia in August 1987, the region was in an uproar. The first brotherhood march into Forsyth County had been turned back by a crowd of rock-hurling racists. More than 20,000 people rallied to a second brotherhood march the following week. In turn Klansmen, white supremacists, and other hate groups were holding rallies at the Forsyth County Courthouse in Cumming. Even Oprah Winfrey had flown into town to devote a show to the turmoil in Forsyth County. Although the Wetherfords lived in Hall County, they were only about a mile from the border with Forsyth and the controversy was starting to lap around them. Within days of Debbie's arrival, the Klan, which had marched in Forsyth County, planned another march and rally in Gainesville, the Hall County seat.

"I decided that I wanted to go and see this Klan demonstration and I wanted to take my children," Debbie said. "I think this is what my grandmother did for me. In some ways she opened me up to seeing the effects of hate and so I wanted to take my kids. It's a perfect way to show what the face of hate looks like." It was also, Debbie said, a chance for her children "to understand me and who I am and where I came from."

As they watched from the fifth floor of an office building, Debbie noticed that some of the spectators turned their backs as the Klan walked by. Sometimes it was a single person. In other places groups of people turned their backs in a silent protest.

"In that flash of a moment I said is it really enough to recognize it? Is it just enough to really work to understand? Is it enough to turn your back on it? I think that was the point I said, no, I need to be able to find my voice. I need to be able to figure out a way to reverse my family history."

When she returned home to New Jersey, she began taking courses in mediation and conflict resolution. In time she and a friend started a non-profit corporation that provided mediation services. Later she worked as a volunteer mediator for the court system in New Jersey. When she had dropped out of the University of Georgia to get married, she had planned to be an elementary school teacher. Now as she reworked her life, she also began taking classes at Rutgers University in sociology and criminal justice. And at every opportunity she went to seminars and classes in race relations. Which was how in 2000 she found herself sitting in a course provided by the New Jersey attorney general's office on racial diversity. The man offering the course was a career prosecutor, a black man named Robin Parker.

On first meeting her, Robin Parker didn't particularly like Debbie Vermaat. It was nothing she did. But even though Debbie has spent more than two decades of living in the North, her voice now and again slips into a soft southern drawl. For Robin that sound was an alarm bell.

He would tell no one that day. He would not tell Debbie until long after the training session. Neither could have guessed the other's secret, but just as Debbie struggled with the legacy thrust upon her family, Robin's family had inherited its own pain rooted in a similar past. And though neither person had planned it, they were about to make peace with their past and with each other.

Today, Debbie only remembers bits and pieces of what she said in the training session. Each participant was asked a series of questions, what exactly she can no longer recall. But whatever it was, one question broke the silence she had maintained for years. She started with Mae's murder and the lynching that followed. She knows she talked about her family's hatred of blacks and her suspicions about what various family members may have done. There were probably other things like her own childhood, but she is not sure. What she remembers clearly is that she was telling this for the first time to a roomful of people, both black and white, and wondering at every step of the way what they would think of her when she was done. She was so emotionally spent when it was over, she did not trust herself to drive home. And as she talked, slipping occasionally into the southern cadences of her childhood, Robin recalls that, "she pushed right up against all of my stuff." That "stuff" was every bit as forbidding as the story of Mae Crow.

Robin learned of his family's past when he was about the same age that Debbie had been when her grandmother took her to the place where Mae had been murdered. Only for Robin there were no rocks or other mementoes. There was just Robin's father telling him how his great-grandfather had been lynched one day in Pinson, Tennessee. "My great-grandfather was lynched because he was accused of cavorting with a white woman," Robin said. "The family legend was that he was lynched in the street and his body was left for dead and the family was told, 'Don't move his body for some time.' And that lynching caused my grandfather to be sent away to an aunt." When he was told the story, Robin's reaction was almost identical to Debbie's. "I was stunned and a little bit afraid." Robin remembers thinking, "It could happen to me too."

Life for all blacks in the South at the turn of the century was hard, but in the aftermath of a lynching, it was a nightmare. Robin's grandfather was sent to live with relatives in Cairo, Illinois in poverty so grinding that its memory still haunts the family. When Robin's grandfather died, there was talk of revisiting the house where he grew up. "The shame about living there was so deep," Robin said, "that my aunts were beside themselves and crying and did not even want to see the place that they had grown up. That's how deep the shame was."

But the shame in the Parker family went deeper than the poverty. "There was a sense in which they weren't part of the American dream," Robin explained. Those who survived a lynching, just as those who were victims of a racial cleansing, were branded as outcasts. "Being forced to be poor because you are black and having your relative lynched or mistreated sends this message that, you know, the truth is that folks don't really think that you are worthy. It's that feeling of being outcast that gives them the feeling of shame."

There was, however, something shared in this pain. Both the Parkers and the Crows were each victims of a murder. One family had become the pursuer, the other the pursued. They had wrestled with similar fears and been dogged by shame. And now, through happenstance, the family of one who had been lynched and the family of another who had driven a lynching had come upon each other. In that moment Robin listened closely as Debbie talked, and that made all the difference.

"When I hear someone with a southern accent, it sends up all kinds of red flags," Robin said. "Then to have that same person, Debbie in this case, speak really poignantly, and from where I sit, truthfully about, in some sense, a common experience that we shared made me feel a sense of closeness. All of a sudden my junk, my garbage around people from the South collides with her really hard work in making the elephant visible in talking about the tragedy of the way in which we have been set at odds through no personal fault of each other."

Robin Parker quit his job as a prosecutor and now works full time advising on race relations. He and Debbie became friends, and, in time, he shared with her his family's story of its lynching. He sums up the bond they share: "We have traveled the same road in some sense and we can talk about it."

Then Robin pauses and says very carefully, "Shame is not destiny. And that there is healing and reconciliation that happens by bringing these things to light and that shame is just a point along the way toward real reconciliation." It is, he explains, "the magic of building a relationship out of a place where there could have been nothing but either polite conversation or avoidance."

In that moment is the promise of a different future. That promise was born when Esta looked up in the tree and knew that talking about the rock would not harm us. The once murderous object lodged there hangs over our heads only because, like the child, we think it still threatens us. Clinging to fables or lapsing into silence is the child's way of pretending the rock is not there. What Esta gave to her grandchild was far more than the story of the rock. It was a demonstration that, if we have the courage, we can shape our own destiny. That was Esta's gift.

NOTES

INTRODUCTION

1. Moore, Gary, *Floridian Magazine*, 25 July 1982; *Rosewood Victim v. State of Florida,* Special Masters Report, 24 March 1994.

2. Petrovic, Drazen, "Ethnic Cleansing: An Attempt at Methodology," *European Journal of International Law,* vol. 5, no. 3. Petrovic places the first use of "ethnic cleansing" in 1981, but says it is impossible to determine who first used the term. Petrovic also notes that for the Croats the use of the word "cleansing" was based on the military concept of clearing an area of enemy troops. The idiom *"cist"* means clean, which is to say that some area is not contaminated with the enemy. In the 1991 press conference the Croats used the term "Enicko Ciscenje" or literally "ethnic cleansing." Petrovic, "Ethnic Cleansing," p. 4.

3. Jeszenszky, Geza, "From 'Eastern Switzerland' to Ethnic Cleansing, Is the Dream Still Relevant," Address at Duquesne History Forum, November 17, 2000.

CHAPTER 1

1. The fact that the Declaration of Independence is exactly contrary to Taney's decision—"all men are created equal"—did not make much of an impression on the chief justice. Fehrenbacher, Don E., *Slavery, Law, and Politics: The Dred Scott Case in Historical Perspective* (New York: Oxford University Press, 1981), pp. 187–192.

2. *Historical Census Browser*, University of Virginia Library, 5 May 2003, http://fisher.lib.virginia.edu/collections/stats/histcensus/

3. "The President's Proclamation," *Washington Democrat,* 8 January 1863.

4. Tredway, G. R., "Democratic Opposition to the Lincoln Administration in Indiana," Indiana Historical Bureau, 1973, p. 148.

5. Rehnquist, William, "Civil Liberty and the Civil War: The Indianapolis Treason Trials," Indiana University School of Law—Bloomington, 28 October 1996.

6. Tredway, "Democratic Opposition to the Lincoln Administration in Indiana," pp. 148–149.

7. Ingersoll, Frank A., Letter to his father, August 1861, Lilly Library, Indiana University.

8. "Lieutenant General Heffren," *Indianapolis Journal,* 6 March 183; Tredway, "Democratic Opposition to the Lincoln Administration in Indiana," p. 149.

9. The following account of the meeting between Heffren and Stidger is drawn from the testimony of Stidger at the treason trials of Heffren and his four fellow conspirators as well as Stidger's later account in his self-published book. Where the two accounts differ—the differences are relatively minor—I have chosen to use Stidger's trial testimony, which occurred relatively soon after the events he described. The transcript of this trial can be found in Pitman, Ben, *The Trials for Treason at Indianapolis* (News Publishing Company, 1892).

10. Stidger, Felix G., *Treason History of the Order of Sons of Liberty, Formerly Circle of Honor Succeeded by Knights of the Golden Circle, Afterward Order of American Knights* (self-published, 1903), p. 34; in his account of his meeting with Heffren almost forty years later, Stidger identifies the clothier as Samuel Drom. But census records show a Simon Drom living in Salem at that time.

11. In Stidger's account of the meeting published in his book forty years later he says Drom thought "I was probably the expected messenger."

12. Pitman, *The Trials for Treason at Indianapolis,* p. 106.

13. Ibid.

14. Thornbrough, Emma Lou, *Indiana in the Civil War Era* (Indiana Historical Bureau and Indiana Historical Society, 1965), pp. 200–203.

15. Horan, James D., *Confederate Agent: A Discovery in History* (New York: Crown Publishers, 1954), p. 20.

16. Pitman, *The Trials for Treason at Indianapolis,* p. 33.

17. Ibid., p. 17.

18. Ibid., p. 107.

19. Stidger, *Treason History of the Order of Sons of Liberty,* p. 58

20. Ibid., pp. 118–119; Pitman, p. 126.

21. Stidger, *Treason History of the Order of Sons of Liberty,* pp. 116–117; Horan, *Confederate Agent,* p. 148; Pitman, *The Trials for Treason at Indianapolis,* p. 119.

22. Thornbrough, p. 187; Sylvester, Lorna Lutes, "Oliver P. Morton and Hoosier Politics During the Civil War," Diss. Indiana University, 1968, pp. 205–207.

23. Pitman, *The Trials for Treason at Indianapolis,* pp. 105–106.

24. Minutes of the Blue River Meeting, pp 138–139, Earlham College.

25. Ibid., p. 171.

26. Horace Heffren, "Pioneer Pickings," *Washington Democrat,* 2 May 1877.

27. *Washington Democrat,* 4 December 1862.

28. Manuscript Census Returns, Seventh Census of the United States, Washington County, Indiana, 1860.

29. Warder W. Stevens, *Centennial History of Washington County* (Indianapolis: B. F. Bowen & Co., 1916), pp. 301–302.

30. Kenneth M. Stampp, *Indiana Politics During the Civil War* (Indianapolis: Indiana Historical Bureau, 1949) 92, 163.

31. *Washington Democrat,* 8 January 1863; 22 January 1863.

32. Heffren's paper was originally called the *Democratic Banner of Liberty.* In November 1862 he shortened the name to the *Washington Democrat.* For simplicity's sake it is cited in the text as the *Washington Democrat. Washington Democrat,* 6 November 1862.

33. Ibid., 13 August 1863.

34. "In Darkest Indiana," *The World,* 30 September 1893.

35. Ibid.

36. Trueblood, Elias Hicks, "Reminiscence of the Underground Railroad (So Called)," *Republican Leader,* 6 April 1894.

37. Trueblood, Lillian D., "The Story of John Williams, Colored," *Indiana Magazine of History,* Vol. 30 No. 150.

38. "Secret Political Societies," *Washington Democrat,* 2 April 1863; Pitman, *The Trials for Treason at Indianapolis,* p. 128.

39. Pitman, *The Trials for Treason at Indianapolis,* p. 132.

40. Stidger, *Treason History of the Order of Sons of Liberty,* p. 161.

41. Pitman, *The Trials for Treason at Indianapolis,* p. 106.

42. Ibid., p. 134.

43. Shklar, Judith N., *American Citizenship: The Quest for Inclusion* (Cambridge, Mass.: Harvard University Press, 1991), pp. 8, 37; Keyssar, Alexander, *The Right to Vote: The Contested History of Democracy in the United States* (New York: Basic Books, 2000), p. 5.

CHAPTER 2

1. Young, Evelyn, personal interview, 9 May 2005; Harlmon, Nicole, personal interview, 3 May 2004.

2. Young, Evelyn, personal interview.

3. Glasgow, Marcia, personal interview, 7 July 2005.

4. Young, Evelyn, personal interview.

5. Ibid.

6. Tate, Phil, "The Murder," *Messenger,* March–April 1996, p. 8; *Comanche Chief,* January 1880.

7. "A Woman Murdered and a Negro Lynched," *Town and Country,* 29 July 1886; "Sallie's Story" is a typescript provided the author by the Hulsey family; "Hanged by a Mob," *Austin Daily Statesman,* 27 July 1886; "The Killer Captured," *Waco Daily Examiner,* 26 July 1886.

8. Nabers, Jim, Lightfoot papers, Comanche Box, University of Texas; "A Woman Murdered and a Negro Lynched," *Town and Country,* 29 July 1886.

9. "To Feed the Wolves," *Messenger*, March–April 1996, p. 6.

10. Wells, Eulalia ed., *Blazing the Way: Tales of Comanche County Pioneers* (privately printed, 1942), p. 162; Gould, Frank, *Common Texas Grasses* (College Station: Texas A&M University Press, 1978), p. 74.

11. Rawick, George P., *The American Slave: A Composite Autobiography*, vol. 7 (Westport, Conn.: Greenwood Press, 1979), pp. 2702, 2462.

12. Ibid., p. 2571.

13. Nabers, interview.

14. Foner, Eric, *Reconstruction: America's Unfinished Revolution* (New York: Harper and Row, 1988), p. 198; Wilson, Theodore, *The Black Codes of the South* (Tuscaloosa: University of Alabama Press, 1965), pp. 44–45.

15. Wilson, *Black Codes*, pp. 63–65; Foner, *Reconstruction*, p. 199.

16. Bond, James E., *No Easy Walk to Freedom: Reconstruction and the Ratification of the Fourteenth Amendment* (Westport, Conn.: Praeger Publishers, 1997), p. 213.

17. Wilson, *Black Codes*, pp. 108–111; Smallwood, James, *Time of Hope, Time of Despair* (Port Washington, N.Y.: Associated Faculty Press, 1981), pp. 54–56.

18. Fehrenbach, T. R., *Lone Star: A History of Texas and the Texans* (New York: Free Press, 1968), p. 402; Texas Agricultural Statistics Service, *1866–1989 Texas Historical Crops Statistics*, p. 12; Wilson, *Black Codes*, p. 54.

19. Foner, *Reconstruction*, pp. 209–210; Bond, *No Easy Walk*, p. 213.

20. Wells, Eulalia ed., *Blazing the Way: Tales of Comanche County Pioneers* (Comanche, Tex.: privately printed, 1942), pp. 159–161.

21. At the time of this writing, the Lightfoot papers do not appear in the catalogue of the university's collection but are filed in a folder marked "Comanche County." Nabers, interview.

22. Wells, *Blazing the Way*, p. 160.

23. Ibid.

24. Ibid.

25. Ibid.; Nabers, interview.

26. Nabers, interview.

27. "The Killer Captured," *Waco Daily Examiner*, 27 July 1886; "The Expulsion," *Messenger*, May/June 1996, p. 12.

28. "The Expulsion," *Messenger*, p. 13.

29. Conaway, Tom, Lightfoot papers, Comanche County box, University of Texas Library.

30. Ibid.

31. Ibid.

32. "The Pruitt Murder," *Town and Country*, 24 June 1886.

33. "Regulator-Moderator War," *Handbook of Texas*, Texas State Historical Association, www.tsha.utexas.edu/handbook/online/articles/RR/jcr1.html

34. Nabers, interview; Records of the Assistant Commissioner for the State of Texas, Bureau of Refugees, Freedman and Abandoned Lands, 1865–1869,

National Archives Microfilm Publication M821, Roll 32; Tate, "The Murder," p. 8.

35. Nabers, interview; Wells, *Blazing the Way*, p. 162.

36. Nabers, interview; *Waco Daily Examiner*, 27 July 1886; *Town and Country*, 29 July 1886.

37. The following exchange is reconstructed from the Nabers interview.

38. Sanders, Lula, Widow's Application for a Pension, Texas, December 8, 1952 in the Texas State Archives; Page, Leo, personal interview, 3 September 2003.

39. U.S. Census, District 4, Enumeration District 31, p. 24; *Sanders v. Sanders*, No. 3123, District Court, Comanche County; Page, personal interview.

40. Nabers, interview.

41. Ibid.

42. *Town and Country*, 29 July 1886.

43. Ibid.

44. "The Expulsion," *Messenger*, p. 17; Lightfoot, Billy Bob, "The Negro Exodus from Comanche County, Texas," *Southwestern Historical Quarterly*, January 1953, p. 414.

45. *Town and Country*, 5 August 1886.

46. "The Expulsion," *Messenger*, p. 17.

47. *Town and Country*, 5 August 1886.

48. Ibid.

49. Ibid.

50. Ibid.

51. Correspondence File, Texas Rangers, Texas State Archives.

52. *Report of the Adjutant General of the State of Texas*, December 1886, p. 55.

53. Correspondence File, Texas Rangers, Texas State Archives; *Report of the Adjutant General of the State of Texas*, December 1886, p. 55; *Town and Country*, 16 September 1886.

54. "The Expulsion," *Messenger*, p. 18; Lightfoot, Billy Bob, "The History of Comanche County to 1920," Diss. University of Texas, 1949, p. 186.

55. Young, Evelyn, personal interview.

56. Harlmon, Nicole, personal interview; Glasgow, Marcia, personal interview.

57. Raesz, Becky, personal interview, 9 July 2005.

CHAPTER 3

1. Barclay, R. E., *The Copper Basin—1890 to 1963* (Cole Printing and Thesis Service, 1975), pp. 19–22.

2. *Transactions of the American Mining Engineer*, vol. 25 (New York City, 1896), p. 173.

3. "Miners on the Warpath," *Chattanooga Daily Times*, 30 April 1894.

4. Barclay, *Copper Basin*, p. 21.

5. Ibid., pp. 21–22.

6. "Miners on the Warpath," *Chattanooga Daily Times; Historical Census Browser,* University of Virginia Library, 5 May 2003, http://fisher.lib.virginia.edu/collections/stats/histcensus/

7. Barclay, *Copper Basin,* p. 20; Mandle, Jay, *Not Slave, Not Free: The African American Economic Experience Since the Civil War* (Durham, N.C.: Duke University Press, 1992), p. 58.

8. Novak, Daniel, *The Wheel of Servitude* (Lexington: University Press of Kentucky, 1978), pp. 29–31; Bernstein, David E., "The Law and Economics of Post-Civil War Restriction on Interstate Migration by African-Americans," *Texas Law Review,* March 1998, vol. 76, pp. 781, 789–791.

9. Mandle, Jay, "Continuity and Change: The Use of Black Labor After the Civil War," *Journal of Black Studies,* vol. 21, no. 4, June 1991, pp. 422–423; Rosenbloom, Joshua, "The Extent of the Labor Market in the United States, 1850–1914," National Bureau of Economic Research Working Paper, Cambridge, Mass., 1996, p. 24.

10. Fishback, Price, "Operations of 'Unfettered' Labor Market: Exit and Voice In American Labor Markets at the Turn of the Century," National Bureau of Economic Research, Cambridge, Mass., 1997, p. 24; Andrews, W. T., "The Causes of Negro Migration from the South," *Journal of Negro History,* vol. 63, no. 4.

11. Cohen, William, "Negro Involuntary Servitude in the South, 1865–1940: A Preliminary Analysis," *Journal of Southern History,* vol. 42, no. 1; Mancini, Matthew J. *One Dies, Get Another* (Columbia: University of South Carolina Press, 1996), p. 41.

12. Cohen, "Negro Involuntary Servitude," p. 37.

13. Harris, Carl V., "Reforms in Government Control of Negroes in Birmingham, Alabama, 1890–1920," *Journal of Southern History,* vol. 38, no. 4, p. 581.

14. Harris, "Reforms in Government Control," p. 585.

15. Shlomowitz, Ralph, "'Bound' or 'Free'? Black Labor in Cotton and Sugarcane Farming, 1865–1880," *Journal of Southern History,* vol. 50, no. 4, p. 596.

16. "Negro Emigration," *Atlanta Constitution,* 19 February 1890; "To Test the Law," *Atlanta Constitution,* 9 March 1890; Bernstein, "Law and Economics," p. 784.

17. "Dispersed by Vagrancy Act," *Atlanta Journal,* 12 March 1900; "Negro Exodus from Athens Is Heavy," *Atlanta Constitution,* 7 March 1900; "Negroes Leave by Hundreds," *Atlanta Constitution,* 12 March 1900.

18. "Negro Exodus Comes to Stop," *Atlanta Constitution,* 12 March 1900.

19. Bernstein, "Law and Economics," pp. 814–820.

20. Baker, Ray Stannard, *Following the Color Line* (New York: Harper & Row, 1908), pp. 96–97.

21. Cohen, "Negro Involuntary Servitude," pp. 56–57; Novak, *Wheel of Servitude,* p. 33.

22. White, Walter, Memorandum for Governor Dorsey from Walter F. White, Papers of the NAACP on microfilm, Part 7, reel 10; White, Walter, "The Work of a Mob," *The Crisis*, September 1918, p. 221.

23. "Hamp Smith Murdered; Young Wife Attacked by Negro Farm Hands," *Quitman Free Press*, 24 May 1918.

24. "Sidney Johnson Is Shot to Death," *Atlanta Constitution*, 22 May 1918; Janken, Kenneth Robert, *White: The Biography of Walter White, Mr. NAACP* (New York: New Press, 2003), p. 32.

25. "State of Insurrection Declared in Portions of Lowndes and Brooks," *Atlanta Constitution*, 22 May 1918; White, "The Work of a Mob," p. 221.

26. White, "The Work of a Mob," p. 221.

27. Stover, John, *The Railroads of the South 1865–1900* (Chapel Hill: University of North Carolina Press, 1955), pp. 61, 125; Ayers, Edward L., *The Promise of the New South* (New York: Oxford University Press, 1992), pp. 111–117.

28. Anderson, James D., *The Education of Blacks in the South, 1860–1935* (Chapel Hill: University of North Carolina Press, 1988), pp. 90–91.

29. Whatley, Warren C., "African American Strikebreaking from the Civil War to the New Deal," *Social Science History*, vol. 17, no. 4, pp. 526–527; Rosenbloom, Joshua L., "Strikebreaking and the Labor Market in the United States, 1881–1894," *Journal of Economic History*, vol. 58, no. 1, pp. 184–185.

30. "Murder May End in a Race War," *Freemont Journal*, 11 May 1903; Matthews, John Michael, "The Georgia 'Race Strike' of 1909," *Journal of Southern History*, vol. 40, no. 4, pp. 613–630.

31. Baker, *Following the Color Line*, p. 85.

32. "The Negro in Politics," *Evansville Journal*, 22 December 1900; "Negro Uprising Feared," *New York Times*.

33. The fear of "Negro domination" would prove to be very durable. Writing in the 1950s, William F. Buckley Jr. noted, "It is unpleasant to adduce statistics evidencing the median cultural advancement of the white over Negro; but the statistics are there. . . ." Given what he called the blacks' inferior culture and the fear that there will be "rule by a Negro majority," Buckley said it was only reasonable that, "In the South, the white community is entitled to put forward a claim to prevail politically because, for the time being anyway, the leaders of American civilization are white." Buckley, William F. and Dos Passos, John, *Up from Liberalism* (New York: McDowell, 1959), pp. 127–128.

34. Perman, Michael, *Struggle for Mastery Disenfranchisement in the South* (Chapel Hill: University of North Carolina Press, 2001), pp. 50–59; Foner, Eric, *Reconstruction: America's Unfinished Revolution* (New York: Harper and Row, 1988), pp. 44–45; Ayers, *Promise of the New South*, pp. 52–53.

35. "Hulett Hayden Lynched," *Neosho Times*, 5 July 1894; "The Negro Murderer Is Given Short Shrift," *Springfield Democrat*, 29 June 1894; "A Negro Murderer Lynched by a Mob," *Springfield Daily Republican*, 30 June 1894.

36. "Hulett Hayden Lynched," *Neosho Times*; "Mob Law, Race War, Riot, and Incendiarism," *Carthage Evening News,* 20 August 1901.

CHAPTER 4

1. Brown, James, personal interview, 5 April 2004.

2. "Mob Hangs Murderer of a Young Woman," *Springfield Republican,* 20 August 1901, p. 1; "Pierce City Still Excited," *Springfield Leader Democrat,* 20 August 1901, p. 1; Murray Bishoff, "The Lynching That Changed Southwest Missouri," *Monett Times,* 15 August 1991, p. 1; "Foully Murdered," *Pierce City Empire,* 22 August 1901, p. 3.

3. "Pierce City—The Hustling Little City to the East," *Pierce City Empire,* 17 May 1900, p. 3.

4. A railroad executive named Peirce donated the land for the town, and, as a result, the townspeople adopted his spelling of his name. Over time the town's name has morphed to the more traditional spelling. So as not to confuse the reader, I have used the current spelling throughout the text.

5. A picture of the bridge accompanies the article "Negroes Driven from Southwest Missouri Towns" by Robertus Love in the *St. Louis Post-Dispatch,* 25 August 1901.

6. "Mob Hangs Murderer of a Young Woman," *Springfield Republican,* p. 1; *Springfield Leader Democrat,* 20 August 1901, p. 1; Bishoff, "The Lynching That Changed Southwest Missouri," p. 1; "Foully Murdered," *Pierce City Empire,* p. 3.

7. "Three Negroes Were Killed at Peirce City," *Joplin Globe,* 21 August 1901, p. 1; "Version from Springfield," *Carthage Evening Press,* 21 August 1901, p. 1; Bishoff, "The Lynching That Changed Southwest Missouri," p. 1; *Springfield Leader Democrat,* 20 August 1901, p. 1; "Foully Murdered," *Pierce City Empire,* p. 3

8. *Pierce City Empire,* 8 September 1881, p. 3; *Pierce City Empire,* 15 May 1884, p. 2; *Pierce City Empire,* 15 March 1900, p. 3; *Pierce City Empire,* 4 October 1900, p. 3.

9. "Hulett Hayden Lynched," *Neosho Times,* 5 July 1894, p. 4; "Lynched at Monett," *Springfield Democrat,* 29 June 1894, p. 1; *Mount Vernon Chieftain,* 5 July 1894, p. 3; "Memorabilia of Monett, Missouri" http://freepages.history.rootsweb.com/~cappscreek/jeffries.html

10. *Pierce City Empire,* 27 October 1881, p. 3; *Pierce City Empire,* 2 July 1891, p. 4; *Pierce City Empire,* 4 November 1886, p. 3; "Under Whip," *Pierce City Empire,* 4 June 1891, p. 3.

11. "Pierce City Still Excited," *Springfield Leader-Democrat,* 20 August 1901, p. 1; "After Mr. Lark," *Springfield Leader-Democrat,* 21 August 1901, p. 1.

12. "Fled for Life," *Springfield Republican,* 23 August 1901, p. 7; Love, "Negroes Driven from Southwest Missouri Towns," p. 1.

13. "Pierce City Still Excited," *Springfield Leader Democrat*, 20 August 1901, p. 1; "Foully Murdered," *Pierce City Empire*, p. 3; "Pierce City's Side of the Story," *Pierce City Empire*, 5 September 1901, p. 3.

14. "Fled for Life," *Springfield Republican*, p. 7; Love, "Negroes Driven from Southwest Missouri Towns," p. 1; "Report in Full," *Springfield Republican*, 31 August 1901, p. 5.

15. Love, "Negroes Driven from Southwest Missouri Towns," p. 1; "Three Negroes Were Killed at Pierce City," *Joplin Globe*, p. 1; "Report in Full," *Springfield Republican*, p. 5.

16. "Hung," *Empire*, 22 August 1901, p. 3

17. "Mob Law, Race War, Riot, and Incendiarism," *Carthage Evening News*, August 20, 1901, p. 1; "Pierce City Still Excited," *Springfield Leader Democrat*, 20 August 1901, p. 1; Bishoff, "The Lynching That Changed Southwest Missouri," p. 1.

18. "Pierce City Still Excited," *Springfield Leader Democrat*, 20 August 1901, p. 1; "Mob Hangs Murderer of a Young Woman," *Springfield Republican*, August 20, 1901, p. 1; "Mob Law, Race War, Riot, and Incendiarism," *Carthage Evening News*, p. 1; "Three Negroes Were Killed at Pierce City," *Joplin Globe*, p. 1.

19. "Three Negroes Were Killed at Pierce City," *Joplin Globe*, p. 1.

20. "Mob Hangs Murderer of a Young Woman," *Springfield Republican*, 20 August 1901, p. 1; "Mob Law, Race War, Riot, and Incendiarism," *Carthage Evening News*, p. 1; "Three Negroes Were Killed at Pierce City," *Joplin Globe*, p. 1.

21. "After Mr. Lark," *Springfield Leader-Democrat*, p. 1; "Pierce City Still Excited," *Springfield Leader*, 20 August 1901, p. 1.

22. The reporter from the Carthage newspaper arrived just as the mob had hustled Godley to the hotel. The account of the lynching is taken from this compelling first-person narrative.

23. "Mob Law, Race War, Riot, and Incendiarism," *Carthage Evening News*.

24. Ibid.

25. "The Strawberry Letters," *Lawrence County Historical Society Bulletin*, October 1985.

26. Love, "Negroes Driven from Southwest Missouri Towns," p. 1; "Fled for Life," *Springfield Republican*, p. 7.

27. In the adjutant general's report of the lynching, he claims the mob broke in the armory and stole the guns at the same time as they assaulted the jail. He then claims that, when members of the National Guard realized what had happened, they moved through the mob to retrieve the rifles. This contradicts every other account and, at best, seems farfetched.

28. Love, "Negroes Driven from Southwest Missouri Towns."

29. Ibid.

30. Ibid.

31. "Mob Law, Race War, Riot, and Incendiarism," *Carthage Evening News*.

32. "Mob at Pierce City Dispersed Last Night," *Springfield Republican*, 21 August 1901; "Mob Law, Race War, Riot, and Incendiarism," *Carthage Evening News*; "The Strawberry Letters."

33. "Mob Law, Race War, Riot, and Incendiarism," *Carthage Evening News*.

34. "Getting Rid of Negroes," *Pittsburgh Daily Headlight*, 23 August 1901; "Good Negro Movement," *Leader-Democrat*, 23 August 1901.

35. "Fled for Life," *Springfield Republican*, p. 7.

36. Love, "Negroes Driven from Southwest Missouri Towns," p. 1.

37. "Drove Negroes Out," *Carthage Evening Press*, 27 August 1901, p. 5.

38. "The Stroud Mob," *Stroud Messenger*, 30 August 1901, p. 3; "Not So Bad As Reported," *Stroud Star*, 30 August 1901, p. 4; "He Would Uphold the Mobbers," *Stroud Messenger*, 6 September 1901, p. 7.

39. "The Strawberry Letters"; "Peirce City All Nervous," *Carthage Evening Press*, 23 August 1901, p. 2.

40. "Peirce City's Side of the Story," *Weekly Empire*, 5 September 1901, p. 3.

41. "The Strawberry Letters."

42. Brown, Miriam Keast, *The Story of Peirce City, Missouri 1870–1970* (Pierce City, Mo.: 1970), p. 47.

43. Brown, James, personal interview, 26 March 2004.

44. Bishoff, Murray, personal interview, 5 April 2004.

CHAPTER 5

1. "Fired by Masked Mob," *Washington Post*, 2 December 1906; "Midnight Raiders Destroy Two Plants," *Louisville Courier-Journal*, 13 November 1906; "Masked Mob Plies Torch," *Louisville Courier-Journal*, 1 December 1906.

2. "Fired by Masked Mob," *Washington Post*; "Midnight Raiders Destroy Two Plants," *Louisville Courier-Journal*; "Masked Mob Plies Torch," *Louisville Courier-Journal*.

3. Hawk, Emory Q. and Snavely, Tipton R., *Economic History of the South*, ed. Carl Wittke (New York: Prentice-Hall, Inc., 1934), pp. 450–476.

4. "Immigration and Quarantine Conference Will Assemble This Morning," *Nashville American*, 12 November 1906.

5. Berthoff, Rowland T., "Southern Attitudes Toward Immigration, 1865–1914," *Journal of Southern History*, vol. 17, no. 3, pp. 328–331 and 341.

6. "Immigration to the South Proves Main Theme of Discussion," *Nashville American*, 13 November 1906.

7. Ibid.

8. Ibid.

9. Collins, William J., "When the Tide Turned: Immigration and the Delay of the Great Black Migration," *Journal of Economic History*, vol. 57, no. 3, pp. 607–608.

10. "The Immigration Convention," *Louisville Courier-Journal*, 14 November 1906.

11. "Threats Made Against Ayres," *Louisville Courier-Journal*, 3 December 1906.

12. Lyle, Eugene P. Jr., "They That Ride by Night," *Hampton's Magazine*, vol. XXII, no. 2, pp. 178–185.

13. Waldrep, Christopher, *Night Riders, Defending Community in the Black Patch, 1890–1915* (Durham, N.C.: Duke University Press, 1993), pp. 67–68.

14. "Threats Made Against Ayres," *Louisville Courier-Journal*; "Will Resist Payment," *Louisville Courier-Journal*, 2 December 1906.

15. Waldrep, *Night Riders*, pp. 141–143.

16. Ibid., p. 143.

17. Interview notes of Max Bohanon, *Commonwealth of Kentucky vs. Marvin Farley and Tom Chiles*, 1908, Marshall County Courthouse.

18. *Champion vs. Champion*, Lyon County Court, Kentucky State Archives.

19. Waldrep, *Night Riders*, p. 146.

20. "Burnett Phelps Takes Stand in Own Defense at Benton—Verdict Is Expected Tomorrow Morning," *Paducah Evening Sun*, 17 June 1908.

21. Interview notes of Mary and Steve Whitefield, *Commonwealth of Kentucky vs. Marvin Farley and Tom Chiles*, 1908, Marshall County Courthouse.

22. Ibid.

23. Interview notes of W. W. Holland, *Commonwealth of Kentucky vs. Marvin Farley and Tom Chiles*.

24. Interview notes of Mary and Steve Whitefield, *Commonwealth of Kentucky vs. Marvin Farley and Tom Chiles*.

25. Interview notes of Fred Holden, J. C. Hicks, Joe Washburn, and G. Thomas, *Commonwealth of Kentucky vs. Marvin Farley and Tom Chiles*.

26. Lyle, Eugene P. Jr., "Night Riding in the Black Patch," *Hampton's Magazine*, vol. XXII, no. 3, p. 348; Cunningham, Bill, *On Bended Knees* (Kuttawa, Ky.: McClanahan, 1983), pp. 72–77.

27. Stafford, Louise, personal interview, 16 June 2004.

28. "Burnett Phelps Takes Stand in Own Defense at Benton," *Paducah Evening Sun*.

29. Interview notes of Walter Clone, *Commonwealth of Kentucky vs. Marvin Farley and Tom Chiles*.

30. Ibid.

31. Interview notes of Brooks Gaines, *Commonwealth of Kentucky vs. Marvin Farley and Tom Chiles*.

32. Ibid.; "Shot Six Negroes," *Hopkinsville Kentuckian*, 12 March 1908; "Negroes Given Hot Time in Marshall County," *Daily Messenger* (Mayfield, Ky.), 11 March 1908.

33. Interview notes of Brooks Gaines, *Commonwealth of Kentucky vs. Marvin Farley and Tom Chiles*.

34. Ibid.; "Burnett Phelps Takes Stand in Own Defense at Benton," *Paducah Evening Sun*.

35. Interview notes of Arthur Griffin, *Commonwealth of Kentucky vs. Marvin Farley and Tom Chiles.*

36. "Big Verdicts in Birmingham Case," *Paducah Evening Sun,* 9 April 1909; "Burnett Phelps Takes Stand in Own Defense at Benton," *Paducah Evening Sun.*

37. Goriely, Alain and McMillen, Tyler, "Shape of a Cracking Whip," *Physical Review Letter,* vol. 88, no. 24, pp. 244301–1 to 244301–3.

38. "Burnett Phelps Takes Stand in Own Defense at Benton," *Paducah Evening Sun;* "Big Verdicts in Birmingham Case," *Paducah Evening Sun,* 3 April 1909.

39. Interview notes of Arthur Griffin and Belle Terry *Commonwealth of Kentucky vs. Marvin Farley and Tom Chiles.*

40. "Big Verdicts in Birmingham Case," *Paducah Evening Sun.*

41. Interview notes of Robert Overby, *Commonwealth of Kentucky vs. Marvin Farley and Tom Chiles;* "Confessed Night Rider on Stand in Benton Trials Names Members and Leaders of Birmingham Mob," *Paducah Evening Sun,* 16 June 1908.

42. Interview notes of Alex Terry, *Commonwealth of Kentucky vs. Marvin Farley and Tom Chiles.*

43. "Negroes Shot and Whipped," *Louisville Courier-Journal,* 11 March 1908.

44. "Lawless Bands Ride by Night," *Louisville Courier-Journal,* 24 March 1908; "Warn Negroes to Leave Calhoun," *Louisville Courier-Journal,* 11 March 1908; "Negro Taken Out and Murdered by Night Riders at Golden Pond," *Hopkinsville Kentuckian,* 26 March 1908; "Judge Lightfoot to Investigate Warning Letters," *Paducah Evening Sun,* 31 March 1908; "Negroes Leaving," *Louisville Courier-Journal,* 28 March 1908.

45. "Negroes Leaving," *Louisville Courier-Journal.*

46. "Death Ends Long Legal Career of Judge W. M. Reed," *Paducah Evening Sun,* 1 October 1925.

47. Flournoy, J. C., letter to Gov. Augustus E. Wilson, 21 March 1908, Wilson Papers, Filson Historical Society, Louisville.

48. Crumbaugh, W. L., letters to Gov. Augustus E. Wilson, 19 March 1908, Wilson Papers, Filson Historical Society, Louisville.

49. Ibid.

50. "Benton Mecca of Men on Horseback Today, According to Reports from Between Rivers, Their Rendezvous," *Paducah Evening Sun,* 25 March 1908; "Night Riders Try to Intimidate Foreman of Marshall Grand Jury by Visiting His Home Last Night," *Paducah Evening Sun,* 31 March 1908; "Attempt to Intimidate Foreman of Grand Jury," *Daily News-Democrat,* 31 March 1908.

51. "Forced to Leave Home by Night Rider Threats," *Daily News-Democrat,* 31 March 1908.

52. "Own Land and Can Not Leave Before Warrants Served," *Paducah Evening Sun,* 2 April 1908.

53. "Eleven White Cappers Indicted in Marshall," *Daily News-Democrat,* 2 April 1908.

54. "Eight More of Marshall White Cappers Caught," *Daily News-Democrat,* 5 April 1908.

55. Ibid.

56. "No Indictments for Night Rider Warnings Found," *Paducah Evening Sun,* 15 April 1908.

57. "Phelps Jury Is Hung," *Daily News-Democrat,* 19 June 1908; "Alleged Captain Marshall County Night Riders Promptly Acquitted of Complicity in Birmingham Raid," *Paducah Evening Sun,* 20 June 1908.

58. "Judge Reed Will Summons Venire from McCracken County to Try Other Alleged Night Rider Cases," *Paducah Evening Sun,* 23 June 1908.

59. "Dr Champion Member of Mob," *Louisville Courier-Journal,* 25 June 1908.

60. "Burnett Phelps Takes Stand in Own Defense at Benton," *Paducah Evening Sun;* "Burnett Phelps Fate Is With Twelve Men," *Paducah Evening Sun,* 18 June 1908.

61. "Confessed Night Rider on Stand in Benton Trials Names Members and Leaders of Birmingham Mob," *Paducah Evening Sun,* 16 June 1908.

62. "Dr. Champion Member of Birmingham Mob," *Lexington (Ky.) Leader,* 25 June 1908; "Confessed Night Rider on Stand in Benton Trials Names Members and Leaders of Birmingham Mob," *Paducah Evening Sun.*

63. "Burnett Phelps Fate Is With Twelve Men," *Paducah Evening Sun.*

64. "Hung Jury," *Louisville Courier-Journal,* 27 June 1908; "Convicted of Night Riding, Dr. Champion Is Given One Year in State Penitentiary by Jury of M'Cracken County Citizens," *Paducah Evening Sun,* 27 June 1908.

65. Stafford, Louise, personal interview, 16 June 2004.

66. Champion, Emelius, letter to Gov. Augustus E. Wilson, 6 October 1909, Wilson Papers, Filson Historical Society, Louisville; Crumbaugh, W. L., letter to Gov. Augustus E. Wilson, 3 October 1909, Wilson Papers.

67. Champion, Emelius, letter to Gov. Augustus E. Wilson, 6 October 1909, Wilson Papers.

68. Wilson, Augustus, letter to Dr. Emelius Champion, 13 October 1909, Wilson Papers, Filson Historical Society, Louisville; Champion, Emelius, letter to Gov. Augustus E. Wilson, 1 December 1909, Wilson Papers.

69. Wilson, Augustus, letter to Judge W. L. Crumbaugh, 4 December 1909, Wilson Papers, Filson Historical Society, Louisville.

70. *Historical Census Browser,* University of Virginia Library, 5 May 2003, http://fisher.lib.virginia.edu/collections/stats/histcensus/; Cunningham, William, personal interview, 16 June 2004.

71. Cunningham, William, personal interview.

CHAPTER 6

1. "Against Racism," *Harrison Daily Times,* 15 January 2006; *Historical Census Browser,* University of Virginia Library, 5 May 2003, http://fisher.lib.virginia.edu/

collections/stats/histcensus/; U.S. Census Bureau, STF 1, 2000 census, Boone County, Arkansas.

2. "Drive Negroes from Harrison," *Arkansas Gazette,* 6 October 1905.

3. Ibid.

4. Froelich, Jacqueline, and Zimmerman, David, "Total Eclipse: The Destruction of the African American Community of Harrison, Arkansas, in 1905 and 1909," *Arkansas Historical Quarterly,* vol. LVIII, no. 2, pp. 134–136.

5. Editorial, *Rogers Democrat,* 11 October 1906.

6. "Severely Whipped," *Marshall Mountain Wave,* 14 October 1905.

7. Woodward, C. Vann, *The Strange Career of Jim Crow,* commemorative edition (New York: Oxford University Press, 2001), pp. 67–74.

8. Arsenault, Raymond, *The Wild Ass of the Ozarks: Jeff Davis and the Social Bases of Southern Politics* (Philadelphia: Temple University Press, 1984), pp. 40–43, 205–206.

9. Rea, Ralph R., *Boone County and Its People* (Press-Argus, 1955), p. 141; Watkins, Loren, "Some History of Boone County, Arkansas," *Boone County Historian,* vol. VII, no. 1, p. 283.

10. Watkins, "Some History of Boone County, Arkansas," p. 283.

11. "Woman of 60 Assault Victim," *Arkansas Gazette,* 19 January 1909; "Heinous Assault Made by Black Brute on Aged Woman in Own Home," *Republican,* 19 January 1909.

12. "Heinous Assault," *Republican;* "Charles Stinnett Is Found Guilty," *Arkansas Gazette,* 23 January 1909; Froelich and Zimmerman, "Total Eclipse," p. 152.

13. "Negroes Leave Boone County," *Arkansas Gazette,* 29 Jan 1909; *History of Boone County, Arkansas* (Paducah, Ky.: Turner Publishing Company, 1998), p. 49.

14. "Locals Lament Racism," *Harrison Daily Times,* 26 January 2003.

15. Kelly, Wayne, personal interview, 5 May 2006

16. "Racism Claims Quite Doubtful," *Harrison Daily Times,* 17 November 2002.

17. "That's Just Harrison," *Northwest Arkansas Times,* 8 November 2002.

18. Holcomb, George, personal interview, 28 April 2006.

19. Holcomb, George: "Young Athletes Felt Racial Intimidation," *Harrison Daily Times,* 24 January 2003; "Racist Image Haunts Town," *Harrison Daily Times,* 24 January 2003; "Locals Lament Racism," *Harrison Daily Times,* 26 January 2003; "Professor Concerned About Harrison," *Harrison Daily Times,* 26 January 2003; "Klan Leader Claims Harrison's 'Traditional Culture' Enticing," *Harrison Daily Times,* 26 January 2003.

20. Griffith, Mary, "Racism in Harrison," email to *Harrison Daily Times,* 26 January 2003.

21. Hoffman, Scott, "Re: task force," email to Wayne Kelly, 17 January 2005.

CHAPTER 7

1. Nash, Lillie, personal interview, 7 October 2004.

2. Crowe, Charles, "Racial Massacre in Atlanta September 22, 1906," *Journal of Negro History*, vol. 54, no. 2; Perman, Michael, *Struggle for Mastery: Disenfranchisement in the South 1888–1908* (Chapel Hill: University of North Carolina Press, 2001), pp. 281–297; Crowe, Charles, "Racial Violence and Social Reform-Origins of the Atlanta Riot of 1906," *Journal of Negro History*, vol. 53, no. 3, p. 251.

3. Dean, H. H., letter to Gov. Joseph M. Brown, 2 September 1912, Papers of Governor Brown, Georgia State Archives, Atlanta, Georgia.

4. "Troops Rushed to Cumming in Autos to Check Race Riot," *Atlanta Journal,* 7 September 1912; "State Trooper Rescue Negroes at Cumming, GA," *Atlanta Constitution,* 8 September 1912.

5. "Negro Is Rushed in Fast Machine to Fulton Towers," *Atlanta Constitution,* 10 September 1912; Shadburn, Don, *The Cottonpatch Chronicles: Reflection on Cherokee History, People, Places, and Events in Forsyth County, Georgia* (D L Shadburn, 2003), pp. 198–200.

6. Shadburn, *Cottonpatch Chronicles,* p. 197; "Troops on Guard as Two Rapists are Convicted," *Atlanta Constitution,* 4 October 1912.

7. "Cumming Negro Lynched by Mob," *Atlanta Constitution,* 11 September 1912; "Cumming Jail Stormed and Mob Takes Negro and Strings Him Up," *Atlanta Journal,* 11 September 1912.

8. "Cumming Negro Lynched by Mob," *Atlanta Constitution;* Shadburn, *Cottonpatch Chronicles,* p. 241.

9. "Four Atlanta Companies Will Go to Cumming," *Atlanta Journal,* 2 October 1912; "Curious Crowds Greet Prisoners at Buford," *Atlanta Journal,* 3 October 1912; "Bayonets Guard Blacks As Trial at Cumming Begins," *Atlanta Journal,* 4 October 1912.

10. "Troops on Guard as Two Rapists Are Convicted," *Atlanta Constitution,* 4 October 1912; Shadburn, *Cottonpatch Chronicles,* p. 216.

11. *Dahlonega Nugget,* 11 October 1912.

12. Ibid.; interview of the family of J. C. Beard, audiocassette, 1987. Forsyth County box, The King Center Archives, Atlanta, Georgia.

13. Interview of the family of Spencer Thornton, audiocassette, 1987. Forsyth County box, The King Center Archives, Atlanta, Georgia.

14. *Dahlonega Nugget,* 11 October 1912.

15. Battle, Annette, audiocassette, 1987. Forsyth County box, The King Center Archives, Atlanta, Georgia; Bowen, Cleveland, audiocassette, 1987. Forsyth County box, The King Center Archives, Atlanta, Georgia; Bell, Bobbie, audiocassette, 1987. Forsyth County box, The King Center Archives, Atlanta, Georgia.

16. "Gainesville Negroes Are Driven from Job," *Atlanta Constitution,* 11 October 1912; *Dahlonega Nugget,* 18 October 1912; *The Crisis,* March 1913, p. 247.

17. Bowers, Michael, "Report of the Attorney General to the Governor, the Department of Community Affairs and the Cumming-Forsyth County Bi-Racial Community Relations Committee," 1987, p. 4.

18. "Resolution Adopted by Mass Meeting of the Citizens of the Town of Cumming at Court House of Forsyth County Wednesday October 16, 1912," Papers of Governor Joseph Brown, Georgia State Archives, Atlanta, Georgia.

19. Brown, Joseph M., letter to C. L. Harris and J. F. Nichols, 21 October 1912, Papers of Governor Joseph Brown, Georgia State Archives, Atlanta, Georgia.

20. Bagley, Garland C., *History of Forsyth County, Georgia,* vol. II, pp. 622–623.

21. "Mob Burns Protecting Fence for View of Double Hanging," *Atlanta Constitution,* 26 October 1912.

22. Bagley, *History of Forsyth County,* pp. 620–622.

23. "Troops Protect Negro Prisoners," *Atlanta Constitution,* 25 October 1912; "Severe Censure for Sheriff Reid," *Atlanta Constitution,* 5 November 1912.

24. "Severe Censure for Sheriff Reid," *Atlanta Constitution.*

25. "Mob Burns Protecting Fence for View of Double Hanging," *Atlanta Constitution;* Shadburn, *History of Forsyth County,* pp. 226–227.

26. Photo of Forsyth hanging, 1912, in author's collection.

27. Cook, Garrett sells property to George W. Oliver, Deed Book 2, p. 101, Forsyth County Courthouse, Cumming, Georgia; Brown, A. G. sells property to Edmundson & Pirkle, Deed Book 1, p. 573, Forsyth County Courthouse, Cumming, Georgia; Crosby, Robert sells property to W. W. Pirkle, Deed Book 1, p. 576, Forsyth County Courthouse, Cumming, Georgia; Pirkle, W. W. sells property to Luther Roper, Deed Book 3, p. 585, Forsyth County Courthouse, Cumming, Georgia; Halsey, C. W sells property to W. W. Pirkle, Deed Book 3, p. 493, Forsyth County Courthouse, Cumming, Georgia.

28. Willingham, Thomas sells property to William Davis Deed Book X, p. 104, Forsyth County Courthouse, Cumming, Georgia; Davis, William mortgages property to W. A. Edmundson, Deed Book X, p. 190, Forsyth County Courthouse, Cumming, Georgia; Davis, William sells property to Maggie Hayse, Deed Book 3, p. 40, Forsyth County Courthouse, Cumming, Georgia; Hayse, Maggie sells property to John D. Black, Deed Book 5, p. 215, Forsyth County Courthouse, Cumming, Georgia.

29. Kellogg, Joe mortgages property to B. P. Roper, Deed Book 1, p. 575, Forsyth County Courthouse, Cumming, Georgia; Kellogg, Joe mortgages property to L. D. Stephens, Deed Book 1, p. 582, Forsyth County Courthouse, Cumming, Georgia; Kellogg, Joe sells property to B. P. Roper Deed Book 3, p. 215, Forsyth County Courthouse, Cumming, Georgia.

30. Long, Clem conveys property to Nannie Carter, Deed Book U, p. 157, Forsyth County Courthouse, Cumming, Georgia.

31. Appendix A contains a summary of black-owned land in Forsyth County at the time of the 1912 racial cleansing and what happened to it; Kemp, C. T. sells property to Alex Hunter, Deed Book, p. 565, Forsyth County Courthouse, Cumming, Georgia; Hunter, Alex sells property to J. L. Black, Deed Book 1, p. 447, Forsyth County Courthouse, Cumming, Georgia.

32. Battle, Annette, audiocassette, 1987. Forsyth County box, The King Center Archives, Atlanta, Georgia.

33. 1912 Tax Roll for Forsyth County, Georgia State Archives, Atlanta, Georgia; 1913 Tax Roll for Forsyth County, Georgia State Archives, Atlanta, Georgia; 1914 Tax Roll for Forsyth County, Georgia State Archives, Atlanta, Georgia; 1915 Tax Roll for Forsyth County, Georgia State Archives, Atlanta, Georgia.

34. Evans, J. D. sells property to Martha Bailey, Deed Book Z, p. 539 Forsyth County Courthouse, Cumming, Georgia; 1913 Tax Roll for Forsyth County, Georgia State Archives, Atlanta, Georgia, p. 80; Mathis, H. G. sells property to D. F. Skinner, Deed Book 3, p. 357, Forsyth County Courthouse, Cumming, Georgia; Higgins, Terrell, *Affidavit in Support of Title,* Deed Book 295, p. 309; Buice, Glen, *Affidavit in Support of Title,* Deed Book 295, p. 311; Bruce, Lee, *Affidavit in Support of Title,* Deed Book 295, p. 310..

35. Bowen, A. G. and Susannah sell property to D. H. Webb, Deed Book 1, p. 422, Forsyth County Courthouse, Cumming, Georgia; Bowen, Kirby, R. E. sells property to George W. Pirkle, Deed Book 25, p. 375, Forsyth County Courthouse, Cumming, Georgia.

36. Buice, N. J. sells property to Morgan Strickland, Deed Book Z, p. 498, Forsyth County Courthouse, Cumming.

37. Anderson, Helen, audiocassette, 1987. Forsyth County box, The King Center Archives, Atlanta, Georgia.

38. Ibid.

39. Ibid.

40. Bell, Bobbie, audiocassette, 1987. Forsyth County box, The King Center Archives, Atlanta, Georgia.

41. "Gov. Brown Urged to Protect Negro Laborers," *Atlanta Journal,* 16 December 1912.

42. *Historical Census Browser,* University of Virginia Library, 5 May 2003, http://fisher.lib.virginia.edu/collections/stats/histcensus/

43. "Gov. Brown Urged to Protect Negro Laborers," *Atlanta Journal.*

44. "Georgia in Terror of Night Riders," *New York Times,* 26 December 1912.

45. Historical Census Browser, University of Virginia Library, 5 May 2003, *http://fisher.lib.virginia.edu/collections/stats/histcensus/*

46. "Dynamite Put Under Homes of Negroes," *News-Herald,* 20 February 1913.

47. The description of the march is based of a television news videotape in the author's possession.

48. "Forsyth County Past and Present: In Forsyth County It's a Battleground for 'Us' And 'Them'," *Atlanta Journal-Constitution,* 25 February 1987.

49. Carter, Dean, personal interview, 25 January 2005.

50. Walraven, Wesley, personal interview, 25 January 2005.

51. Ibid.

52. "Forsyth Event Sober Celebrants," *Atlanta Journal and Constitution,* 18 January 1987.

53. "Cumming Deplores Racial Harrassment [*sic*]," *Atlanta Constitution,* 8 May 1968; "Lily-White Forsyth Looks Ahead—Racial Change Is Blowing in the Wind," *Atlanta Journal,* 8 November 1977; U.S. Census, Forsyth County, Georgia, 1980; "Assault Case Goes to Forsyth Jurors," *Atlanta Constitution,* 20 November 1980; Crowe, Melvin, personal interview, 1 March 2005.

54. "400 Rowdies Spoil World's View of Forsyth County," *Atlanta Journal-Constitution,* 24 January 1987; "Forsyth: For Shame," *Atlanta Journal-Constitution,* 19 January 1987.

55. "20,000 March on Forsyth County: 60 Arrests Mark Day of Tension; 1,000 Turn Out in Counter Protest," *Atlanta Journal-Constitution,* 25 January 1987; "6 Appointed to Biracial Panel: Harris Names 1 White, 5 Blacks to Investigate Forsyth County Unrest," *Atlanta Constitution,* 18 February 1987.

56. "Bowers Probing Ownership of Land by Blacks in Forsyth, Compensation," *Atlanta Constitution,* 23 April 1987; Bowers, Michael, "Report of the Attorney General to the Governor. . . ," pp. 4–5.

57. "Tale of White Forsyth Not Fully Factual," *Atlanta Journal-Constitution,* 28 June 1987.

58. Ibid.

59. Ibid.

60. Ibid.

61. "Story on Black Exodus from Forsyth Misses Mark," *Atlanta Journal-Constitution,* 5 July 1987; "No Racism Remedies in Past," *Atlanta Journal,* 4 December 1987.

62. "No Racism Remedies in Past" *Atlanta Journal.*

63. Spears, Brian, Memo to the Executive Committee of the Coalition to End Fear and Intimidation in Forsyth County, 11 November 1987, in the author's possession; Spears, Brian et al., "Report of the Legal Redress Committee to the Coalition Against Fear and Intimidation in Forsyth County," 23 October 1987. The report is not numbered, but the section on land titles from which this information is drawn is called "Title Examination Report."

64. Spears, Brian et al., "Report of the Legal Redress Committee. . . ."

65. Ibid.

66. Transcript of the Bi-Racial Committee Meeting, Forsyth County box, The King Center Archives, Atlanta, Georgia 1 April 1987, p. 33.

67. Ibid., p. 90.

68. Shadburn, Don, personal interview; Transcript of the Bi-Racial Committee Meeting, 22 April 1987, Forsyth County box, The King Center Archives, Atlanta, Georgia p. 33.

69. Transcript of the Bi-Racial Committee Meeting, 22 April 1987, p. 103.

70. Report of Cumming/Forsyth County Biracial Committee, 22 December 1987, p. 2–8.

71. Ibid., pp. 2–22 to 2–26.

72. Ibid., p. 2–13.

73. Ibid., p. 2–7.

74. "Forsyth Report Will Have Little Impact, Blacks Say; Let County Solve Its Race Problems, Harris Suggests," *Atlanta Constitution,* 23 December 1987.

75. "Cumming Store Rejects Black Workers; Winn-Dixie Issues Public Apology for July 29 Incident," *Atlanta Constitution,* 5 August 1993; U.S. Census Bureau, STF 1, 1990 census, Forsyth County, Georgia; "Past Racial Tensions Ebb," *Atlanta Journal-Constitution,* 8 July 2002.

76. "Past Racial Tensions Ebb," *Atlanta Journal-Constitution.*

77. Bramblett, Annette, *Forsyth County History Stories,* (Charleston, S.C.: Arcadia Publishing, 2002), p. 146.

78. Ibid., pp. 147–148.

79. Ledbetter, Linda, personal interview, 27 January 2005.

CHAPTER 8

1. "Erwin Mob Shoots and Burns Body of Negro Who Attacked Girl," *Bristol Herald Courier,* 21 May 1918.

2. Alexander, Mary, personal interview, 13 March 2003.

3. Ovington, Mary White, "How NAACP Began," http://www.naacp.org/about/history/howbegan; Crouthamel, James L., "The Springfield Race Riot of 1908," *Journal of Negro History,* vol. 45, no. 3, pp. 168–170; Weinberg, Arthur and Lila, eds., *The Muckrackers* (Urbana: University of Illinois Press, 1961), pp. 233–237.

4. Weinberg, *The Muckrackers,* pp. 238–239.

5. Ovington, Mary White, *The Walls Came Tumbling Down* (New York: Harcourt Brace, 1947; reprint, New York: Arno Press and New York Times, 1969), pp. 102–104.

6. Ibid., p. 107; Greene, Harry Washington, *Holders of Doctorates Among American Negroes* (Boston: Meador Publishing Company), p. 26; Record, Wilson, "Negro Intellectual Leadership in the National Association for the Advancement of Colored People," *Phylon,* vol. 17, no. 4, p. 381.

7. "Negroes Flee from Forsyth," *Atlanta Constitution,* 13 October 1912; "Georgia in Terror of Night Riders," *New York Times,* 26 December 1912.

8. *The Crisis,* October 1912, p. 275; *The Crisis,* November 1912, p. 13.

9. "Negroes Flee from Forsyth," *Atlanta Constitution*; "Ask Aid to End Crime in Forsyth," *Atlanta Constitution,* 18 October 1912.

10. *The Crisis,* February 1913, p. 169.

11. *The Crisis,* March 1913, p. 247.

12. *The Crisis,* April 1913, p. 273.

13. *Unicoi County, Tennessee and Its People: 1875–1995* (Marceline, Mo.: Walsworth, 1995), p. 1.

14. Helton, William H., *Around Home in Unicoi County* (Johnson City, Tenn.: Overmountain Press, 1987), pp. 38–39.

15. Ibid., pp. 426–427.

16. "Triple Tragedy at Erwin on Sunday When Negro Runs Wild," *Johnson City Staff*, 20 May 1918; "Erwin Mob Shoots and Burns Body of Negro Who Attacked Girl," *Bristol Herald Courier*, 21 May 1918.

17. Helton, *Around Home in Unicoi County*, pp. 425–427.

18. NAACP Papers, Library of Congress, Container C–367, Folder 7.

19. "The Erwin Lesson," *Johnson City Staff*, 23 May 1918.

20. "That Erwin Mob," *Knoxville Journal and Tribune*, 24 May 1918.

21. Ovington, *The Walls Came Tumbling Down*, pp. 153–154.

22. Bond, Julian, personal interview, 2 February 2005; DeLeon, David, ed., *Leaders from the 1960s: A Biographical Sourcebook of American Activism* (Westport, Conn.: Greenwood Press, 1994), pp. 44–45.

CHAPTER 9

1. Thomas, T. D., sworn statement given 19 January 1920, Gov. Edwin P. Morrow, Rejected Petitions, Box 5, File 177 Kentucky Department for Libraries and Archives.

2. Killenger, Blake, oral history, 28 June 1977, Kentucky Oral History Commission.

3. Snyder, J. B., letter to Judge H. H. Tye, 5 January 1920, Gov. Edwin P. Morrow, Rejected Petitions, Box 5, File 177 Kentucky Department for Libraries and Archives; Scholl, C. L., letter to Judge H. H. Tye, 26 January 1920, Gov. Edwin P. Morrow, Rejected Petitions, Box 5, File 177 Kentucky Department for Libraries and Archives.

4. Everman, H. E., "Corbin: A Complex Railroad 'Boom' Town, 1895–1930," paper presented at the Ohio Valley Historical Conference, October 2001, pp. 1–3.

5. Wright, George C., "The Forced Removal of Afro-Americans from Rural Kentucky," *Reflections*, vol. 1, no. 1, p. 4; Everman, "Corbin: A Complex Railroad 'Boom' Town, 1895–1930," pp. 5–7.

6. "Petition to His Excellency, Governor Edwin P. Morrow," undated Gov. Edwin P. Morrow Rejected Petitions, Box 5, File 177 Kentucky Department for Libraries and Archives.

7. Stansberry, W. R., oral history, 29 June 1977, Kentucky Oral History Commission; Garrett, John, 28 June 1977, Kentucky Oral History Commission; Little, Oscar, 25 June 1977, Kentucky Oral History Commission.

8. Killenger, oral history.

9. "Stabbed and Robbed on Way from Work," *Corbin Times*, 31 October 1919.

10. Stansberry, oral history.

11. Fugate, William, sworn statement given 24 January 1920, Gov. Edwin P. Morrow, Rejected Petitions, Box 5, File 177, Kentucky Department for Libraries and Archives.

12. Ibid.

13. Tye, Alex, sworn statement given 23 January 1920, Gov. Edwin P. Morrow, Rejected Petitions, Box 5, File 177. Kentucky Department for Libraries and Archives.

14. Fugate, sworn statement.

15. Turner, John, sworn statement given 21 January 1920, Gov. Edwin P. Morrow, Rejected Petitions, Box 5, File 177. Kentucky Department for Libraries and Archives/

16. Fugate, sworn statement.

17. Turner, sworn statement.

18. Ibid.

19. Walker, Alfred, oral history, 28 June 1977, Kentucky Oral History Commission.

20. Good, Tom, sworn statement given 22 January 1920, Gov. Edwin P. Morrow, Rejected Petitions, Box 5, File 177, Kentucky Department for Libraries and Archives.

21. Thomas, T. D., sworn statement given 19 January 1920, Gov. Edwin P. Morrow, Rejected Petitions, Box 5, File 177, Kentucky Department for Libraries and Archives; Killenger, oral history.

22. Walker, J. A., sworn statement given 20 January 1920, Gov. Edwin P. Morrow, Rejected Petitions, Box 5, File 177, Kentucky Department for Libraries and Archives.

23. Killenger, oral history; "Negroes Driven from Corbin by Mob of Whites," *Lexington Herald,* 1 November 1919.

24. Tye, sworn statement.

25. Early, Bill, oral history, 28 June 1977, Kentucky Oral History Commission.

26. Jones, Will, sworn statement given 20 January 1920, Gov. Edwin P. Morrow, Rejected Petitions, Box 5, File 177, Kentucky Department for Libraries and Archives; Miles, O. A., sworn statement given 19 January 1920, Gov. Edwin P. Morrow, Rejected Petitions, Box 5, File 177, Kentucky Department for Libraries and Archives.

27. Wilburn, H. H., sworn statement given 24 January 1920, Gov. Edwin P. Morrow, Rejected Petitions, Box 5, File 177, Kentucky Department for Libraries and Archives; Good, sworn statement; Edwards, B. J., sworn statement given 24 January 1920, Gov. Edwin P. Morrow, Rejected Petitions, Box 5, File 177, Kentucky Department for Libraries and Archives.

28. Killenger, oral history.

29. "Negroes Driven from Corbin by Mob of Whites," *Lexington Herald.*

30. Tye, sworn statement.

31. Ibid.; "Negroes Driven from Corbin by Mob of Whites," *Lexington Herald;* Stansberry, oral history.

32. Manuscript Census Returns, Fourteenth Census of the United States, Laurel and Whitley Counties, Kentucky, 1920.

33. Frakes, Peter, sworn statement given 23 January 1920, Gov. Edwin P. Morrow, Rejected Petitions, Box 5, File 177, Kentucky Department for Libraries and

Archives; Snyder, Joseph B. Letter to Governor Edwin P. Morrow, 6 December 1920, Gov. Edwin P. Morrow, Rejected Petitions, Box 5, File 177 Kentucky Department for Libraries and Archives; "Petition to His Excellency, Governor Edwin P. Morrow."

34. Livingston, Glenda, personal interview, 15 June 2004.

35. Ibid.

36. Ibid.

37. Ibid.

38. Ibid.

39. Livingston, Shawn, personal interview, 14 June 2004.

40. Livingston, Glenda, personal interview.

41. Dizney, Allen, personal interview, 16 February 2006.

42. Henson, Robby, Personal interview, 30 June 2006.

CHAPTER 10

1. "Four Arrests Made and Wet Equipment Is Seized in Raids," *Daily Clintonian*, 4 January 1923; "Six Men Caught in Federal Drag Net Today; Four Thurs.," *Daily Clintonian*, 5 January 1923; "Stills and 'Mule' Are Seized in City and Mining Camps," *Daily Clintonian*, 9 January 1923; "All Negroes Driven from Indiana Town," *New York Times*, 21 January 1923; "Blanford," *Hoosier State*, 24 January 1923.

2. "Two Serbians Kill in Blanford Affray," *Daily Clintonian*, 29 January 1923.

3. Lester, J. C. and Wilson, D. L., *Ku Klux Klan: Its Origin, Growth and Disbandment* (Neale Publishing Company, 1905), pp. 52–64.

4. Ibid., pp. 73–74.

5. Ezell, John Samuel, *The South Since 1865* (New York: Macmillan, 1963), p. 95; for a different view of the Klan's disbanding see Kennedy, Stetson, *After Appomattox: How the South Won the War* (Gainesville: University Press of Florida, 1995), pp. 91.

6. Higham, John, *Strangers in the Land: Patterns of American Nativism, 1860–1925* (New Brunswick: Rutgers University Press, 1955), pp. 286–287; Cutlip, Scott M., *The Unseen Power: Public Relations, a History* (Lawrence Erlbaum Associates, 1994), pp. 373–374, 377–381; "Ku Klux Klan Meets at Night on Stone Mountain," *Atlanta Journal*, 28 November 1915.

7. When scholar Leonard J. Moore matched the Klan members in Richmond, Indiana chapter with their religious affiliation, he found 12 percent were Quakers. Richmond is also the home of Earlham College, a Quaker school. Two of its students were on the Klan rolls for Richmond. One of the Klan recruiters on campus was Tom Barr, an Earlham alumnus and son of Daisy Douglas Barr, a Quaker minister. Mrs. Barr, in addition to being a Quaker minister was also a Klan member. She joined the Klan in 1922 and rose to national prominence as Klan Kluckeress. Lipset, Seymour Martin and Raab, Earl, *The Politics of Unreason: Right Wing*

Extremism in America, 1790–1970 (New York: Harper and Row, 1970), pp. 117; Moore, Leonard J., *Citizen Klansmen: The Ku Klux Klan in Indiana, 1921–1928* (Chapel Hill: University of North Carolina Press, 1991), p. 73; Chalmers, David M., *Hooded Americanism: The History of the Ku Klux Klan* (New York: Doubleday, 1965), p. 33.

8. "Why You Should Become a Klansman," Indiana Historical Society, Pamphlet Collection.

9. "Why the Klu [*sic*] Klux Klan Has Been Revived," *Atlanta Journal,* 9 January 1921.

10. Ibid.

11. Ibid.

12. Manuscript Census Returns, Eleventh Census of the United States, Vermillion County, Indiana, 1890; Manuscript Census Returns, Thirteenth Census of the United States, Vermillion County, Indiana, 1920.

13. "Must Watch Bolshevism," *Daily Clintonian,* 17 February 1919.

14. "Bolsheviki Propaganda Scattered in City," *Daily Clintonian,* 20 February 1919.

15. "Anarchist Literature Scattered in Night," *Daily Clintonian,* 24 April 1919; "Some Soviets Plan to Seize Women Also," *Daily Clintonian,* 24 April 1919.

16. "Palmer Warns 'Red' in U.S.," *Daily Clintonian,* 19 June 1919.

17. "Federal Men Take Six Clinton Radicals," *Daily Clintonian,* 3 January 1920; "Second Raid Made on Radicals in Clinton," *Daily Clintonian,* 5 January 1920.

18. "All Are Americans Here," *Daily Clintonian,* 14 November 1918.

19. "All Reds Are Foreigners," *Daily Clintonian,* 3 May 1919; Editorial, *Daily Clintonian,* 13 February 1919.

20. Ibid.

21. "Booze Traffickers Are Caught in Net; Joe Trunko, Patketta And Carlvetta Nabbed," *Daily Clintonian,* 21 June 1919; "Booze Haulers Are Nabbed at Dana," *Daily Clintonian,* 27 January 1919.

22. "Shoots Wife, Kills Self," *Daily Clintonian,* 13 March 1919; "Crime Wave Follows War," *Daily Clintonian,* 13 March 1919; "Look at Facts Calmly," *Daily Clintonian* 10 March 1919.

23. Moore, *Citizen Klansmen,* p. 50.

24. "AN ACT to authorize the formation of companies for the detection and apprehension of Horse Thieves and other felons, and defining their powers," Chapter 51, The Revised Statutes of the State of Indiana passed at the Thirty-Sixth Session of the General Assembly; *Journal* National Horse Thief Detective Association, Fifty-Sixth Annual Session, p. 9; *Journal* National Horse Thief Detective Association, Sixty-Third Annual Session, p. 14; *Journal* National Horse Thief Detective Association, Sixty-Fourth Annual Session, p. 14.

25. "Ku Klux Morons Police Indiana! State Reaping Whirlwind from Klan's Revival of old 'Horse Thief' Law," *Tolerance,* 5 August 1923; "Labor Sore at Horsethief Bodies," *Hammond Times,* 31 August 1923.

26. Skorich, Eli, personal interview, 16 March 2005.

27. Ibid.

28. "Trouble at Blanford Likely to Be Averted," *Indianapolis News*, 20 January 1923; "Assault Stirs Race Trouble in Blanford," *Daily Clintonian*, 20 January 1923.

29. "All Negroes Driven from Indiana Town," *New York Times*, 21 January 1923; "Negroes Begin Exit After Ultimatum by White Miners," *Indianapolis Star*, 21 January 1923; *Historical Census Browser*, University of Virginia Library, 5 May 2003, http://fisher.lib.virginia.edu/collections/stats/histcensus/

30. "Report All Quiet at Blanford After Race Strife," *Daily Clintonian*, 22 January 1923.

31. Ibid.

32. Manuscript Census Returns, Thirteenth Census of the United States, Vermillion County, Indiana, 1920.

33. Skorich, personal interview; "Trouble at Blanford Likely to Be Averted," *Indianapolis News.*

34. "M'Cray Orders I.N.G. Officer to Blanford," *Indianapolis News*, 24 January 1923.

35. "Two Serbians Killed in Blanford Affray," *Daily Clintonian*, 29 January 1923.

36. Ibid.; "Two Serbs Killed by Sheriff and Deputies," *Hoosier State*, 31 January 1923.

37. "Ed Sturm Explodes Story As to Start of Trouble," *Daily Clintonian*, 1 February 1923.

38. Ku Klux Klan officers, 1925, *Indiana Historical Society*, Indianapolis, Indiana.

39. Skorich, personal interview.

40. VanSant, Jon, personal interview, 26 April 2005.

CHAPTER 11

1. Hise, Lloyd, personal interview, 29 July 2005.

2. Ibid.

3. Ibid.

4. Ibid.

5. Ibid.

6. Jennings, Elvira, personal interview, 27 July 2005; *Historical Census Browser*, University of Virginia Library, 5 May 2003, http://fisher.lib.virginia.edu/collections/stats/histcensus/; "In Retrospect," *Mitchell News-Journal*, 9 May 1985; *Lenoir Topic*, 16 December 1886.

7. McClellan, Georgia, personal interview, 29 July 2005.

8. Sheppard, Muriel Early, *Cabins in the Laurel* (Chapel Hill: University of North Carolina Press, 1991), p. 131; "Political Enemies and Allies," University of North Carolina Press, 1994 www.ibiblio.org/uncpress/ncbooks/3politics.html

9. Sheppard, *Cabins in the Laurel*, pp. 131–132.

10. Ibid., p. 131.

11. McClellan, personal interview.

12. "Another Guard Outfit Is Ordered to Spruce Pine by General Metts; Situation Appears More Serious," *Asheville Citizen*, 1 October 1923.

13. "Little Mountain Town Quiet After Stirring Events," *Asheville Times*, 30 September 1923.

14. Sheppard, *Cabins in the Laurel*, p. 132; "Little Mountain Town Quiet After Stirring Events," *Asheville Times*, 30 September 1923; McClellan, personal interview.

15. "Little Mountain Town Quiet After Stirring Events," *Asheville Times*.

16. Ibid.; "Spruce Pine Mob Drives Negroes out of the Town," *Asheville Citizen*, 28 September 1923; Sheppard, *Cabins in the Laurel*, p. 133

17. Sheppard, *Cabins in the Laurel*, p. 132; "Little Mountain Town Quiet After Stirring Events," *Asheville Times*.

18. "Troop Is Called to Spruce Pine," *Asheville Times*, 28 September 1923; O'Brien, P. H., letter to Governor Cameron Morrison, 27 September 1923, Papers of Governor Morrison, North Carolina State Archives, Raleigh, N.C.

19. "Spruce Pine Mob Drives Negroes out of the Town," *Asheville Citizen;* "Spruce Pine Negroes Forcibly Deported by Armed Mob in Cars," *Asheville Times*, 27 September 1923.

20. "The Red Shirt Movement in North Carolina 1898–1900," *Journal of Negro History*, vol. 62, no. 2, pp. 178–179; Luebke, Paul, *Tar Heel Politics: Myths and Realities* (Chapel Hill: University of North Carolina Press, 1990), pp. 9–14; "North Carolina Politics Between the Wars," University of North Carolina Press, 1994 www.ibiblio.org/uncpress/ncbooks/3politics.html

21. "National Guard Outfits Arrive at Spruce Pine; Deported Negroes to Return to Highway Work Today," *Asheville Citizen*, 29 September 1923; "More Men and Supplies to Be Sent to Spruce Pine to Aid in Preserving Order," *Asheville Times*, 29 September 1923; Morrison, Governor Cameron, Telegram to A. N. Fuller, T. W. Dayton, Dr. Charles A. Peterson, and Dan W. Adams, 27 September 1923, Papers of Governor Morrison, North Carolina State Archives, Raleigh, N.C.; Adjutant General's Department, "Special Orders No. 317–1/2 27," September 1923, Papers of Governor Morrison, North Carolina State Archives, Raleigh, N.C.; "Governor Acts Quietly to Quell Disorder," *Asheville Citizen*, 29 September 1923.

22. "Spruce Pine Mob Drives Negroes out of the Town," *Asheville Citizen*.

23. "More Men and Supplies to Be Sent to Spruce Pine to Aid in Preserving Order," *Asheville Times;* "Troops Patrol Village Streets," *Asheville Times*, 30 September 1923; "Troops Arrival Is Surprise to the Citizenship," *Asheville Citizen*, 29 September 1923.

24. "Trial Negro Four Days and Nights Over Mountains," *Sunday Citizen*, 30 September 1923; "Was Walking on Railroad Track," *Asheville Times*, 30 September 1923.

25. "Was Eating Crackers When Officers Came," *Sunday Citizen*, 30 September 1923.

26. "Negro Is Being Taken to the States Prison," *Sunday Citizen*, 30 September 1923; Morrison, Governor Cameron, Telegram to sheriff of Mitchell County, 1 October 1923, Papers of Governor Morrison, North Carolina State Archives, Raleigh, N.C.; Morrison, Governor Cameron, Telegram to General Metts, 1 October 1923, Papers of Governor Morrison, North Carolina State Archives, Raleigh, N.C.; Griffith, John, Telegram to Governor Cameron Morrison, 2 October 1923, Papers of Governor Morrison, North Carolina State Archives, Raleigh, N.C.; Morrison, Governor Cameron, Telegram to Judge T. B. Finley, 4 October 1923, Papers of Governor Morrison, North Carolina State Archives, Raleigh, N.C.; White, Walter, Telegram to Governor Cameron Morrison, 28 September 1923, Papers of Governor Morrison, North Carolina State Archives, Raleigh, N.C.; Morrison, Governor Cameron, Telegram to Walter White, 28 September 1923, Papers of Governor Morrison, North Carolina State Archives, Raleigh, N.C.

27. "John Goff Captured," *Asheville Times,* 30 September 1923; "Another Guard Outfit Is Ordered to Spruce Pine by General Metts; Situation Appears More Serious," *Asheville Times;* "Attempt Made to Have the Mayor of Town Ousted," *Asheville Citizen,* 1 October 1923; "Little Mountain Town Quiet After Stirring Events," *Asheville Times.*

28. "Another Guard Outfit Is Ordered to Spruce Pine by General Metts; Situation Appears More Serious," *Asheville Times;* Bailey, Lloyd Richard Sr., ed., *The Heritage of the Toe River Valley Volume IV Area News, 1777–1949* (Walsworth Publishing, 2004), p. 229

29. Rusher, James Thomas, *Until He Is Dead* (Boone, N.C.: Parkway Publishers, 2003), pp. 23, 38–39; "True Bills Are Lodged Against 77 Mitchell Men," *Asheville Citizen*, 23 October 1923.

30. "John Goss to Pay Death Penalty on Sept. 26 for Act," *Asheville Citizen,* 23 October 1923.

31. "Goss Before Death in Electric Chair, Makes Confession of Crime," *Asheville Times,* 7 December 1923.

32. Sheppard, *Cabins in the Laurel*, p. 135.

33. Burleson, J. E., Letter to Governor Cameron Morrison, 8 October 1923, Papers of Governor Morrison, North Carolina State Archives, Raleigh, N.C.

34. Hise, personal interview.

35. McClellan, personal interview.

CHAPTER 12

1. Moore, Caruth Shaver, *Early History of Sharp County* (self-published, 1979). This does not have page numbers, but blacks are mentioned in the sections "Yanks

Befriended by a Southern Gentlewoman" and "The Story of Private Acie Ladd"; Lankford, Rose Mary, *The History of Evening Shade* (Ash Flat, Ark.: Sharp County Historical Society, 2003).

2. "Negroes Leaving; Mysterious Threats Have Driven Almost Every Negro from Evening Shade," *Sharp County Record*, 28 December 1906.

3. "The Negro Trouble," *Sharp County Record*, 4 January 1907.

4. *Sharp County Record*, 12 April 1907; *Sharp County Record*, 7 June 1907.

5. "Dined with a Negro," *Sharp County Record*, 25 October 1901.

6. *Sharp County Record*, 7 June 1907.

7. Ibid.

8. *Historical Census Browser*, University of Virginia Library, 5 May 2003, http://fisher.lib.virginia.edu/collections/stats/histcensus/

9. Manuscript Census Returns, Twelfth Census of the United States, Magoffin County, Kentucky, 1900.

10. Manuscript Census Returns, Thirteenth Census of the United States, Magoffin County, Kentucky, 1910.

11. *1900 Magoffin County Kentucky Census* (Magoffin County Historical Society, 1984), p. 66; *1900 Magoffin County Kentucky Census* (Magoffin County Historical Society, 1984), p. 66; *1910 Magoffin County Kentucky Census* (Magoffin County Historical Society, 1986), pp. 244–245; ibid., p. 23.

12. *1900 Magoffin County Kentucky Census*, p. 66; *1910 Magoffin County Kentucky Census*, p. 236; Sheet 11B, Lakeville Precinct, Manuscript Census Returns, Fourteenth Census of the United States, Magoffin County, Kentucky, 1920.

13. Werner Sollors, ed., *Interracialism: Black-White Intermarriage in American History, Literature, and Law* (New York: Oxford University Press, 2000), p. 191; Plecker, W. A., "Shall America Remain White?" *Virginia Health Bulletin,* November 1925, vol. XVII, Extra No. 12; Smith, J. Douglas, *Managing White Supremacy: Race, Politics, and Citizenship in Jim Crow Virginia* (Chapel Hill: University of North Carolina Press, 2002), pp. 89–90.

14. Smith, p. 91; "The Black-and-White World of Walter Ashby Plecker: How An Obscure Bureaucrat Tried To Eradicate Virginia's 'Third Race'," *Virginian-Pilot*, 18 August 2004; Cook, Samuel, *Monacans and Miners: Native American and Coal Mining Communities in Appalachia* (Lincoln: University of Nebraska Press, 2000), p. 110.

15. *Historical Census Browser*, University of Virginia Library, 5 May 2003.

16. *State of Tennessee; Eleventh Annual Report of the Mining Department* (Willians Printing Co., 1901), p. 12; *State of Tennessee; Twenty-First Annual Report Of The Mining Department* (Willians Printing Co., 1912), p. 32; Manuscript Census Returns, Thirteenth Census of the United States, Scott County, Tennessee, 1910.

17. *Historical Census Browser*, University of Virginia Library, 5 May 2003.

18. "Lynched at Elk Valley," *Knoxville Journal and Tribune*, 25 June 1903.

19. "A Negro Lynched," *Clinton Gazette*, 27 June 1903.

20. Manuscript Census Returns, Twelfth Census of the United States, Scott County, Tennessee, 1900; Manuscript Census Returns, Thirteenth Census of the United States, Scott County, Tennessee, 1910.

21. "Amid Criticism of Federal Efforts, Charges of Racism Are Lodged," *New York Times*, 5 September 2005; "Katrina Words," *New York Times*, 18 September 2005.

22. Runsick, Elmer, personal interview, 25 March 2004.

APPENDIX A:
BLACK POPULATION
COLLAPSES

The following list represents just a sample of the black population collapse that can be found in census figures. The sudden disappearance of the black population in a county does not necessarily mean that there was a racial cleansing. The drop could have resulted from such things as the boundary lines of a county being redrawn or the reassignment of a black railroad crew. But, based on my research for this book, I am certain that in some of these counties whites attacked blacks and the dramatic population drop represents another expulsion.

ARKANSAS

County	Year	Total population	Black population	Change in black population (%)
CARROLL	1890	17,288	82	0.00
	1900	18,848	166	102.44
	1910	16,829	66	–60.24
	1920	17,786	82	24.24
	1930	15,820	25	–69.51
CLAY	1890	12,200	43	0.00
	1900	15,886	9	–79.07
	1910	23,690	10	11.11
	1920	27,276	3	–70.00
	1930	27,278	10	233.33
CLEBURNE	1890	7,884	49	0.00
	1900	9,628	11	–77.55
	1910	11,903	7	–36.36
	1920	12,696	1	–85.71
	1930	11,373	3	200.00

GREENE	1890	12,908	161	0.00
	1900	16,979	81	−49.69
	1910	23,852	40	−50.62
	1920	26,105	32	−20.00
	1930	26,127	22	−31.25
JOHNSON	1890	16,758	631	0.00
	1900	17,448	620	−1.74
	1910	19,698	517	−16.61
	1920	21,062	329	−36.36
	1930	19,289	366	11.25
MARION	1890	10,390	32	0.00
	1900	11,377	38	18.75
	1910	10,203	0	−100.00
	1920	10,154	0	0.00
	1930	8,876	1	0.00
POLK	1890	9,283	46	0.00
	1900	18,352	177	284.78
	1910	17,216	46	−74.01
	1920	16,412	9	−80.43
	1930	14,857	3	−66.67
SALINE	1890	11,311	1,484	0.00
	1900	13,122	1,920	29.38
	1910	16,657	1,833	−4.53
	1920	16,781	451	−75.40
	1930	15,660	558	23.73
SCOTT	1890	12,635	31	0.00
	1900	13,183	104	235.48
	1910	14,302	22	−78.85
	1920	13,232	10	−54.55
	1930	11,803	13	30.00
SEARCY	1890	9,664	28	0.00
	1900	11,988	16	−42.86
	1910	14,825	104	550.00
	1920	14,590	24	−76.92
	1930	11,056	1	−95.83
STONE	1890	7,043	113	0.00
	1900	8,100	79	−30.09
	1910	8,946	94	18.99
	1920	8,779	15	−84.04
	1930	7,993	15	0.00
	2000	11,499	9	−40.00

GEORGIA

County	Year	Total population	Black population	Change in black population (%)
BANKS	1890	8,562	1,563	0.00
	1900	10,545	2,097	34.17
	1910	11,244	2,321	10.68
	1920	11,814	2,548	9.78
	1930	9,703	963	−62.21
DADE	1890	5,707	1,093	0.00
	1900	4,578	438	−59.93
	1910	4,139	291	−33.56
	1920	3,918	230	−20.96
	1930	4,146	206	−10.43
HABERSHAM	1890	11,573	1,589	0.00
	1900	13,604	1,792	12.78
	1910	10,134	711	−60.32
	1920	10,730	615	−13.50
	1930	12,748	685	11.38
TOWNS	1890	4,064	74	0.00
	1900	4,748	71	−4.05
	1910	3,932	15	−78.87
	1920	3,937	0	−100.00
	1930	4,346	0	0.00
GILMER	1890	9,074	69	0.00
	1900	10,198	77	11.59
	1910	9,237	71	−7.79
	1920	8,406	38	−46.48
	1930	7,344	12	−68.42
UNION	1890	7,749	165	0.00
	1900	8,481	128	−22.42
	1910	6,918	64	−50.00
	1920	6,455	46	−28.13
	1930	6,340	47	2.17

INDIANA

County	Year	Total population	Black population	Change in black population (%)
DUBOIS	1890	20,253	93	0.00
	1900	20,357	19	−79.57
	1910	19,843	9	−52.63

	1920	19,915	7	–22.22
	1930	20,553	3	–57.14
GREENE	1890	24,379	169	0.00
	1900	28,530	133	–21.30
	1910	36,873	85	–36.09
	1920	36,770	48	–43.53
	1930	31,481	13	–72.92
HANCOCK	1890	17,829	92	0.00
	1900	19,189	114	23.91
	1910	19,030	125	9.65
	1920	17,210	47	–62.40
	1930	16,605	28	–40.43
MORGAN	1890	18,643	114	0.00
	1900	20,457	106	–7.02
	1910	21,182	94	–11.32
	1920	20,010	51	–45.74
	1930	19,424	8	–84.31
PIKE	1890	18,544	56	0.00
	1900	20,486	146	160.71
	1910	19,684	133	–8.90
	1920	18,684	137	3.01
	1930	16,361	51	–62.77
SPENCER	1890	22,060	1,388	0.00
	1900	22,407	1,321	–4.83
	1910	20,676	837	–36.64
	1920	18,400	562	–32.86
	1930	16,713	438	–22.06
WARRICK	1890	21,161	614	0.00
	1900	22,239	715	16.45
	1910	21,911	456	–36.22
	1920	19,862	366	–19.74
	1930	18,230	382	4.37

KANSAS

County	Year	Total population	Black population	Change in black population (%)
GREENWOOD	1890	16,309	168	0.00
	1900	16,196	66	–60.71
	1910	16,060	32	–51.52
	1920	14,715	36	12.50
	1930	19,235	34	–5.56

HODGEMAN	1890	2,395	155	0.00
	1900	2,032	125	–19.35
	1910	2,930	67	–46.40
	1920	3,734	108	61.19
	1930	4,157	55	–49.07
OSBORNE	1890	12,083	106	0.00
	1900	11,844	118	11.32
	1910	12,827	69	–41.53
	1920	12,441	24	–65.22
	1930	11,568	26	8.33
PHILLIPS	1890	12,581	72	0.00
	1900	11,182	84	16.67
	1910	11,811	42	–50.00
	1920	10,714	34	–19.05
	1930	9,819	27	–20.59
STAFFORD	1890	8,520	190	0.00
	1900	9,829	170	–10.53
	1910	12,510	127	–25.29
	1920	11,559	114	–10.24
	1930	10,460	37	–67.54

KENTUCKY

County	Year	Total population	Black population	Change in black population (%)
CARTER	1890	17,204	137	0.00
	1900	20,228	143	4.38
	1910	21,966	110	–23.08
	1920	22,474	59	–46.36
	1930	23,839	53	–10.17
ESTILL	1890	10,836	581	0.00
	1900	11,669	223	–61.62
	1910	12,273	106	–52.47
	1920	15,569	204	92.45
	1930	17,079	145	–28.92
GALLATIN	1890	4,611	497	0.00
	1900	5,163	565	13.68
	1910	4,697	274	–51.50
	1920	4,664	241	–12.04
	1930	4,437	184	–23.65
JOHNSON	1880	9,155	103	0.00
	1890	11,027	84	–18.45

	1900	13,730	1	−98.81
	1910	17,482	47	4,600.00
	1920	19,622	67	42.55
	1930	22,968	46	−31.34
LEE	1890	6,205	459	0.00
	1900	7,988	271	−40.96
	1910	9,531	234	−13.65
	1920	11,918	235	0.43
	1930	9,729	140	−40.43
LESLIE	1890	3,964	32	0.00
	1900	6,753	75	134.38
	1910	8,976	132	76.00
	1920	10,097	98	−25.76
	1930	10,765	19	−80.61
MAGOFFIN	1890	9,196	160	0.00
	1900	12,006	136	−15.00
	1910	13,654	54	−60.29
	1920	13,859	51	−5.56
	1930	15,719	44	−13.73
	2000	13,332	20	−54.55
MCLEAN	1890	9,887	786	0.00
	1900	12,448	874	11.20
	1910	13,241	750	−14.19
	1920	12,502	602	−19.73
	1930	11,072	315	−47.67
WOLFE	1890	7,180	122	0.00
	1900	8,764	97	−20.49
	1910	9,864	56	−42.27
	1920	8,783	18	−67.86
	1930	8,425	6	−66.67

MISSOURI

County	Year	Total population	Black population	Change in black population (%)
ADAIR	1890	17,417	303	0.00
	1900	21,728	316	4.29
	1910	22,700	216	−31.65
	1920	21,404	106	−50.93
	1930	19,436	113	6.60

ANDREW	1890	16,000	249	0.00
	1900	17,332	220	−11.65
	1910	15,282	130	−40.91
	1920	14,075	95	−26.92
	1930	13,469	42	−55.79
CALDWELL	1890	15,152	374	0.00
	1900	16,656	430	14.97
	1910	14,605	278	−35.35
	1920	13,849	148	−46.76
	1930	12,509	102	−31.08
CAMDEN	1890	10,040	97	0.00
	1900	13,113	95	−2.06
	1910	11,582	46	−51.58
	1920	10,474	31	−32.61
	1930	9,142	13	−58.06
CEDAR	1890	15,620	127	0.00
	1900	16,923	45	−64.57
	1910	16,080	13	−71.11
	1920	13,933	0	−100.00
	1930	11,136	1	0.00
CHRISTIAN	1890	14,017	92	0.00
	1900	16,939	117	27.17
	1910	15,832	51	−56.41
	1920	15,252	20	−60.78
	1930	13,169	6	−70.00
CLARK	1890	15,126	170	0.00
	1900	15,383	142	−16.47
	1910	12,811	50	−64.79
	1920	11,874	32	−36.00
	1930	10,254	23	−28.13
DE KALB	1890	14,539	110	0.00
	1900	14,418	127	15.45
	1910	12,531	64	−49.61
	1920	11,694	76	18.75
	1930	10,270	38	−50.00
IRON	1890	9,119	320	0.00
	1900	8,716	248	−22.50
	1910	8,563	179	−27.82
	1920	9,458	82	−54.19
	1930	9,642	129	57.32

MILLER	1890	14,162	228	0.00
	1900	15,187	190	−16.67
	1910	16,717	96	−49.47
	1920	15,567	52	−45.83
	1930	16,728	89	71.15
PERRY	1890	13,237	492	0.00
	1900	15,134	440	−10.57
	1910	14,898	228	−48.18
	1920	14,434	107	−53.07
	1930	13,707	99	−7.48
POLK	1890	20,339	163	0.00
	1900	23,255	185	13.50
	1910	21,561	138	−25.41
	1920	20,351	44	−68.12
	1930	17,803	20	−54.55
WAYNE	1890	11,927	104	0.00
	1900	15,309	115	10.58
	1910	15,181	23	−80.00
	1920	13,012	9	−60.87
	1930	12,243	9	0.00
WEBSTER	1890	15,177	167	0.00
	1900	16,640	116	−30.54
	1910	17,377	87	−25.00
	1920	16,609	53	−39.08
	1930	16,148	21	−60.38

NORTH CAROLINA

County	Year	Total population	Black population	Change in black population (%)
GRAHAM	1890	3,313	25	0.00
	1900	4,343	153	512.00
	1910	4,749	0	−100.00
	1920	4,872	5	0.00
	1930	5,841	1	−80.00
	2000	7,993	15	1,400.00

OHIO

County	Year	Total population	Black population	Change in black population (%)
ADAMS	1880	24,005	343	0.00
	1890	26,093	406	18.37
	1900	26,328	277	−31.77
	1910	24,755	184	−33.57
	1920	22,403	79	−57.07
	1930	20,381	74	−6.33
DEFIANCE	1890	25,769	107	0.00
	1900	26,387	63	−41.12
	1910	24,498	23	−63.49
	1920	24,549	28	21.74
	1930	22,714	26	−7.14
MORROW	1880	19,072	143	0.00
	1890	18,120	115	−19.58
	1900	17,879	56	−51.30
	1910	16,815	56	0.00
	1920	15,570	36	−35.71
	1930	14,489	24	−33.33
PUTNAM	1880	23,713	94	0.00
	1890	30,188	62	−34.03
	1900	32,525	58	−6.45
	1910	29,972	26	−55.17
	1920	27,751	28	7.69
	1930	25,074	1	−96.43
VINTON	1880		212	0.00
	1890	16,045	203	−4.25
	1900	15,330	91	−55.17
	1910	13,096	213	134.07
	1920	12,075	42	−80.28
	1930	10,287	218	419.05
WILLIAMS	1890	24,897	35	0.00
	1900	24,953	54	54.29
	1910	25,198	5	−90.74
	1920	24,627	7	40.00
	1930	24,316	11	57.14
WYANDOT	1890	21,722	82	0.00
	1900	21,125	63	−23.17
	1910	20,760	21	−66.67
	1920	19,481	14	−33.33
	1930	19,036	11	−21.43

TENNESSEE

County	Year	Total population	Black population	Change in black population (%)
CAMPBELL	1890	13,486	559	0.00
	1900	17317	616	10.20
	1910	27387	1887	206.33
	1920	28265	1272	−32.59
	1930	26827	606	−52.36
GRUNDY	1890	6345	438	0.00
	1900	7802	315	−28.08
	1910	8322	143	−54.60
	1920	9753	145	1.40
	1930	9717	155	6.90
SCOTT	1900	9,794	366	0.00
	1910	12947	97	−73.50
	1920	13411	16	−83.51
	1930	14080	15	−6.25

TEXAS

County	Year	Total population	Black population	Change in black population (%)
BANDERA	1890	3,795	126	0.00
	1900	5,332	99	−21.43
	1910	4,921	34	−65.66
	1920	4,001	18	−47.06
	1930	3,784	11	−38.89
BLANCO	1890	4,649	210	0.00
	1900	4,703	224	6.67
	1910	4,311	350	56.25
	1920	4,063	169	−51.71
	1930	3,842	133	−21.30
GILLESPIE	1890	7,056	108	0.00
	1900	8,229	106	−1.85
	1910	9,447	116	9.43
	1920	10,015	57	−50.86
	1930	11,020	128	124.56
MAVERICK	1890	3,698	142	0.00
	1900	4,066	195	37.32
	1910	5,151	96	−50.77

	1920	7,418	74	−22.92
	1930	6,120	18	−75.68
MONTAGUE	1890	18,863	87	0.00
	1900	24,800	26	−70.11
	1910	25,123	27	3.85
	1920	22,200	1	−96.30
	1930	19,159	3	200.00
PARKER	1890	21,682	671	0.00
	1900	25,823	867	29.21
	1910	26,331	693	−20.07
	1920	23,382	337	−51.37
	1930	18,759	279	−17.21

VIRGINIA

County	Year	Total population	Black population	Change in black population (%)
CRAIG	1890	3,835	149	0.00
	1910	4,711	207	38.93
	1920	4,100	95	−54.11
	1930	3,562	15	−84.21
FREDERICK	1890	17,880	2,228	0.00
	1900	13,239	753	−66.20
	1910	12,787	694	−7.84
	1920	12,461	499	−28.10
	1930	13,167	458	−8.22
ROANOKE	1890	30,101	9,005	0.00
	1900	15,837	3,846	−57.29
	1910	19,623	3,525	−8.35
	1920	22,395	2,877	−18.38
	1930	35,289	3,269	13.63
ROCKINGHAM	1890	31,299	2,814	0.00
	1900	33,527	2,634	−6.40
	1910	34,903	2,335	−11.35
	1920	30,047	1,012	−56.66
	1930	29,709	890	−12.06

WEST VIRGINIA

County	Year	Total population	Black population	Change in black population (%)
CALHOUN	1890	8,155	81	0.00
	1900	10,266	83	2.47
	1910	11,258	80	–3.61
	1920	10,268	36	–55.00
	1930	10,866	12	–66.67
DODDRIDGE	1890	12,183	131	0.00
	1900	13,689	25	–80.92
	1910	12,672	8	–68.00
	1920	11,976	1	–87.50
	1930	10,488	20	1,900.00
JACKSON	1890	19,021	87	0.00
	1900	22,987	115	32.18
	1910	20,956	26	–77.39
	1920	18,658	12	–53.85
	1930	16,124	4	–66.67
LINCOLN	1890	11,246	211	0.00
	1900	15,434	63	–70.14
	1910	20,491	30	–52.38
	1920	19,378	61	103.33
	1930	19,156	42	–31.15

APPENDIX B:
BLACK FORSYTH COUNTY
LANDOWNERS

Listed below are the black Forsyth County landowners, the properties they owned in 1912, and the dates of the properties' disposition. This is a compilation of the 1912 Forsyth County Tax Roll as well as information from deeds that I found in the county's courthouse.

Forsyth County is divided into forty-acre land lots which are each given a unique number. In cases where I could determine a land lot, the lot number is listed. In some instances, however, the land lot number on the tax roll is not listed or is unreadable, or the tax rolls and deed information do not agree. For example, Joe Kellogg is shown as being taxed on one set of lots, but deeds show him selling a different set. In such cases I've used the number from the deeds. If I could not determine the land lot number, I've listed the number of acres owned.

Individual owners	District	Land Lot(s)	Date sold
Allen, Hugh	Cumming	246, 263	No sale found
Bagley, William	Bells	468, 470	No sale found
Bailey, George and Martha	Rolands	745	No sale found
Beard, Mollie	Chattahoochee	542, 557, 559, 626	10/12/1915
Beard, Betty	Chattahoochee	558, 625	12/12/1912
Black, A. J.	Cumming	1179, town lot	No sale found
Black, J. L.	Cumming	Town lot	11/6/1915
Bowen, H. T.	Vickery	45 acres	No sale found
Brown, A. G.	Cumming	85, 162, town lot	10/19/1912
Bugg, Laura	Chattahoochee	633	No sale found
Burress, Agnes J.	Cumming	Town lot	No sale found
Cantrell, H. W.	Cumming	Town lot	No sale found
Cantrell, Kanzadie	Rolands	20 acres	No sale found
Carter, John	Big Creek	575	No sale found

307

Cook , Garett	New Bridge	1180	10/11/1912
Craft, J. P.	Chattahoochee	634	No sale found
Crosby, Robert	Not Listed	502, 507	10/29/1912
Davis, William	Cumming	Town lot	1/1/1913
Goss, J. M.	Rolands	Town lot	No sale found
Graham, Charles	Cumming	834	3/25/1913
Graham, Rachel	Cumming	1032	7/15/1947
Graham, Thomas	Cumming	7 acres	1/4/1920
Greenlee, A. G.	Vickery	Town lot	No sale found
Hansard, Isham	Cumming	58	No sale found
Harkness, Cicero	Cumming	152	12/20/1912
Harkness, Clemmie	Cumming	136	12/20/1912
Harrell, Andy	Vickery	1163	1/12/1916
Harrell, Ray	Vickery	Town lot	No sale found
Harrison, Andy	Big Creek	635	3/29/1919
Hill, Robert	Bells	537	10/26/1912
Houston, C. H.	Cumming	Town lot	No sale found
Hunter, Alex	Cumming	78, 140, 177	12/2/1912
Hunter, Charles	Cumming	65	11/8/1912
Hunter, George	Cumming	77	No sale found
Hunter, Warren	Cumming	80, 81	11/23/1912
Jenks, Phillis	Bells	537, 544	6/16/1913
Kellog, Joe	Cumming	1058, 1057, 1104, 1128, 1129, 1176	7/2/1914
Kellog, Henry	Cumming	Town lot	No sale found
Kellog, Henry (Bud)	Cumming	3 acres	No sale found
Maxey, George	Vickery	482	No sale found
McClure, Steve	Cumming	Town lot	No sale found
Merritt, Gus	Cumming	152	12/20/1912
Moore, Andy	Vickery	Town lot	No sale found
Nuckolls, R. D.	Cumming	5 acres	No sale found
Pool, Mark	Vickery	Town lot	No sale found
Roper, T. R.	Rolands	586	No sale found
Smith, A. G.	Cumming	Town lot	No sale found
Strickland, Morgan	Big Creek	1012	No sale found
Strickland, Thomas	Big Creek	1206	3/16/1915
Strickland, James	Big Creek	990, 1000	2/5/1943
Strickland, J. W.	Big Creek	452, 613, 654, 716, 775	No sale found
Thompson, W. A.	Cumming	Town lot	No sale found
Watson, H. E.	Big Creek	921, 922	No sale found
Webb, David H.	Cumming	35	No sale found
Wilson, Benjamin	Vickery	169, 194, 239, 668, 669	No sale found
Wingo, C. H.	Chestatee	895	No sale found

| Wingo, S. C. | Rolands | 20 acres, town lot | No sale found |
| Woodliff, Emily | Cumming | 5 acres of lot 32 | 4/23/1913 |

CHURCHES AND ORGANIZATIONS

M. E. Church	10/12/1916
Stoney Point Church	5/10/1930
Shady Grove Church	10/12/1916
Cummings Baptist Church	11/20/1916
Sawnee Mountain Sunday School	12/5/1918
Mutual Aid Society	1/26/1918
New Bethel Colored Baptist Church	1/17/1921

ACKNOWLEDGEMENTS

When a book is published, it has a sense of inevitability about it. The idea for the book presents itself. The author plunges ahead writing one chapter after another. The result is so compelling that someone is bound to publish it. And, what now graces a bookshelf, is the product of a rational and deliberate process. It is a comforting story. Too bad it is not true.

This book is as much a result of luck or chance as anything I have done. Partly I have had the outrageous good fortune to find documents, oral histories and letters that no one should have assumed existed. It happened so often that at times I could have sworn I heard the Gods laughing.

But the greater share of my luck as been in finding people only too willing to help me. Without them, this book would not exist. The one person who was by my side every step of the way was Joanne Linhard, my friend, partner, and confidant. She read endless drafts, endured long absences, encouraged me at every turn and never wavered.

The two other people who were critical in the creation of this book are Judy Reustle of Springfield, Missouri and Elizabeth Connor in Atlanta, Georgia. While they helped with the research, that does not begin to do justice to their contributions. They acted as a sounding board for my often far-fetched ideas, critiqued the manuscript and in some very dark moments were a bright light. While Judy initially worked on the Pierce City chapter, her hand can be found everywhere in this book. She was the one who found the affidavits detailing the Corbin expulsion and she was also the person who unearthed the sole surviving account of the Sharp County racial cleansing. Elizabeth, on the other hand, helped me to rework the writing in nearly every chapter. In addition to her encyclopedic knowledge of just about everything, she has an uncanny eye for the telling anecdote. When she was not marking up the manuscript, she was hunting through archives and court houses for crucial documents.

Their work was complimented by people who assisted me in nearly every county I researched. While some people wish to remain anonymous, I am indebted to the late Coy Robbins Jr. and Willie Harlen who were crucial in researching Washington County, Indiana. In Comanche County Margaret Waring's help was invaluable along with that of Ruth Cottrell. Ken Rush helped me unravel the intricacies of copper mining in Polk County. Murray Bishoff, as well as being unbelievably kind and generous, is a walking database of Lawrence County history. Judge Bill Cunningham in Marshal County, Kentucky helped me to find one of the last surviving children of a Night Rider and Jennifer Jones, who runs the post office in Blanford, Indiana was my guide for nearly every interview I did there. John Martin Smith and Jon VanSant provided documents, lists and even legal research on the Horse Thief Detective Association and the Klan in Indiana. Dr. Robert Weise of Eastern Kentucky University took me on a tour of eastern Kentucky and helped me research Magoffin County.

Once I finished my research, numerous people agreed to read and comment on my manuscript. Among them are Dr. Diana Jergovic, Dr. Judy Sylvester at Louisiana State University, attorney Felicia Nestor, Jessica Jaspin, Lars-Marten Nagel, and Steve Sternberg at *USA Today*. I am particularly indebted to Felicia and Steve for their help with "Esta's Gift."

A manuscript, no matter how good, is of little use without a publisher. Again fate intervened in the form of Robert O'Harrow Jr. at the Washington Post and Dr. David Garrow of Cambridge University. When I mentioned my book to O'Harrow, unbidden he talked with the people at the Center for Investigative Reporting (CIR). They, in turn, found me my agent, Amy Rennert, and helped finance my research. In similar fashion, after I interviewed Dr. Garrow, he became so interested in the project that he called Lara Heimert at Basic

Books and recommended she look at my manuscript. At that point the Gods were clapping their hands with glee.

Lara Heimert is the editor most writers only dream about. She is funny, smart, supportive and as she likes to say just "a smidge demanding." She pretends that, when she edits a book, she puts a writer through hell. In fact, Lara is the patient tutor drawing out the best in her students.

To these people and others I cannot name, I give my thanks. Together I think we did something important.

BIBLIOGRAPHY

BOOKS

1900 Magoffin County Kentucky Census. The Magoffin County Historical Society, 1984.

1910 Magoffin County Kentucky Census. The Magoffin County Historical Society, 1986.

Anderson, James D. *The Education of Blacks in the South, 1860–1935*. Chapel Hill: University of North Carolina Press, 1988.

Arsenault, Raymond. *The Wild Ass of the Ozarks: Jeff Davis and the Social Bases of Southern Politics*. Philadelphia: Temple University Press, 1984.

Ayers, Edward L. *The Promise of the New South*. New York: Oxford University Press, 1992.

Bagley, Garland C. *History of Forsyth County, Georgia Volume II*.

Bailey, Lloyd Richard Sr., ed. *The Heritage of the Toe River Valley Volume IV Area News, 1777–1949*. Marceline, MO: Walsworth Publishing Co., 2004.

Baker, Ray Stannard. *Following the Color Line*. New York: Harper & Row, 1964.

Barclay, R. E. *The Copper Basin—1890 to 1963*. Knoxville: Barclay, 1975.

Blee, Kathleen M. *Women of the Klan: Racism and Gender In The 1920s*. Berkeley: University of California Press, 1991.

Bond, James E. *No Easy Walk to Freedom: Reconstruction and the Ratification of the Fourteenth Amendment*. Westport: Praeger Publishers, 1997.

Bramblett, Annette. *Images Of America Forsyth County, Twentieth Century Changes*. Arcadia Publishing, 2002.

Brown, Miriam Keast. *The Story of Peirce City, Missouri 1870–1970*. Pierce City, 1970.

Chalmers, David M. *Hooded Americanism: The First Century of the Ku Klux Klan*. Garden City: Doubleday, 1965.

Cook, Samuel. *Monacans and Miners: Native American and Coal Mining Communities in Appalachia*. Lincoln: University of Nebraska Press, 2000.

Cunningham, Bill. *On Bended Knees: The Night Rider Story*. Nashville: McClanahan Publishing House, 1983.

Cutlip, Scott M. *The Unseen Power: Public Relations, a History*. Hillsdale: Lawrence Erlbaum Associates, 1994.

Ezell, John Samuel. *The South Since 1865*. New York: Macmillan, 1963.

Fehrenbach, T. R. *Lone Star: A History of Texas and the Texans*. New York: Macmillan, 1968.

Fehrenbacher, Don E. *Slavery, Law, and Politics: The Dred Scott Case in Historical Perspective*. New York: Oxford University Press, 1981.

Foner, Eric. *Reconstruction: America's Unfinished Revolution*. New York: Harper & Row, 1988.

Friedman, David M. *A Mind of Its Own: The Cultural History of the Penis*. New York: Free Press, 2001.

Gould, Frank. *Common Texas Grasses*. College Station: Texas A & M University Press, 1978.

Greene, Harry Washington. *Holders of Doctorates Among American Negroes*. Boston: Meador Publishing Company, 1946.

Hamm, Thomas. *Earlham College: a history, 1847–1997*. Bloomington: Indiana University Press, 1997.

Helton, William W. *Around Home in Unicoi County*. Johnson City: Overmountain Press, 1994.

Higham, John. *Strangers in the Land: Patterns of American Nativism 1860–1925*. New Brunswick: Rutgers University Press, 1955.

Horan, James D. *Confederate Agent: A Discovery in History*. New York: Crown Publishers, 1954.

Janken, Kenneth Robert. *White: The Biography of Walter White, Mr. NAACP*. New York: The New Press, 2003.

Kennedy, Stetson. *After Appomattox: How the South Won the War*. Gainesville: University Press of Florida, 1995.

Keyssar, Alexander. *The Right To Vote: the Contested History of Democracy In the United States*. New York: Basic Books, 2000.

Lankford, Rose Mary. *The History of Evening Shade*. Sharp County Historical Society, 2003.

Lester, J. C. and Wilson, D. L. *Ku Klux Klan: Its Origin, Growth and Disbandment*. New York: The Neale Publishing Company, 1905.

Luebke, Paul. *Tar Heel Politics: Myths and Realities*. Chapel Hill: University of North Carolina Press, 1990.

Mancini, Matthew J. *One Dies, Get Another*. Columbia: University of South Carolina Press, 1996.

Mandle, Jay. *Not Slave, Not Free: The African American Economic Experience Since the Civil War*. Durham: Duke University Press, 1992.

Moore, Caruth Shaver. *Early History of Sharp County*. Evening Shade: C. S. Moore, 1979.

Moore, Leonard J. *Citizen Klansmen: The Ku Klux Klan in Indiana, 1921–1928*. Chapel Hill: University of North Carolina Press, 1991.

Novak, Daniel. *The Wheel of Servitude*. Lexington: University Press of Kentucky, 1978.

Ovington, Mary White. *The Walls Came Tumbling Down*. New York: Arno Press, 1969.

Perman, Michael. *Struggle for Mastery Disenfranchisement in the South*. Chapel Hill: University of North Carolina Press, 2001.

Pittman, Ben. *The Trials for Treason at Indianapolis*. Salem: The News Publishing Company, 1892.

Rawick, George P. *The American Slave: A Composite Autobiography, vol. 7*. Westport: Greenwood Press, 1979.

Rea, Ralph R. *Boone County and Its People*. Van Buren: Argus Press, 1955.

Rusher, James Thomas. *Until He is Dead*. Boone: Parkway Publishers Inc., 2003.

Shadburn, Don. *The Cottonpatch Chronicles: Reflection on Cherokee History, People, Places, and Events in Forsyth County, Georgia*. Cumming: D. L. Shadburn, 2003.

Sheppard, Muriel. *Early Cabins In The Laurel*. Chapel Hill: The University of North Carolina Press, 1991.

Shklar, Judith N. *American Citizenship: The Quest for Inclusion*. Cambridge: Harvard University Press, 1991.

Smallwood, James. *Time of Hope, Time of Despair*. Port Washington: National University Publishers, 1981.

Smith, J. Douglas. *Managing White Supremacy: Race, Politics, and Citizenship in Jim Crow Virginia*. Chapel Hill: University of North Carolina Press, 2002.

Sollors, Werner, ed. *Interracialism: Black-White Intermarriage in American History, Literature, and Law*. New York: Oxford, 2000.

Stampp, Kenneth M. *Indiana Politics during the Civil War*. Indianapolis: Indiana Historical Bureau, 1949.

Stidger, Felix G. *Treason History of the Order of Sons of Liberty, Formerly Circle of Honor Succeeded by Knights of the Golden Circle, Afterward Order of American Knights*. New York: Felix G., 1903.

Stover, John. *The Railroads of the South 1865–1900*. Chapel Hill: University of North Carolina Press, 1955.

Thornbrough, Emma Lou. *Indiana in the Civil War Era*. Indianapolis: Indiana Historical Bureau, 1965.

Tredway, G. R. *Democratic Opposition to the Lincoln Administration in Indiana*. Indianapolis: Indiana Historical Bureau, 1973.

Waldrep, Christopher. *Night Riders: Defending Community in the Black Patch, 1890–1915*. Durham: Duke University Press, 1993.

Weinberg, Arthur and Lila Weinberg, eds. *The Muckrackers*. New York: Simon and Schuster, 1961.

Wells, Eulalia, ed. *Blazing the Way: Tales of Comanche County Pioneers*. Blanket: 1942.

Wilson, Theodore. *The Black Codes of the South*. Birmingham: University of Alabama, 1965.

Woodward, C. Vann. *The Strange Career of Jim Crow*. New York: Oxford University Press, 2002.

MAGAZINES

Hoover, Dwight. "Daily Douglas Barr: From Quaker to Klan 'Kluckeress.'" *Indiana Magazine of History*, June 1991.

Lyle, Eugene P., Jr. "They That Ride By Night." *Hampton's Magazine* 12, no. 2.

Trueblood, Lillie D. "The Story of John Williams, Colored." *Indiana Magazine of History*, vol 30, no. 150.

White, Walter. "The Work of a Mob." *The Crisis*, September 1918.

Wright, George C. "The Forced Removal of Afro-Americans From Rural Kentucky." *Reflections* 1, no. 1.

NEWSPAPERS

Arkansas Gazette
Asheville Citizen
Asheville Times
Atlanta Constitution
Atlanta Journal
Atlanta Journal-Constitution
Austin Daily Statesman
Bristol Herald
Carthage Evening News
Chattanooga Daily Times
Comanche Chief
Corbin Times
Courier-Journal
Dahlonega Nugget
Daily Clintonian
Daily Messenger
Daily News-Democrat
Evansville Journal
Freemont Journal
Hammond Times
Harrison Daily Times
Hoosier State
Hopkinsville Kentuckian
Houston Telegraph

Indianapolis Journal
Indianapolis News
Indianapolis Star
Johnson City Staff
Joplin Globe
Knoxville Journal & Tribune
Lenoir Topic
Lexington Herald
Lexington Leader
Louisville Courier-Journal
Marshall Mountain Wave
Messenger
Mitchell News-Journal
Monett Times
Mount Vernon Chieftan
Nashville American
Neosho Times
News-Herald
New York Times
Northwest Arkansas Times
Paducah Evening Sun
Pierce City Empire
Pittsburgh Daily Headlight
Quitman Free Press
Republican
Republican Leader
Rogers Democrat
St. Louis Post-Dispatch
Sharp County Record
Springfield Democrat
Springfield Leader Democrat
Springfield Daily Republican
Stroud Messenger
Stroud Star
Sunday Citizen
Tolerance
Town and Country
Virginian-Pilot
Waco Daily Examiner
Washington Democrat
Washington Post
World

INTERVIEWS

Alexander, Mary.

Bishoff, Murray. April 5, 2004.

Bond, Julian. February 2, 2005.

Brown, James. March 26, 2004.

Carter, Dean. January 25, 2005.

Crowe, Melvin. March 1, 2005.

Cunningham, William. June 16, 2005.

Dizney, Allen. February 16, 2006.

Glasgow, Marcia. July 7, 2005.

Harlmon, Nicole. May 3, 2004.

Henson, Robby.

Hise, Lloyd. July 29, 2005.

Holcomb, George. April 28, 2006.

Jennings, Elvira. July 27, 2005.

Kelly,Wayne. May 5, 2006.

Ledbetter, Linda.

Livingston, Glenda. June 15, 2004.

Livingston, Shawn. June 14, 2004.

McClellan, Georgia. July 29, 2005.

Nash, Lillie. October 7, 2004.

Page, Leo. September 3, 2003.

Raesz, Becky. July 9, 2005.

Runsick, Elmer. March 25, 2004.

Shadburn, Don.

Skorich, Eli. March 16, 2005.

Stafford, Louise. June 16, 2004.

Van Sant, Jon. April 26, 2005.

Walraven, Wesley. January 25, 2005.

Young, Evelyn. May 9, 2005.

ORAL HISTORIES

Anderson, Helen. Audiocassette, 1987. Forsyth County box, The King Center Archives, Atlanta, Georgia.

Battle, Annette. Audiocassette, 1987. Forsyth County box, The King Center Archives, Atlanta, Georgia.

Interview of the family of J. C. Beard. Audiocassette, 1987. Forsyth County box, The King Center Archives, Atlanta, Georgia.

Bell, Bobbie. Audiocassette, 1987. Forsyth County box, The King Center Archives, Atlanta, Georgia.

Bowen, Cleveland. Audiocassette, 1987. Forsyth County box, The King Center Archives, Atlanta, Georgia.

Conaway, Tom. Lightfoot papers. Comanche County box, University of Texas Library.

Early, Bill. Oral history, June 28, 1977, Kentucky Oral History Commission.

Garrett, John. Oral history, June 28, 1977, Kentucky Oral History Commission.

Killenger, Blake. Oral history, June 28, 1977, Kentucky Oral History Commission.

Little, Oscar. Oral history, June 25, 1977, Kentucky Oral History Commission.

Nabers, Jim. Lightfoot papers, Comanche County box, University of Texas.

Stansberry, W. R. Oral history, June 29, 1977, Kentucky Oral History Commission.

Interview of the family of Spencer Thornton. Audiocassette, 1987. Forsyth County box, The King Center Archives, Atlanta, Georgia.

Walker, Alfred. Oral history, June 28, 1977, Kentucky Oral History Commission.

JOURNALS

American Institute of Mining Engineers. *Transactions of the American Institute of Mining Engineers* 25 (1895).

Andrews, W. T. "The Causes of Negro Migration from the South." *Journal of Negro History* 63, no. 4 (1978): 366–372.

Bernstein, David E. "The Law and Economics of Post-Civil War Restriction on Interstate Migration by African-Americans." *Texas Law Review* 76 (March 1998): 781.

Berthoff, Rowland T. "Southern Attitudes Toward Immigration, 1865–1914." *Journal of Southern History* 17 (August 1951): 328–360.

Cohen, William, "Negro Involuntary Servitude in the South, 1865–1940: A Preliminary Analysis." *Journal of Southern History* 42 (February 1976): 31–60.

Collins, William J. "When the Tide Turned: Immigration and the Delay of the Great Black Migration." *Journal of Economic History* 57 (September 1997): 607–632.

Crouthamel, James L. "The Springfield Race Riot of 1908." *Journal of Negro History* 45, no. 3 (July 1960): 164–181.

Crowe, Charles. "Racial Massacre in Atlanta September 22, 1906." *Journal of Negro History* 54, no. 2 (April 1969): 150–173.

_____. "Racial Violence and Social Reform: Origins of the Atlanta Riot of 1906." *Journal of Negro History* 53, no. 3 (July 1968): 254.

Fishback, Price V. "Operations of 'Unfettered' Labor Market: Exit and Voice in American Labor Markets at the Turn of the Century." *Journal of Economic Literature* 36 (June 1998): 722–765.

Froelich, Jacqueline and David Zimmerman. "Total Eclipse: The Destruction of the African American Community of Harrison, Arkansas, in 1905 and 1909." *Arkansas Historical Quarterly* 58, no. 2 (Summer 1999): 133–159.

Goriely, Alain and Tyler McMillen. "Shape of A Cracking Whip." *Physical Review Letters* 88, no. 244301 (2002).

Harris, Carl V. "Reforms in Government Control of Negroes in Birmingham, Alabama, 1890–1920." *The Journal of Southern History* 38, no. 4 (1972): 567–600.

Lightfoot, Billy Bob. "The Negro Exodus from Comanche County, Texas." *The Southwestern Historical Quarterly* 56 (January 1953): 405–416.

Mandle, Jay. "Continuity and Change, the Use of Black Labor After the Civil War." *Journal of Black Studies* 21, no. 4 (June 1991): 414–427.

Matthews, John Michael. "The Georgia 'Race Strike' of 1909." *Journal of Southern History* 40, no. 4 (November 1974): 613–630.

Record, Wilson. "Negro Intellectual Leadership in the National Association for the Advancement of Colored People." *Phylon* 17, no. 4 (4th Quarter, 1956): 375–389.

Rosenbloom, Joshua L. "The Extent of the Labor Market in the United States, 1850–1914." *Social Science History* 22, no. 3 (Autumn 1998): 287–318.

_____. "Strikebreaking and the Labor Market in the United States, 1881–1894." *Journal of Economic History* 58, no. 1 (1998): 183–205.

Shlomowitz, Ralph. "'Bound' or 'Free'? Black Labor in Cotton and Sugarcane Farming, 1865–1880." *Journal of Southern History* 50, no. 4 (November 1984): 569–596.

Watkins, Loren. "Some History of Boone County, Arkansas." *Boone County Historian* 8 (1978): 282–288.

Whatley, Warren C. "African American Strikebreaking from the Civil War to the New Deal." *Social Science History* 17, no. 4 (Winter 1993): 525–558.

SPEECHES

Rehnquist, William. "Civil Liberty and the Civil War: The Indianapolis Treason Trials." October 28, 1996, Indiana University School of Law, Bloomington.

LETTERS AND E-MAILS

Brown, Joseph M. Letter to C. L. Harris and J. F. Nichols. October 21, 1912. Papers of Gov. Joseph Brown. Georgia State Archives, Atlanta.

Burlesaon, J. E. Letter to Gov. Cameron Morrison. October 8, 1923. Papers of Gov. Morrison. North Carolina State Archives, Raleigh.

Champion, Emelius. Letter to Gov. Augustus E. Wilson. October 6, 1909. Wilson Papers. Filson Historical Society, Louisville, KY.

Crumbaugh, W. L. Letters to Gov. Augustus E. Wilson. March 19, 1908. Wilson Papers. Filson Historical Society, Louisville, KY.

Dean, H. H. Letter to Gov. Joseph M. Brown. September 2, 1912. Papers of Gov. Brown. Georgia State Archives, Atlanta.

Flournoy, J. C. Letter to Gov. Augustus E. Wilson. March 21, 1908. Wilson Papers. Filson Historical Society, Louisville, KY

Griffith, John. Telegram to Gov. Cameron Morrison. October 12, 1923. Papers of Gov. Morrison. North Carolina State Archives, Raleigh.

Griffith, Mary. "Racism in Harrison." E-mail to *Harrison Daily Times*, January 26, 2003.

Hoffman, Scott. "Re: task force." E-mail to Wayne Kelly, January 17, 2005.

Ingersoll, Frank A. Letter to his father. August 1861. Lilly Library, Indiana University, Bloomington.

Morrison, Cameron. Telegram to sheriff of Mitchell County. October 1, 1923. Papers of Gov. Morrison. North Carolina State Archives, Raleigh.

_____. Telegram to Judge T. B. Finley. October 4, 1923. Papers of Gov. Morrison. North Carolina State Archives, Raleigh.

_____. Telegram to General Metts. October 1, 1923. Papers of Gov. Morrison. North Carolina State Archives, Raleigh.

_____. Telegram to A. N. Fuller, T. W. Dayton, Dr. Charles A. Peterson, and Dan W. Adams. September 27, 1923. Papers of Gov. Morrison. North Carolina State Archives, Raleigh.

_____. Telegram to Walter White. September 28, 1923. Papers of Gov. Morrison. North Carolina State Archives, Raleigh.

O'Brien, P. H. Letter to Gov. Cameron Morrison. September 27, 1923. Papers of Gov. Morrison. North Carolina State Archives, Raleigh.

Scholl, C. L. Letter to Judge H. H. Tye. January 26, 1920. Gov. Edwin P. Morrow Rejected Petitions, box 5, file 177. Kentucky Department for Libraries and Archives, Frankfort.

Snyder, Joseph B. Letter to Judge H. H. Tye. January 5, 1920. Gov. Edwin P. Morrow Rejected Petitions, box 5, file 177. Kentucky Department for Libraries and Archives, Frankfort.

_____. Letter to Governor Edwin P. Morrow. December 6, 1920. Gov. Edwin P. Morrow Rejected Petitions, box 5, file 177. Kentucky Department for Libraries and Archives, Frankfort.

White, Walter. Telegram to Gov. Cameron Morrison. September 28, 1923. Papers of Gov. Morrison. North Carolina State Archives, Raleigh.

Wilson, Augustus. Letter to Dr. Emelius Champion. October 13, 1909. Wilson Papers. Filson Historical Society, Louisville, KY.

DISSERTATIONS

Lightfoot, Billy Bob. *The History of Comanche County to 1920*. Diss. University of Texas.

Sylvester, Lorna Lutes. *Oliver P. Morton and Hoosier Politics During the Civil War*. Diss. Indiana University, 1968.

PAPERS

Adjutant General's Department. "Special Orders No. 317–1/2 27." Papers of Gov. Morrison. North Carolina State Archives, Raleigh. September 1923.

Bi-Racial Committee. Meeting transcript, April 22, 1987. Forsyth County box, The King Center Archives, Atlanta, GA.

_____. Meeting transcript, April 1, 1987. Forsyth County box, The King Center Archives, Atlanta, GA.

Blue River Meeting minutes. Earlham College, Richmond, IN.

Edwards, B. J. Sworn statement given January 24, 1920. Gov. Edwin P. Morrow Rejected Petitions, box 5, file 177. Kentucky Department for Libraries and Archives, Frankfort.

Everman, H. E. "Corbin: A Complex Railroad 'Boom' Town, 1895–1930." Paper presented at the Ohio Valley Historical Conference, October 2001.

Fugate, William. Sworn statement given January 24, 1920. Gov. Edwin P. Morrow Rejected Petitions, box 5, file 177. Kentucky Department for Libraries and Archives, Frankfort.

Frakes, Peter. Sworn statement given January 23, 1920. Gov. Edwin P. Morrow Rejected Petitions, box 5, file 177. Kentucky Department for Libraries and Archives, Frankfort.

Good, Tom. Sworn statement given January 22, 1920. Gov. Edwin P. Morrow Rejected Petitions, box 5, file 177. Kentucky Department for Libraries and Archives, Frankfort.

Griffin, Arthur. Interview notes. *Commonwealth of Kentucky v. Marvin Farley and Tom Chiles*, 1908. Marshall County Courthouse, Benton, KY.

Gaines, Brooks. interview notes *Commonwealth of Kentucky v. Marvin Farley and Tom Chiles*, 1908. Marshall County Courthouse, Benton, KY.

Hick, J. C. Interview notes. *Commonwealth of Kentucky v. Marvin Farley and Tom Chiles*, 1908. Marshall County Courthouse, Benton, KY.

Holden, Fred. Interview notes. *Commonwealth of Kentucky v. Marvin Farley and Tom Chiles*, 1908. Marshall County Courthouse, Benton, KY.

Holland, W. W. Interview notes. *Commonwealth of Kentucky v. Marvin Farley and Tom Chiles*, 1908. Marshall County Courthouse, Benton, KY.

Jones, Will. Sworn statement given January 20, 1920. Gov. Edwin P. Morrow Rejected Petitions, box 5, file 177. Kentucky Department for Libraries and Archives, Frankfort.

National Horse Thief Detective Association. *Journal.* 56th Annual Session.

_____. *Journal.* 63rd Annual Session.

_____. *Journal.* 64th Annual Session.

Klone, Walter. Interview notes. *Commonwealth of Kentucky v. Marvin Farley and Tom Chiles*, 1908. Marshall County Courthouse, Benton, KY.

Ku Klux Klan officers. *Indiana Historical Society*, 1925. Indianapolis, IN.

Lawrence County Historical Society Bulletin. "The Strawberry Letters." October 1985.

Miles, O. A. Sworn statement given January 19, 1920. Gov. Edwin P. Morrow Rejected Petitions, box 5, file 177. Kentucky Department for Libraries and Archives, Frankfort.

"Resolution Adopted By Mass Meeting of the Citizens of the Town of Cumming at Court House of Forsyth County Wednesday October 16, 1912." Papers of Gov. Joseph Brown. Georgia State Archives, Atlanta.

Overby, Robert. Interview notes. *Commonwealth of Kentucky v. Marvin Farley and Tom Chiles*, 1908. Marshall County Courthouse, Benton, KY.

"Petition to His Excellency, Governor Edwin P. Morrow." Gov. Edwin P. Morrow Rejected Petitions, box 5, file 177. Kentucky Department for Libraries and Archives, Frankfort.

Spears, Brian. Memo to the Executive Committee of the Coalition to End Fear and Intimidation in Forsyth County. November 11, 1987.

Spears, Brian et al. "Report of the Legal Redress Committee to the Coalition Against Fear and Intimidation in Forsyth County." October 23, 1987.

Terry, Alex. Interview notes. *Commonwealth of Kentucky v. Marvin Farley and Tom Chiles*, 1908. Marshall County Courthouse, Benton, KY.

Terry, Belle. Interview notes. *Commonwealth of Kentucky v. Marvin Farley and Tom Chiles,* 1908. Marshall County Courthouse, Benton, KY.

Thomas, T. D. Sworn statement given January 19, 1920. Gov. Edwin P. Morrow Rejected Petitions, box 5, file 177. Kentucky Department for Libraries and Archives, Frankfort.

Thomas, G. Interview notes. *Commonwealth of Kentucky v. Marvin Farley and Tom Chiles*, 1908. Marshall County Courthouse, Benton, KY.

Turner, John. Sworn statement given January 21, 1920. Gov. Edwin P. Morrow Rejected Petitions, box 5, file 177. Kentucky Department for Libraries and Archives, Frankfort.

Tye, Alex. Sworn statement given January 23, 1920. Gov. Edwin P. Morrow Rejected Petitions, box 5, file 177. Kentucky Department for Libraries and Archives, Frankfort.

Walker, J. A. Sworn statement given January 20, 1920. Gov. Edwin P. Morrow Rejected Petitions, box 5, file 177. Kentucky Department for Libraries and Archives, Frankfort.

Washburn, Joe. Interview notes. *Commonwealth of Kentucky v. Marvin Farley and Tom Chiles*, 1908. Marshall County Courthouse, Benton, KY.

White, Walter. Memorandum for Gov. Dorsey from Walter F. White, Papers of the NAACP on microfilm, part 7, reel 10.

Whitefield, Mary. Interview notes. *Commonwealth of Kentucky v. Marvin Farley and Tom Chiles*, 1908. Marshall County Courthouse, Benton, KY.

Whitefield, Steve. Interview notes. *Commonwealth of Kentucky v. Marvin Farley and Tom Chiles*, 1908. Marshall County Courthouse, Benton, KY.

Wilburn, H. H. Sworn statement given January 24, 1920. Gov. Edwin P. Morrow Rejected Petitions, box 5, file 177. Kentucky Department for Libraries and Archives, Frankfort.

GOVERNMENT PUBLICATIONS

Forsyth County. *1912 Tax Roll*. Georgia State Archives, Atlanta.

_____. *1913 Tax Roll*. Georgia State Archives, Atlanta.

_____. *1914 Tax Roll*. Georgia State Archives, Atlanta.

_____. *1915 Tax Roll*. Georgia State Archives, Atlanta.

Bowers, Michael. "Report of the Attorney General to the Governor, the Department of Community Affairs and the Cumming-Forsyth County Bi-Racial Community Relations Committee." 1987.

Lyon County Court. *Champion v. Champion*. Kentucky State Archives, Benton.

Manuscript Census Returns, 1900. 12th Census of the United States, Magoffin County, KY.

Manuscript Census Returns, 1910. 13th Census of the United States, Magoffin County, KY.

Manuscript Census Returns, 1910. 13th Census of the United States, Scott County, TN.

Manuscript Census Returns, 1900. 12th Census of the United States, Scott County, TN.

Manuscript Census Returns, 1910. 13th Census of the United States, Scott County, TN.

Manuscript Census Returns, 1890. 11th Census of the United States, Vermillion County, IN.

Manuscript Census Returns, 1920. 13th Census of the United States, Vermillion County, IN.

Manuscript Census Returns, 1860. 7th Census of the United States, Washington County, IN.

Manuscript Census Returns, 1920. 14th Census of the United States, Laurel and Whitley Counties, KY.

Plecker, W. A. "Shall America Remain White?" *Virginia Health Bulletin* 17, extra no. 12 (November 1925).

State of Indiana. *The Revised Statutes of the State of Indiana*. Indianapolis: J. P. Chapman, state printer, 1852.

State of Tennessee. *Eleventh Annual Report of the Mining Department*. Willians Printing Co, 1901.

_____. *Twenty-First Annual Report of the Mining Department*. Willians Printing Co, 1912.

Texas Rangers. Correspondence file. Texas State Archives, Austin.

U.S. Census Bureau. 1980 census, Forsyth County, GA.

_____. 2000 census, Boone County, AR.

INDEX